Samuel Johnson, Peter Peterson

Life of Pope

Samuel Johnson, Peter Peterson

Life of Pope

ISBN/EAN: 9783744674263

Printed in Europe, USA, Canada, Australia, Japan

Cover: Foto ©Lupo / pixelio.de

More available books at **www.hansebooks.com**

JOHNSON'S
LIFE OF POPE

BY

PETER PETERSON, D.Sc.

PROFESSOR OF ORIENTAL LANGUAGES, ELPHINSTONE COLLEGE, BOMBAY

London

MACMILLAN AND CO., Limited

NEW YORK: THE MACMILLAN COMPANY

1899

All rights reserved

GLASGOW: PRINTED AT THE UNIVERSITY PRESS
BY ROBERT MACLEHOSE AND CO.

NOTE

THE notes marked C.D.P. and enclosed in square brackets have been supplied by Mr. C. D. Punchard, who has also drawn up the summary on pages ix. to xvi.

CONTENTS

	PAGE
SUMMARY OF JOHNSON'S LIFE OF POPE,	ix
JOHNSON'S LIFE OF POPE,	1
NOTES,	111
INDEX,	183

SUMMARY OF JOHNSON'S LIFE OF POPE.

1. **Life of Pope—**

i. *Early years*: Born in 1688 of Papist parents—delicate constitution, gentle and sweet disposition.

ii. *Education*: Excluded from best schools on account of religion; taught by his aunt, by Romish priests, at private schools; went to London to study French and Italian.

iii. *Early poems*: A lampoon at school; *Ode on Solitude* at twelve; *Thebais* at fourteen; Chaucer's *Tales* and *Silence* about the same time.

iv. *Early friends*: Dryden, a slight acquaintance; Sir William Trumbal at Binfield; Wycherley, the poet, offended by Pope's free criticism; Mr. Cromwell, received many letters from Pope; Walsh, advised Pope to practise correctness. At seventeen he began to frequent Will's coffee-house, and to read diligently for improvement and instruction. Tonson, the famous bookseller, published Pope's *Pastorals* in his *Miscellany* (1709).

v. *From 1709 to 1715. Essay on Criticism*: Praised by Addison and Warburton; considered by Dennis (the critic) as an attack on himself, Dennis attacked Pope in an abusive pamphlet. *The Messiah*, corrected by Steele, published in the *Spectator*; *Verses on the Unfortunate Lady* written. The *Rape of the Lock*, written at the request of Mr. Caryl to conciliate an offended lady. Addison praised the incomplete poem, and advised Pope not to alter it. Pope assumed that this advice was caused by jealousy. Years after Dennis criticised the poem. *The Temple of Fame* published after being written two years. *Eloisa to Abelard* excels all other similar compositions. *Windsor Forest* is said to have offended Addison, but evidently but little as Pope wrote a Prologue to Addison's *Cato*, and a reply to Dennis's remarks on *Cato*. A comparison of the *Pastorals* of Philips and Pope in the *Guardian* increased Pope's hostility to Addison. About this time Pope studied painting under Jervas.

vi. *The Iliad*: In 1713 Pope solicited a subscription to a translation with notes, in six volumes, at six guineas. Lintot bought the work. Other editions were published in Holland. Critics questioned Pope's qualifications as a translator, but he used other translations freely, and was assisted by Broome, Fenton, Jortin, and Parnell. The work was completed in 1718, and brought Pope above five thousand pounds. This success procured Pope friends. Pope read parts to Lord Halifax, who offered Pope favours; Mr. Craggs offered him a pension; both offers were declined. The manuscripts in the British Museum show Pope's careful method of work. The success of Pope put an end to his friendship with Addison. Adherents of each promoted rivalry between these two literary chiefs. Jervas tried to re-establish their friendship; Swift promoted the subscription to the *Iliad*, thereby perhaps offending Addison; Steele procured an interview between the rivals, but it proved stormy, and they parted in mutual rage. Addison praised a rival translation by Tickell, giving it his preference. The public condemned Tickell. Pope relates that he threatened Addison by letter, and sent him a sketch of his *Satire on Addison*. Atterbury saw these verses and advised Pope to exercise his talent in satire.

vii. *Pope's homes*: Born in London; brought up at Binfield (Berkshire), whither his father had retired at the Revolution. In 1715 the Binfield estate was sold, and Pope bought a house at Twickenham. Vines, quincunx, and grotto were his delight. His father died in 1717, his mother in 1733.

viii. *Minor Works, 1720-1727*: An edition of Shakespeare (1721), published by Tonson, criticised by Theobald; translation of the *Odyssey*, published by Lintot (1725). (Pope gave evidence at Atterbury's trial in 1723.) Friendship with Spence arose out of cool and candid criticism of the *Odyssey*. The upsetting of a coach nearly proved fatal to Pope, and led to a consolatory letter from Voltaire. *Art of Sinking in Poetry*, published in the Miscellanies of Pope and Swift.

ix. *The Dunciad*: A satire on all writers who had attacked Pope. Theobald was chief Dunce. Success secured by the replies of those who thought themselves attacked. Pope relates the "war of the Dunces." Walpole presented the *Dunciad* to the King. A later edition gave names of those attacked. Dennis replied by attacking the *Rape of the Lock*. To some objectors Pope apologised.

x. *Later life (1731-1744)*: The poem on *Taste* caused an accusation of ingratitude to the Duke of Chandos, and Pope apologised under the name of Cleland.

Curll published some of Pope's letters, and Pope prosecuted, but he is suspected of encouraging this publication as a pretext for publishing all his letters. The letters contain few matters of interest, but are excellent specimens.

Essay on Man, published at intervals in 1733-4. The author's name was suppressed till all had appeared. Bolingbroke ridiculed the system of morality in this essay, declaring that Pope did not understand the doctrines he was propagating. Crousaz read the French translations, criticised the Essay, and declared it opposed to revealed religion. Warburton defended Pope against Crousaz, and was rewarded by Pope's interest, and a legacy of his works.

Epistles—to Lord Bathurst, on *The Use of Riches*, in praise of Kyrl, the Man of Ross; to Lord Cobham, on the *Characters of Men*, enunciating Pope's theory of the Ruling Passion; to a Lady on the *Characters of Women*, said to contain no character from life, but describing the Duchess of Marlborough as Atossa; to Arbuthnot, an epistle containing the Satire on Addison, but not Addison's name. The last-named epistle formed a Prologue to *Imitations of Horace*.

Memoirs of the Scriblerus Club were commenced by Pope, Swift, and Arbuthnot in concert, but the writers separated and the work was not completed.

A new *Dunciad* was published in 1742, attacking Cibber, the Poet Laureate, who had ridiculed Pope's drama, *Three Hours after Marriage*, laughed off the stage in 1717. Pope and Cibber attacked each other in successive pamphlets, the former losing more credit than the latter.

xi. *Death and subsequent events*: Worn out by disease, ceased work in 1743; attended by Dr. Thomson, Lord Bolingbroke, Lord Marchmont, and Dodsley; neglected by Martha Blount. Died in May, 1744. Left his papers to Bolingbroke, whom he asked to print a few copies of *The Patriot King* for friends. Dodsley produced a complete earlier edition which Bolingbroke burnt. Warburton apologised for Pope's deception. A contemptuous legacy was left to Allen of Bath.

2. **Personal appearance and habits.**—Small, deformed; face pleasing, eyes animated; a victim to headache, sensitive to cold, and in need of constant attendance. A valetudinarian, and a very troublesome guest, monopolising all the servants.

3. **Character.**—Indulgent to his appetite, but pretended the reverse. Fond of secrecy and slyness. Not brilliant in company, has left no witty sayings. Fretful, resentful, rarely jocular, never merry. Eminently frugal, niggardly to his guests, but fond of ridiculing poverty. Proud of his acquaintance with men of rank, but not servile; never flattered for gain. His letters show liberality, gratitude, constancy, tenderness; but they seem premeditated and artificial, hence too favourable to himself. He professed (*a*) contempt for his own poetry, but this was not sincere; (*b*) insensibility to criticism, but every pamphlet disturbed his quiet; (*c*) contempt for Kings, but was flattered by a Prince's attentions; (*d*) contempt for the world, but strove to please mankind; (*e*) scorn of the great, but boasted of living among them. His own importance is often in his mind, his letters show him insensible to excellence in others. As a friend he was liberal and faithful;

zealous and constant. He professed the Roman Catholic religion but was not scrupulously pious.

4. **Intellectual character.**—Characterised by good sense; possessed genius, activity, and ambition of mind, a strong and exact memory, unwearied diligence. He laboured for pleasure, was never negligent, never impatient. His work was voluntary, his subjects chosen by himself. His publications were never hasty.

5. **Dryden and Pope compared.**—Dryden wrote to please the people, with little consideration, when occasion called; never attempted to improve what was good. Pope desired to excel, considered and reconsidered his pieces, corrected and improved even after publication.

Dryden had more education, larger range of mind, more general notions. Dryden's knowledge was more dignified. Pope's was more certain.

Dryden's prose style is capricious and varied. Pope's cautious and uniform.

Dryden's genius was superior, but his performances hasty. Pope's genius was very high, and his performances careful.

Dryden's flights are higher, and often surpass expectation. Pope's are more uniform, but never below expectation.

6. **Works of Pope criticised—**

i. *Pastorals*: Composed with close thought, show literature rather than wit, powerful in language, skilful in metre.

ii. *Temple of Fame*: Splendid, luxuriant in ornaments; skilful in allegory, correct in imagery; but has little relation to real life.

iii. *Messiah*: Excels the *Pollio*, because taken from the Bible.

iv. *Unfortunate Lady*: Treats suicide with respect, in parts animated, in others tender; the tale is not skilfully told, and is inconsistent.

v. *Ode for St. Cecilia's Day*: Above all others except Dryden's. The third stanza is the best. Pope was ignorant of music.

vi. *Essay on criticism*: Pope's greatest work. The simile of the Alps is its greatest beauty; another celebrated paragraph deals with sound as an echo of the sense. Johnson gives examples of Pope's success in observing the principle he lays down.

vii. *Rape of the Lock*: Most attractive of all ludicrous compositions; supernatural agents happily introduced; new things are made familiar; familiar things are made new; the purpose is to laugh at the little unguarded follies of the female sex; Dennis says it lacks a moral, and that the machinery is superfluous.

viii. *Eloise to Abelard*: Happy production, judiciously chosen subject; excites interest because the characters deserve notice.

ix. *The Iliad*: The Greeks had no translations; the Italians were very diligent translators; Cicero and Germanicus left behind some Latin specimens; Terence translated Menander; the French translated industriously; Virgil borrowed from Homer, Pope from Dryden; Pope's version "tuned the English tongue." Critics objected that Pope's Homer was not Homerical; this is the necessary result of change of time, custom, and language. Many beauties in Pope's version are not found in the original. The purpose of a writer is to be read; criticism which objects to this may be ignored. The notes add to the pleasure given by the translation.

x. *The Dunciad*: Suggested by *MacFlecknoe*: had a moral design, but was petulant and malignant; contains many beauties, but marred by grossness of the images.

xi. *Essay on Man*: Subject not proper for poetry—poet not master of the subject. From the nature of the Supreme Being he deduces mankind, and questions whether mankind is in the wrong place. He very wisely tells us much that every man knows. The essay shows predominant genius, splendid imagery, seductive eloquence—disguising penury of knowledge, and vulgarity of sentiment. Not a felicitous composition—shows examples of unpolished lines, harsh diction, imperfectly expressed thoughts, inelegant levity.

xii. *Characters of Men and Women*: Successful speculation upon human life; superior to Boileau's *Satire*.

xiii. *Epistles*: Warburton has tried to find a train of thought connecting these Epistles. The best passages are on Good Sense, the End of the Duke of Buckingham, and the poet's own Character.

7. **Pope's genius.**—Pope possessed in due proportion the qualities which constitute genius : (*a*) inventive faculty (*Rape of the Lock*, *Essay on Criticism*); (*b*) imagination (*Eloisa*, *Windsor Forest*, *Epistles*); (*c*) judgment; (*d*) the colours of language.

8. **Characteristics of Pope's verse.**—(*a*) melodious metre, censured for being too uniformly musical; (*b*) frequent triplets and Alexandrines; (*c*) few double rhymes, and no expletives; (*d*) happy combination of words, poetical elegance of phrases (Watts).

9. **Letters to Mr. Bridges.**

10. **Criticism of thirteen Epitaphs.**

POPE.

ALEXANDER POPE was born in London, May 22, 1688, of parents whose rank or station was never ascertained: we are informed that they were of *gentle blood*; that his father was of a family of which the Earl of Downe was the head; and that his mother was the daughter of William Turner, Esquire, of York, who had likewise three sons, one of whom had the honour of being killed, and the other of dying, in the service of Charles the First; the third was made a general officer in Spain, from whom the sister inherited what sequestrations and forfeitures had left in the family.

This, and this only, is told by Pope; who is more willing, as I have heard observed, to show what his father was not, than what he was. It is allowed that he grew rich by trade; but whether in a shop or on the Exchange was never discovered till Mr. Tyers told, on the authority of Mrs. Racket, that he was a linen-draper in the Strand. Both parents were papists.

Pope was from his birth of a constitution tender and delicate; but is said to have shown remarkable gentleness and sweetness of disposition. The weakness of his body continued through his life; but the mildness of his mind perhaps ended with his childhood. His voice when he was young was so pleasing, that he was called in fondness the *little Nightingale*.

Being not sent early to school, he was taught to read by an aunt; and when he was seven or eight years old, became a lover of books. He first learned to write by imitating printed books; a species of penmanship in which he retained great excellence through his whole life, though his ordinary hand was not elegant. When he was about eight, he was placed in Hampshire, under Taverner, a Romish priest, who, by a method very rarely practised, taught him the Greek and Latin rudiments together. He was now first regularly initiated in poetry by the perusal of Ogylby's Homer, and Sandys' Ovid. Ogylby's assistance he never repaid with any praise; but of Sandys he declared, in his notes to the Iliad, that English poetry owed much of its present beauty to his translations. Sandys very rarely attempted original composition.

From the care of Taverner, under whom his proficiency was considerable, he was removed to a school at Twyford, near Winchester, and again to another school about Hydepark Corner; from which he used sometimes to stroll to the play-house; and was so delighted with theatrical exhibitions, that he formed a kind of play from Ogylby's Iliad, with some verses of his own intermixed, which he persuaded his schoolfellows to act, with the addition of his master's gardener, who personated Ajax.

At the two last schools he used to represent himself as having lost part of what Taverner had taught him; and on his master at Twyford he had already exercised his poetry in a lampoon. Yet under those masters he translated more than a fourth part of the Metamorphoses. If he kept the same proportion in his other exercises, it cannot be thought that his loss was great. He tells of himself, in his poems, that he *lisp'd in numbers*; and used to say, that he could not remember the time when he began to make verses. In the style of fiction it might have been said of him as of Pindar, that when he lay in his cradle, *the bees swarmed about his mouth.*

About the time of the Revolution, his father, who was undoubtedly disappointed by the sudden blast of popish prosperity, quitted his trade, and retired to Binfield in Windsor Forest, with about twenty thousand pounds; for which, being conscientiously determined not to entrust it to the government, he found no better use than that of locking it up in a chest, and taking from it what his expenses required; and his life was long enough to consume a great part of it, before his son came to the inheritance.

To Binfield, Pope was called by his father when he was about twelve years old; and there he had for a few months the assistance of one, Deane, another priest, of whom he learned only to construe a little of Tully's Offices. How Mr. Deane could spend, with a boy who had translated so much of Ovid, some months over a small part of Tully's Offices, it is now vain to enquire. Of a youth so successfully employed, and so conspicuously improved, a minute account must be naturally desired; but curiosity must be contented with confused, imperfect, and sometimes improbable intelligence. Pope, finding little advantage from external help, resolved thenceforward to direct himself, and at twelve formed a plan of study, which he completed with little other incitement than the desire of excellence. His primary and principal purpose was to be a poet, with which his father accidentally concurred, by proposing subjects, and obliging him to correct his performances by many revisals; after which the old gentleman, when he was satisfied, would say, *these are good rhymes*. In his perusal of the English poets, he soon distinguished the versification of Dryden, which he considered as the model to be studied, and was impressed with such veneration for his instructor, that he persuaded some friends to take him to the coffee-house which Dryden frequented, and pleased himself with having seen him.

Dryden died May 1, 1701, some days before Pope was twelve; so early must he therefore have felt the power of

harmony, and the zeal of genius. Who does not wish that Dryden could have known the value of the homage that was paid him, and foreseen the greatness of his young admirer?
The earliest of Pope's productions is his Ode on Solitude, written before he was twelve, in which there is nothing more than other forward boys have attained, and which is not equal to Cowley's performances at the same age. His time was now spent wholly in reading and writing. As he read the classics, he amused himself with translating
10 them; and at fourteen made a version of the first book of the Thebais, which, with some revision, he afterwards published. He must have been at this time, if he had no help, a considerable proficient in the Latin tongue.
By Dryden's Fables, which had then been not long published, and were much in the hands of poetical readers, he was tempted to try his own skill in giving Chaucer a more fashionable appearance, and put January and May, and the Prologue of the Wife of Bath, into modern English. He translated likewise, the Epistle of Sappho
20 to Phaon, from Ovid, to complete the version, which was before, imperfect; and wrote some other small pieces, which he afterwards printed. He sometimes imitated the English poets, and professed to have written at fourteen, his poem upon Silence, after Rochester's Nothing. He had now formed his versification, and in the smoothness of his numbers surpassed his original: but this is a small part of his praise; he discovers such acquaintance both with human life and public affairs, as is not easily conceived to have been attainable by a boy of fourteen in Windsor Forest.
30 Next year, he was desirous of opening to himself new sources of knowledge, by making himself acquainted with modern languages; and removed for a time to London, that he might study French and Italian, which, as he desired nothing more than to read them, were by diligent application soon despatched. Of Italian learning he does not appear to have ever made much use in his subsequent studies.

He then returned to Binfield, and delighted himself with his own poetry. [He tried all styles, and many subjects. He wrote a comedy, a tragedy, an epic poem, with panegyrics on all the princes of Europe ; and, as he confesses, *thought himself the greatest genius that ever was.* Self-confidence is the first requisite to great undertakings ; he, indeed, who forms his opinion of himself in solitude, without knowing the powers of other men, is very liable to error; but it was the felicity of Pope to rate himself at his real value.]

Most of his puerile productions were, by his maturer judgment, afterwards destroyed ; Alcander, the epic poem, was burnt by the persuasion of Atterbury. The tragedy was founded on the legend of St. Genevieve. Of the comedy there is no account. Concerning his studies it is related, that he translated Tully on Old Age ; and that, besides his books of poetry and criticism, he read Temple's Essays, and Locke on Human Understanding. His reading, though his favourite authors are not known, appears to have been sufficiently extensive and multifarious ; for his early pieces show, with sufficient evidence, his knowledge of books.

He, that is pleased with himself, easily imagines that he shall please others. Sir William Trumbal, who had been ambassador at Constantinople, and secretary of state, when he retired from business, fixed his residence in the neighbourhood of Binfield. Pope, not yet sixteen, was introduced to the statesman of sixty, and so distinguished himself, that their interviews ended in friendship and correspondence. Pope was, through his whole life, ambitious of splendid acquaintance, and he seems to have wanted neither diligence nor success in attracting the notice of the great ; for, from his first entrance into the world, and his entrance was very early, he was admitted to familiarity with those whose rank or station made them most conspicuous.

From the age of sixteen, the life of Pope, as an author, may be properly computed. He now wrote his Pastorals, which were shown to the poets and critics of that time; as they well deserved, they were read with admiration, and many praises were bestowed upon them and upon the Preface, which is both elegant and learned in a high degree: they were, however, not published till five years afterwards.

Cowley, Milton, and Pope are distinguished among the English poets by the early exertion of their powers; but the
10 works of Cowley alone were published in his childhood, and therefore of him only can it be certain that his puerile performances received no improvement from his maturer studies.

At this time began his acquaintance with Wycherley, a man who seems to have had among his contemporaries his full share of reputation, to have been esteemed without virtue, and caressed without good-humour. Pope was proud of his notice; Wycherley wrote verses in his praise, which he was charged by Dennis with writing to himself, and they
20 agreed for a while to flatter one another. It is pleasant to remark how soon Pope learned the cant of an author, and began to treat critics with contempt, though he had yet suffered nothing from them. But the fondness of Wycherley was too violent to last. His esteem of Pope was such, that he submitted some poems to his revision; and when Pope, perhaps proud of such confidence, was sufficiently bold in his criticisms, and liberal in his alterations, the old scribbler was angry to see his pages defaced, and felt more pain from the detection than content from the amendment of his faults.
30 They parted; but Pope always considered him with kindness, and visited him a little time before he died.

Another of his early correspondents was Mr. Cromwell, of whom I have learned nothing particular but that he used to ride a-hunting in a tye-wig. He was fond, and perhaps vain, of amusing himself with poetry and criticism; and sometimes sent his performances to Pope, who did not forbear such remarks as were now-and-then unwelcome. Pope, in his turn, put the juvenile version of Statius into his hands for correction.

Their correspondence afforded the public its first knowledge of Pope's Epistolary Powers; for his Letters were given by Cromwell to one Mrs. Thomas; and she, many years afterwards, sold them to Curll, who inserted them in a volume of his Miscellanies.

Walsh, a name yet preserved among the minor poets, was one of his first encouragers. His regard was gained by the Pastorals, and from him Pope received the counsel by which he seems to have regulated his studies. Walsh advised him to correctness, which, as he told him, the English poets had hitherto neglected, and which therefore was left to him as a basis of fame; and, being delighted with rural poems, recommended to him to write a pastoral comedy, like those which are read so eagerly in Italy; a design which Pope probably did not approve, as he did not follow it.

Pope had now declared himself a poet; and thinking himself entitled to poetical conversation, began at seventeen to frequent Will's, a coffee-house on the north side of Russell-street in Convent-garden, where the wits of that time used to assemble, and where Dryden had, when he lived, been accustomed to preside. During this period of his life he was indefatigably diligent, and insatiably curious; wanting health for violent, and money for expensive pleasures, and having certainly excited in himself very strong desires of intellectual eminence, he spent much of his time over his books; but he read only to store his mind with facts and images, seizing all that his authors presented with undistinguishing voracity, and with an appetite for knowledge too eager to be nice. In a mind like his, however, all the faculties were at once involuntarily improving. Judgement is forced upon us by experience. He, that reads many books must compare one opinion or one style with another; and, when he compares, must necessarily distinguish, reject, and prefer. But the account given by himself of his studies was, that from fourteen to twenty he read only for amusement, from twenty to twenty-seven for improvement and instruction; that in the first part of this time, he desired only to know, and in the second he endeavoured to judge.

The Pastorals, which had been for some time handed about among poets and critics, were at last printed (1709) in Tonson's Miscellany, in a volume which began with the Pastorals of Philips, and ended with those of Pope.

The same year was written the Essay on Criticism; a work which displays such extent of comprehension, such nicety of distinction, such acquaintance with mankind, and such knowledge both of ancient and modern learning, as are not often attained by the maturest age and longest experience. It was published about two years afterwards; and, being praised by Addison in the Spectator, with sufficient liberality, met with so much favour as enraged Dennis, "who," he says, "found himself attacked, without any manner of provocation on his side, and attacked in his person instead of his writings, by one who was wholly a stranger to him, at a time when all the world knew he was persecuted by fortune; and not only saw that this was attempted in a clandestine manner, with the utmost falsehood and calumny, but found that all this was done by a little affected hypocrite, who had nothing in his mouth at the same time but truth, candour, friendship, good-nature, humanity, and magnanimity."

How the attack was clandestine is not easily perceived, nor how his person is depreciated; but he seems to have known something of Pope's character, in whom may be discovered an appetite to talk too frequently of his own virtues. The pamphlet is such as rage might be expected to dictate. He supposes himself to be asked two questions; whether the Essay will succeed, and who or what is the author.

Its success he admits to be secured by the false opinions

then prevalent; the author he concludes to be *young and raw.*

"First, because he discovers a sufficiency beyond his little ability, and hath rashly undertaken a task infinitely above his force. Secondly, while this little author struts, and affects the dictatorian air, he plainly shows that at the same time he is under the rod; and, while he pretends to give laws to others, is a pedantic slave to authority and opinion. Thirdly, he hath, like schoolboys, borrowed both from living and dead. Fourthly, he knows not his own mind, and frequently contradicts himself. Fifthly, he is almost perpetually in the wrong."

All these positions he attempts to prove by quotations and remarks; but his desire to do mischief is greater than his power. He has, however, justly criticised some passages. In these lines,

> There are whom Heaven has bless'd with store of wit,
> Yet want as much again to manage it;
> For wit and judgement ever are at strife—

it is apparent that *wit* has two meanings, and that what is wanted, though called *wit*, is truly judgement. . . .

In another place, Pope himself allowed that Dennis had detected one of those blunders which are called *bulls.* The first edition had this line:

> What is this wit—
> Where wanted scorn'd; and envied where acquired?

"How," says the critic, "can wit be *scorn'd* where it is not? Is not this a figure frequently employed in Hibernian land? The person that wants this wit may indeed be scorned, but the scorn shews the honour which the contemner has for wit." Of this remark Pope made the proper use, by correcting the passage.

I have preserved, I think, all that is reasonable in Dennis's criticism; it remains that justice be done to his delicacy.

"For his aquaintance (says Dennis) he names Mr. Walsh, who had by no means the qualification which this author reckons absolutely necessary to a critic, it being very certain that he was, like this Essayer, a very indifferent poet; he loved to be well-dressed; and I remember a little young gentleman whom Mr. Walsh used to take into his company as a double foil to his person and capacity.—Enquire, between Sunninghill and Oakingham, for a young, short, squab gentleman, the very bow of the God of Love, and tell me whether he be a proper author to make personal reflections?—He may extol the ancients, but he has reason to thank the gods that he was born a modern; for had he been born of Grecian parents, and his father consequently had by law had the absolute disposal of him, his life had been no longer than that of one of his poems, the life of half a day.— Let the person of a gentleman of his parts be never so contemptible, his inward man is ten times more ridiculous; it being impossible that his outward form, though it be that of downright monkey, should differ so much from human shape as his unthinking immaterial part does from human understanding." Thus began the hostility between Pope and Dennis, which, though it was suspended for a short time, never was appeased. Pope seems, at first, to have attacked him wantonly; but though he always professed to despise him, he discovers, by mentioning him very often, that he felt his force or his venom.

Of this Essay, Pope declared, that he did not expect the sale to be quick, because *not one gentleman in sixty, even of liberal education, could understand it.* The gentlemen, and the education of that time, seem to have been of a lower character than they are of this. He mentioned a thousand copies as a numerous impression.

Dennis was not his only censurer: the zealous papists thought the monks treated with too much contempt, and Erasmus too studiously praised; but to these objections he had not much regard.

The Essay has been translated into French by Hamilton, author of the Comte de Grammont, whose version was never printed; by Robotham, secretary to the King for Hanover, and by Resnel; and commented by Dr. Warburton, who has discovered in it such order and connection as was not perceived by Addison, nor, as is said, intended by the author.

Almost every poem, consisting of precepts, is so far arbitrary and immethodical, that many of the paragraphs may change places with no apparent inconvenience; for of two or more positions, depending upon some remote and general principle, there is seldom any cogent reason why one should precede the other. But for the order in which they stand, whatever it be, a little ingenuity may easily give a reason. *It is possible,* says Hooker, *that, by long circumduction, from any one truth all truth may be inferred.* Of all homogeneous truths at least, of all truths respecting the same general end, in whatever series they may be produced, a concatenation by intermediate ideas may be formed, such as, when it is once shown, shall appear natural; but if this order be reversed, another mode of connection equally specious may be found or made. Aristotle is praised for naming Fortitude first of the cardinal virtues, as that without which no other virtue can steadily be practised; but he might, with equal propriety, have placed Prudence and Justice before it; since without Prudence, Fortitude is mad; without Justice, it is mischievous. As the end of method is perspicuity, that series is sufficiently regular that avoids obscurity; and where there is no obscurity, it will not be difficult to discover method.

In the Spectator was published the Messiah, which he first submitted to the perusal of Steele, and corrected in compliance with his criticisms. It is reasonable to infer, from his Letters, that the verses on the Unfortunate Lady, were written about the time when his Essay was published. The lady's name and adventures I have sought

with fruitless enquiry. I can therefore tell no more than
I have learned from Mr. Ruffhead, who writes with the
confidence of one who could trust his information. She was
a woman of eminent rank and large fortune, the ward of an
uncle, who, having given her a proper education, expected
like other guardians that she should make at least an equal
match; and such he proposed to her, but found it rejected in
favour of a young gentleman of inferior condition.

Having discovered the correspondence between the two
10 lovers, and finding the young lady determined to abide by her
own choice, he supposed that separation might do what can
rarely be done by arguments, and sent her into a foreign
country, where she was obliged to converse only with those
from whom her uncle had nothing to fear. Her lover took
care to repeat his vows; but his letters were intercepted and
carried to her guardian, who directed her to be watched
with still greater vigilance; till of this restraint she grew so
impatient, that she bribed a woman-servant to procure her a
sword, which she directed to her heart.

20 From this account, given with evident intention to raise
the lady's character, it does not appear that she had any
claim to praise, nor much to compassion. She seems to have
been impatient, violent, and ungovernable. Her uncle's
power could not have lasted long; the hour of liberty and
choice would have come in time. But her desires were too
hot for delay, and she liked self-murder better than suspense.

Nor is it discovered that the uncle, whoever he was,
is with much justice delivered to posterity as *a false*
30 *guardian*; he seems to have done only that for which a
guardian is appointed; he endeavoured to direct his niece
till she should be able to direct herself. Poetry has not
often been worse employed than in dignifying the amorous
fury of a raving girl.

Not long after, he wrote the Rape of the Lock, the most
airy, the most ingenious, and the most delightful of all his

JOHNSON'S LIFE OF POPE. 13

compositions, occasioned by a frolic of gallantry, rather too familiar, in which Lord Petre cut off a lock of Mrs. Arabella Fermor's hair. This, whether stealth or violence, was so much resented, that the commerce of the two families, before very friendly, was interrupted. Mr. Caryl, a gentleman, who, being secretary to King James's queen, had followed his mistress into France, and who being the author of Sir Solomon Single, a comedy, and some translations, was entitled to the notice of a wit, solicited Pope to endeavour a reconciliation by a ludicrous poem, which might bring both 10 the parties to a better temper. In compliance with Caryl's request, though his name was for a long time marked only by the first and last letter, C—l, a poem of two cantos was written (1711), as is said, in a fortnight, and sent to the offended lady, who liked it well enough to show it; and, with the usual process of literary transactions, the author, dreading a surreptitious edition, was forced to publish it.

The event is said to have been such as was desired, the pacification and diversion of all to whom it related, except Sir George Brown, who complained with some bitterness 20 that, in the character of Sir Plume, he was made to talk nonsense. Whether all this be true I have some doubt; for at Paris, a few years ago, a niece of Mrs. Fermor, who presided in an English convent, mentioned Pope's work with very little gratitude, rather as an insult than an honour; and she may be supposed to have inherited the opinion of her family.

At its first appearance, it was termed by Addison *merum sal*. Pope, however, saw that it was capable of improvement; and, having luckily contrived to borrow his 30 machinery from the Rosicrucians, imparted the scheme with which his head was teeming, to Addison, who told him that his work, as it stood, was *a delicious little thing*, and gave him no encouragement to retouch it.

This has been too hastily considered as an instance of Addison's jealousy; for, as he could not guess the conduct of the new design, or the possibilities of pleasure comprised in a fiction of which there had been no examples, he might very reasonably and kindly persuade the author to acquiesce in his own prosperity, and forbear an attempt which he considered as an unnecessary hazard. Addison's counsel was happily rejected. Pope foresaw the future efflorescence of imagery then budding in his mind, and resolved to spare no art, or industry of cultivation. The soft luxuriance of his fancy was already shooting, and all the gay varieties of diction were ready at his hand, to colour and embellish it.

His attempt was justified by its success. The Rape of the Lock stands forward, in the classes of literature, as the most exquisite example of ludicrous poetry. Berkeley congratulated him upon the display of powers more truly poetical than he had shown before; with elegance of description and justness of precepts, he had now exhibited boundless fertility of invention. He always considered the intermixture of the machinery with the action, as his most successful exertion of poetical art. He indeed could never afterwards produce anything of such unexampled excellence. Those performances, which strike with wonder, are combinations of skilful genius with happy casualty; and it is not likely that any felicity, like the discovery of a new race of preternatural agents, should happen twice to the same man.

Of this poem, the author was, I think, allowed to enjoy the praise for a long time without disturbance. Many years afterwards, Dennis published some remarks upon it, with very little force, and with no effect; for the opinion of the public was already settled, and it was no longer at the mercy of criticism.

About this time, he published the Temple of Fame, which, as he tells Steele in their correspondence, he had written two years before; that is, when he was only twenty-two years old, an early time of life for so much learning and so much observation, as that work exhibits. On this poem Dennis afterwards published some remarks, of which the most reasonable is, that some of the lines represent motion as exhibited by sculpture.

Of the Epistle from Eloisa to Abelard, I do not know the date. His first inclination to attempt a composition of that tender kind, arose, as Mr. Savage told me, from his perusal of Prior's Nut-brown Maid. How much he has surpassed Prior's work it is not necessary to mention, when perhaps it may be said with justice, that he has excelled every composition of the same kind. The mixture of religious hope and resignation gives an elevation and dignity to disappointed love, which images merely natural cannot bestow. The gloom of a convent strikes the imagination with far greater force than the solitude of a grove. This piece was, however, not much his favourite in his latter years, though I never heard upon what principle he slighted it.

In the next year (1713) he published Windsor Forest; of which part was, as he relates, written at sixteen, about the same time as his Pastorals, and the latter part was added afterwards: where the addition begins, we are not told. The lines relating to the Peace confess their own date. It is dedicated to Lord Lansdowne, who was then high in reputation and influence among the Tories; and it is said, that the conclusion of the poem gave great pain to Addison, both as a poet and a politician. Reports like this are often spread with boldness very disproportionate to their evidence. Why should Addison receive any particular disturbance from the last lines of Windsor Forest? If contrariety of opinion could poison a politician, he would not live a day; and, as a poet, he must have felt Pope's force of genius much more from many other parts of his works. The pain that Addison might feel, it is not likely that he would confess; and it is certain that he so well suppressed his discontent, that Pope now thought himself his favourite; for having been consulted in the revisal of Cato, he introduced it by a prologue; and, when Dennis published his Remarks, undertook, not indeed to vindicate, but to revenge his friend, by a Narrative of the Frenzy of John Dennis.

There is reason to believe that Addison gave no encouragement to this disingenuous hostility; for, says Pope, in a letter to him, "indeed your opinion, that 'tis entirely to be neglected, would be my own in my own case; but I felt more warmth here than I did when I first saw his book against myself, (though indeed in two minutes it made me heartily merry)." Addison was not a man on whom such
10 cant of sensibility could make much impression. He left the pamphlet to itself, having disowned it to Dennis, and perhaps did not think Pope to have deserved much by his officiousness.

This year was printed in the Guardian the ironical comparison between the Pastorals of Philips and Pope; a composition of artifice, criticism, and literature, to which nothing equal will easily be found. The superiority of Pope is so ingeniously dissembled, and the feeble lines of Philips so skilfully preferred, that Steele, being deceived, was un-
20 willing to print the paper, lest Pope should be offended. Addison immediately saw the writer's design; and, as it seems, had malice enough to conceal his discovery, and to permit a publication, which, by making his friend Philips ridiculous, made him for ever an enemy to Pope.

It appears that about this time, Pope had a strong inclination to unite the art of painting with that of poetry, and put himself under the tuition of Jervas. He was near-sighted, and therefore not formed by nature for a painter: he tried, however, how far he could advance, and sometimes persuaded
30 his friends to sit. A picture of Betterton, supposed to be drawn by him, was in the possession of Lord Mansfield: if this was taken from the life, he must have begun to paint earlier; for Betterton was now dead. Pope's ambition of this new art produced some encomiastic verses to Jervas, which certainly show his power as a poet, but I have been told that they betray his ignorance of painting. He appears

to have regarded Betterton with kindness and esteem; and after his death, published, under his name, a version into modern English of Chaucer's Prologues, and one of his Tales, which, as was related by Mr. Harte, were believed to have been the performance of Pope himself, by Fenton, who made him a gay offer of five pounds, if he would show them in the hand of Betterton.

The next year (1713) produced a bolder attempt, by which profit was sought as well as praise. The poems which he had hitherto written, however they might have diffused his name, had made very little addition to his fortune. The allowance which his father made him, though, proportioned to what he had, it might be liberal, could not be large; his religion hindered him from the occupation of any civil employment, and he complained that he wanted even money to buy books.

He therefore resolved to try how far the favour of the public extended, by soliciting a subscription to a version of the Iliad, with large notes. To print by subscription was, for some time, a practice peculiar to the English. The first considerable work for which this expedient was employed, is said to have been Dryden's Virgil; and it has been tried again with great success when the Tatlers were collected into volumes.

There was reason to believe that Pope's attempt would be successful. He was in the full bloom of reputation, and was personally known to almost all whom dignity of employment or splendour of reputation had made eminent; he conversed indifferently with both parties, and never disturbed the public with his political opinions; and it might be naturally expected, as each faction then boasted its literary zeal, that the great men, who on other occasions practised all the violence of opposition, would emulate each other in their encouragement of a poet who had delighted all, and by whom none had been offended. With those hopes, he offered an English Iliad to subscribers, in six volumes in quarto, for six guineas; a sum, according to the value of money at that

B

time, by no means inconsiderable, and greater than I believe to have been ever asked before. His proposal, however, was very favourably received, and the patrons of literature were busy to recommend his undertaking, and promote his interest. Lord Oxford, indeed, lamented that such a genius should be wasted upon a work not original; but proposed no means by which he might live without it: Addison recommended caution and moderation, and advised him not to be content with the praise of half the nation, when he might be universally favoured.

The greatness of the design, the popularity of the author, and the attention of the literary world, naturally raised such expectations of the future sale, that the booksellers made their offers with great eagerness; but the highest bidder was Bernard Lintot, who became proprietor on condition of supplying, at his own expense, all the copies which were to be delivered to subscribers, or presented to friends, and paying two hundred pounds for every volume.

Of the Quartos it was, I believe, stipulated, that none should be printed but for the author, that the subscription might not be depreciated; but Lintot impressed the same pages upon a small Folio, and paper perhaps a little thinner; and sold exactly at half the price, for half a guinea each volume, books so little inferior to the Quartos, that by a fraud of trade, those Folios, being afterwards shortened by cutting away the top and bottom, were sold as copies printed for the subscribers.

Lintot printed two hundred and fifty on royal paper in Folio for two guineas a volume; of the small folio, having printed seventeen hundred and fifty copies of the first volume, he reduced the number in the other volumes to a thousand. It is unpleasant to relate that the bookseller, after all his hopes and all his liberality, was, by a very unjust and illegal action, defrauded of his profit. An edition of the English Iliad was printed in Holland in duodecimo, and imported clandestinely for the gratification of those who were impatient to read what they could not yet afford to buy. This fraud could only be counteracted by an edition equally cheap and more commodious; and Lintot was compelled to contract his folio at once into a duodecimo, and lose the advantage of an intermediate gradation. The notes, which in the Dutch copies were placed at the end of each book, as they had been in the large volumes, were now subjoined to the text in the same page, and are therefore more easily consulted. Of this edition two thousand five hundred were first printed, and five thousand a few weeks 10 afterwards; but indeed great numbers were necessary to produce considerable profit.

Pope, having now emitted his proposals, and engaged not only his own reputation, but in some degree that of his friends who patronised his subscription, began to be frighted at his own undertaking; and finding himself at first embarrassed with difficulties, which retarded and oppressed him, he was for a time timorous and uneasy, had his nights disturbed by dreams of long journeys through unknown ways, and wished, as he said, *that somebody* 20 *would hang him.* This misery, however, was not of long continuance; he grew by degrees more acquainted with Homer's images and expressions, and practice increased his facility of versification. In a short time he represents himself as despatching regularly fifty verses a day, which would show him by an easy computation the termination of his labour.

His own diffidence was not his only vexation. He that asks a subscription soon finds that he has enemies. All who do not encourage him defame him. He that wants 30 money will rather be thought angry than poor; and he that wishes to save his money conceals his avarice by his malice. Addison had hinted his suspicion that Pope was too much a Tory; and some of the Tories suspected his principles, because he had contributed to the Guardian, which was carried on by Steele.

To those who censured his politics, were added enemies yet more dangerous, who called in question his knowledge of Greek, and his qualifications for a translator of Homer. To these he made no public opposition; but in one of his Letters escapes from them as well as he can. At an age like his, for he was not more than twenty-five, with an irregular education, and a course of life of which much seems to have passed in conversation, it is not very likely that he overflowed with Greek. But when he felt himself
10 deficient he sought assistance; and what man of learning would refuse to help him? Minute enquiries into the force of words are less necessary in translating Homer than other poets, because his positions are general, and his representations natural, with very little dependence on local or temporary customs, on those changeable scenes of artificial life, which, by mingling original with accidental notions, and crowding the mind with images which time effaces, produce ambiguity in diction, and obscurity in books. To this open display of unadulterated nature it must be ascribed,
20 that Homer has fewer passages of doubtful meaning than any other poet either in the learned or in modern languages. I have read of a man, who being, by his ignorance of Greek, compelled to gratify his curiosity with the Latin printed on the opposite page, declared that from the rude simplicity of the lines literally rendered, he formed nobler ideas of the Homeric majesty than from the laboured elegance of polished versions. Those literal translations were always at hand, and from them he could easily obtain his author's sense with sufficient certainty; and among the readers of
30 Homer the number is very small of those who find much in the Greek more than in the Latin, except the music of the numbers.

If more help was wanting, he had the poetical translation of Eobanus Hessus, an unwearied writer of Latin verses; he had the French Homers of La Valterie and Dacier, and the English of Chapman, Hobbes, and Ogylby. With Chapman, whose work, though now totally neglected, seems to have been popular almost to the end of the last century, he had very frequent consultations, and perhaps never translated any passage till he had read his version, which indeed he has been sometimes suspected of using instead of the original.

Notes were likewise to be provided; for the six volumes would have been very little more than six pamphlets without them. What the mere perusal of the text could suggest, Pope wanted no assistance to collect or methodize; but more was necessary; many pages were to be filled, and learning must supply materials to wit and judgement. Something might be gathered from Dacier; but no man loves to be indebted to his contemporaries, and Dacier was accessible to common readers. Eustathius was therefore necessarily consulted. To read Eustathius, of whose work there was then no Latin version, I suspect Pope, if he had been willing, not to have been able; some other was therefore to be found, who had leisure as well as abilities; and he was doubtless most readily employed who would do much work for little money.

The history of the notes has never been traced. Broome, in his preface to his poems, declares himself the commentator *in part upon the Iliad*; and it appears from Fenton's Letter, preserved in the Museum, that Broome was at first engaged in consulting Eustathius; but that after a time, whatever was the reason, he desisted: another man of Cambridge was then employed, who soon grew weary of the work; and a third, that was recommended by Thirlby, is now discovered to have been Jortin, a man since well known to the learned world, who complained that Pope, having accepted and approved his performance, never testified any curiosity to see him, and who professed to have forgotten the terms on which he worked. The terms which Fenton uses are very mercantile: *I think at first sight that his performance is very commendable, and have sent word for him to finish the seventeenth book, and to send it with his demands for his trouble. I have here enclosed the specimen; if the rest come before the return, I will keep them till I receive your order.*

Broome then offered his service a second time, which was probably accepted, as they had afterwards a closer correspondence. Parnell contributed the Life of Homer, which Pope found so harsh, that he took great pains in correcting it; and by his own diligence, with such help as kindness or money could procure him, in somewhat more
10 than five years he completed his version of the Iliad, with the notes. He began it in 1712, his twenty-fifth year, and concluded it in 1718, his thirtieth year. When we find him translating fifty lines a day, it is natural to suppose that he would have brought his work to a more speedy conclusion. The Iliad, containing less than sixteen thousand verses, might have been despatched in less than three hundred and twenty days by fifty verses in a day. The notes, compiled with the assistance of his mercenaries, could not be supposed to require more time than the text. According to this
20 calculation, the progress of Pope may seem to have been slow; but the distance is commonly very great between actual performances and speculative possibility. [It is natural to suppose, that as much as has been done to-day may be done to-morrow; but on the morrow some difficulty emerges, or some external impediment obstructs. Indolence, interruption, business, and pleasure, all take their turns of retardation; and every long work is lengthened by a thousand causes that can, and ten thousand that cannot, be recounted. Perhaps no extensive and multifarious per-
30 formance was ever effected within the term originally fixed in the undertaker's mind. He that runs against Time has an antagonist not subject to casualties.]

The encouragement given to this translation, though report seems to have over-rated it, was such as the world has not often seen. The subscribers were five hundred and seventy-five. The copies for which subscriptions were given, were six hundred and fifty-four ; and only six hundred and sixty were printed. For those copies Pope had nothing to pay ; he therefore received, including the two hundred pounds a volume, five thousand three hundred and twenty pounds four shillings, without deduction, as the books were supplied by Lintot.

By the success of his subscription, Pope was relieved from those pecuniary distresses, with which, notwithstanding his popularity, he had hitherto struggled. Lord Oxford had often lamented his disqualification for public employment, 10 but never proposed a pension. While the translation of Homer was in its progress, Mr. Craggs, then secretary of state, offered to procure him a pension, which, at least during his ministry, might be enjoyed with secrecy. This was not accepted by Pope, who told him, however, that, if he should be pressed with want of money, he would send to him for occasional supplies. Craggs was not long in power, and was never solicited for money by Pope, who disdained to beg what he did not want.

With the product of this subscription, which he had too 20 much discretion to squander, he secured his future life from want, by considerable annuities. The estate of the Duke of Buckingham was found to have been charged with five hundred pounds a year, payable to Pope, which doubtless his translation enabled him to purchase.

It cannot be unwelcome to literary curiosity, that I deduce thus minutely the history of the English Iliad. It is certainly the noblest version of poetry which the world has ever seen ; and its publication must therefore be considered as one of the great events in the annals of Learning. To 30 those who have skill to estimate the excellence and difficulty of this great work, it must be very desirable to know how it was performed, and by what gradations it advanced to correctness. Of such an intellectual process the knowledge has very rarely been attainable ; but happily there remains the original copy of the Iliad, which, being obtained by

Bolingbroke as a curiosity, descended from him to Mallet, and is now by the solicitation of the late Dr. Maty reposited in the Museum. Between this manuscript, which is written upon accidental fragments of paper, and the printed edition, there must have been an intermediate copy, that was perhaps destroyed as it returned from the press.

From the first copy I have procured a few transcripts, and shall exhibit first the printed lines; then, in a smaller print, those of the manuscripts, with all their variations. Those
10 words in the small print which are given in italics are cancelled in the copy, and the words placed under them adopted in their stead.

The beginning of the first book stands thus:

> The wrath of Peleus' son, the direful spring
> Of all the Grecian woes, O Goddess, sing,
> That wrath which hurl'd to Pluto's gloomy reign
> The souls of mighty chiefs untimely slain

> The stern Pelides' *rage*, O Goddess, sing,
>   wrath
20   Of all the woes *of Greece* the fatal spring,
>   Grecian
>   That strewed with *warriors* dead the Phrygian plain,
>   heroes
>   And *peopled the dark hell with heroes* slain;
>   fill'd the shady hell with chiefs untimely

> Whose limbs, unburied on the naked shore,
> Devouring dogs and hungry vultures tore,
> Since great Achilles and Atrides strove;
> Such was the sovereign doom, and such the will of Jove.

30   Whose limbs, unburied on the hostile shore,
>   Devouring dogs and greedy vultures tore,
>   Since first *Atrides* and *Achilles* strove;
>   Such was the sovereign doom, and such the will of Jove.

> Declare, O Muse, in what ill-fated hour
> Sprung the fierce strife, from what offended Power!
> Latona's son a dire contagion spread,
> And heap'd the camp with mountains of the dead;

The King of men his reverend priest defy'd,
And for the King's offence the people dy'd.

> Declare, O Goddess, what offended Power
> Enflamed their *rage*, in that *ill-omen'd* hour;
>   anger   fatal, hapless
> Phœbus himself the *dire* debate procured,
>   fierce
> T' avenge the wrongs his injured priest endured;
> For this the God a dire infection spread,
> And heap'd the camp with millions of the dead: 10
> The King of Men the Sacred Sire defy'd,
> And for the King's offence the people dy'd.

For Chryses sought with costly gifts to gain
His captive daughter from the Victor's chain;
Suppliant the venerable Father stands,
Apollo's awful ensigns grace his hands;
By these he begs, and, lowly bending down,
Extends the sceptre and the laurel crown.

> For Chryses sought by *presents to regain*
>   costly gifts to gain 20
> His captive daughter from the Victor's chain;
> Suppliant the venerable Father stands,
> Apollo's awful ensigns grac'd his hands.
> By these he begs, and, lowly bending down
> *The golden sceptre* and the laurel crown,
> Presents the sceptre
> *For these as ensigns of his God he bare,*
> *The God that sends his golden shafts afar;*
> Then low on earth the venerable man,
> Suppliant before the brother kings began. 30

He sued to all, but chief implored for grace,
The brother kings of Atreus' royal race;
Ye kings and warriors, may your vows be crown'd,
And Troy's proud walls lie level with the ground;
May Jove restore you, when your toils are o'er,
Safe to the pleasures of your native shore.

> To all he sued, but chief implor'd for grace
> The brother kings of Atreus' royal race.

JOHNSON'S LIFE OF POPE.

> Ye *sons of Atreus*, may your vows be crown'd,
>   Kings and warriors
> *Your labours, by the Gods be all your labours crown'd;*
> *So may the Gods your arms with conquest bless,*
> *And* Troy's proud walls *lie* level with the ground;
> Till   laid
> *And crown your labours with deserved success;*
> May Jove restore you, when your toils are o'er,
> Safe to the pleasures of your native shore.

10   But, oh! relieve a wretched parent's pain,
     And give Chryseis to these arms again;
     If mercy fail, yet let my present move,
     And dread avenging Phœbus, son of Jove.

> But, oh! relieve a hapless parent's pain,
> And give my daughter to these arms again;
> *Receive my gifts;* if mercy fails, yet let my present move,
> And fear *the God that deals his darts around,*
>   avenging Phœbus, son of Jove.

     The Greeks, in shouts, their joint assent declare
20   The priest to reverence, and release the fair.
     Not so Atrides; he with kingly pride,
     Repulsed the sacred Sire, and thus reply'd.

> He said, the Greeks their joint assent declare,
> *The father said, the gen'rous Greeks relent,*
> T' accept the ransom, and release the fair;
> *Revere the priest, and speak their joint assent;*
> Not so *the tyrant,* he, with kingly pride,
>   Atrides
> Repuls'd the sacred Sire, and thus reply'd.
30   [Not so the tyrant. DRYDEN.]

Of these lines, and of the whole first book, I am told that there was yet a former copy, more varied, and more deformed with interlineations.

The beginning of the second book varies very little from the printed page, and is therefore set down without any parallel; the few differences do not require to be elaborately displayed.

> Now pleasing sleep had seal'd each mortal eye:
> Stretch'd in their tents the Grecian leaders lie;

Th' Immortals slumber'd on their thrones above,
All but the ever-watchful eye of Jove.
To honour Thetis' son he bends his care,
And plunge the Greeks in all the woes of war.
Then bids an empty phantom rise to sight,
And thus *commands* the vision of the night:
      directs
Fly hence, delusive dream, and, light as air,
To Agamemnon's royal tent repair;
Bid him in arms draw forth th' embattled train,   10
March all his legions to the dusty plain.
Now tell the King 'tis given him to destroy,
Declare ev'n now
The lofty *walls* of wide-extended Troy;
      tow'rs
For now no more the Gods with Fate contend;
At Juno's suit the heavenly factions end.
Destruction *hovers* o'er yon devoted wall,
      hangs
And nodding Ilium waits th' impending fall.   20

Invocation to the catalogue of ships.

   Say, virgins, seated round the throne divine,
   All-knowing Goddesses! immortal Nine!
   Since earth's wide regions, heaven's unmeasured height,
   And hell's abyss, hide nothing from your sight,
   (We, wretched mortals! lost in doubts below,
   But guess by rumour, and but boast we know)
   Oh say what heroes, fired by thirst of fame,
   Or urged by wrongs, to Troy's destruction came!
   To count them all, demands a thousand tongues,   30
   A throat of brass and adamantine lungs.

      Now, Virgin Goddesses, immortal Nine!
      That round Olympus' heavenly summit shine,
      Who see through Heaven and Earth, and Hell profound,
      And all things know, and all things can resound!
      Relate what armies sought the Trojan land,
      What nations follow'd, and what chiefs command;

(For doubtful Fame distracts mankind below,
And nothing can we tell, and nothing know)
Without your aid, to count th' unnumber'd train,
A thousand mouths, a thousand tongues, were vain,

Book V. v. 1.

But Pallas now Tydides' soul inspires,
Fills with her force, and warms with all her fires:
Above the Greeks his deathless fame to raise,
And crown her hero with distinguish'd praise,
High on his helm celestial lightnings play,
10   His beamy shield emits a living ray;
Th' unwearied blaze incessant streams supplies,
Like the red star that fires the autumnal skies.

But Pallas now Tydides' soul inspires,
Fills with her *rage*, and warms with all her fires:
    force
O'er all the Greeks decrees his fame to raise,
Above the Greeks *her warrior's* fame to raise,
    his deathless
And crown her hero with *immortal* praise;
    distinguish'd
20   *Bright from* his beamy *crest* the lightnings play,
High on   helm
From his broad buckler flash'd the living ray;
High on his helm celestial lightnings play,
His beamy shield emits a living ray;
The Goddess with her breath the flame supplies,
Bright as the star whose fires in Autumn rise;
Her breath divine thick streaming flames supplies,
Bright as the star that fires th' autumnal skies;
Th' unwearied blaze incessant streams supplies,
30   Like the red star that fires th' autumnal skies.

When first he rears his radiant orb to sight,
And bath'd in ocean shoots a keener light,
Such glories Pallas on the chief bestow'd,
Such from his arms the fierce effulgence flow'd;
Onward she drives him, furious to engage,
Where the fight burns, and where the thickest rage.

When fresh he rears his radiant orb to sight,
And gilds old Ocean with a blaze of light,

Bright as the star that fires th' autumnal skies,
Fresh from the deep, and gilds the seas and skies:
Such glories Pallas on her chief bestow'd,
Such sparkling rays from his bright armour flow'd,
Such from his arms the fierce effulgence flow'd;
Onward she drives him *headlong* to engage,
      furious
Where the *war bleeds*, and where the *fiercest* rage.
  fight burns   thickest

The sons of Dares first the combat sought, 10
A wealthy priest, but rich without a fault;
In Vulcan's fane the father's days were led,
The sons to toils of glorious battle bred;

  There lived a Trojan—Dares was his name,
  The priest of Vulcan, rich, yet void of blame;
  The sons of Dares first the combat sought,
  A wealthy priest, but rich without a fault.

Conclusion of Book VIII. *v.* 687.

As when the moon, refulgent lamp of night,
O'er Heaven's clear azure spreads her sacred light;
When not a breath disturbs the deep serene, 20
And not a cloud o'ercasts the solemn scene;
Around her throne the vivid planets roll,
And stars unnumber'd gild the glowing pole;
O'er the dark trees a yellower verdure shed,
And tip with silver every mountain's head:
Then shine the vales—the rocks in prospect rise,
A flood of glory bursts from all the skies;
The conscious swains, rejoicing in the sight,
Eye the blue vault, and bless the useful light.
So many flames before proud Ilion blaze, 30
And lighten glimmering Xanthus with their rays;
The long reflections of the distant fires
Gleam on the walls, and tremble on the spires.
A thousand piles the dusky horrors gild,
And shoot a shady lustre o'er the field;

Full fifty guards each flaming pile attend,
Whose umber'd arms by fits thick flashes send;
Loud neigh the coursers o'er their heaps of corn,
And ardent warriors wait the rising morn.

As when in stillness of the silent night,
As when the moon in all her lustre bright,
As when the moon, refulgent lamp of night,
O'er Heaven's *clear* azure *sheds* her *silver* light;
     pure   spreads sacred
As still in air the trembling lustre stood,
And o'er its golden border shoots a flood;
When *no loose gale* disturbs the deep serene,
    not a breath
And *no dim* cloud o'ercasts the solemn scene;
    not a
Around her silver throne the planets glow,
And stars unnumber'd trembling beams bestow;
Around her throne the vivid planets roll,
And stars unnumber'd gild the glowing pole;
Clear gleams of light o'er the dark trees are seen,
     o'er the dark trees a yellow sheds
O'er the dark trees a yellower *green* they shed,
     gleam
     verdure
And tip with silver all the *mountain* heads
     forest
And tip with silver every mountain's head.
The valleys open, and the forests rise,
The vales appear, the rocks in prospect rise,
Then shine the vales, the rocks in prospect rise
All Nature stands reveal'd before our eyes;
A flood of glory bursts from all the skies.
The conscious shepherd, joyful at the sight,
Eyes the blue vault, and numbers every light.
The conscious *swains rejoicing at the sight*,
     shepherds gazing with delight
Eye the blue vault, and bless the *vivid* light,
     glorious
     useful
So many flames before *the navy* blaze,
     proud Ilion
And lighten glimmering Xanthus with their rays
Wide o'er the fields to Troy extend the gleams
And tip the distant spires with fainter beams

The long reflections of the distant fires
Gild the high walls, and tremble on the spires;
Gleam on the walls, and tremble on the spires;
A thousand fires at distant stations bright,
Gild the dark prospect, and dispel the night.

Of these specimens every man who has cultivated poetry, or who delights to trace the mind from the rudeness of its first conceptions to the elegance of its last, will naturally desire a greater number; but most other readers are already tired, and I am not writing only to poets and philosophers.

The Iliad was published volume by volume, as the translation proceeded ; the four first books appeared in 1715. The expectation of this work was undoubtedly high, and every man who had connected his name with criticism, or poetry, was desirous of such intelligence as might enable him to talk upon the popular topic. Halifax, who, by having been first a poet, and then a patron of poetry, had acquired the right of being a judge, was willing to hear some books while they were yet unpublished. Of this rehearsal Pope afterwards gave the following account.

"The famous Lord Halifax was rather a pretender to taste than really possessed of it.—When I had finished the two or three first books of my translation of the Iliad, that Lord desired to have the pleasure of hearing them read at his house. Addison, Congreve, and Garth, were there at the reading. In four or five places, Lord Halifax stopped me very civilly, and with a speech each time of much the same kind, 'I beg your pardon, Mr. Pope ; but there is something in that passage that does not quite please me. Be so good as to mark the place, and consider it a little at your leisure. I am sure you can give it a little turn.'—I returned from Lord Halifax's with Dr. Garth, in his chariot ; and, as we were going along, was saying to the Doctor, that my Lord had laid me under a good deal of difficulty by such loose and general observations ; that I had been thinking over the passages almost ever since, and could not guess at what it was that offended

his lordship in either of them. Garth laughed heartily at my embarrassment: said, I had not been long enough acquainted with Lord Halifax to know his way yet; that I need not puzzle myself about looking those places over and over when I got home. 'All you need do (says he) is to leave them just as they are; call on Lord Halifax two or three months hence, thank him for his kind observations on those passages, and then read them to him as altered. I have known him much longer than you have, and will be
10 answerable for the event.' I followed his advice; waited on Lord Halifax some time after; said, I hoped he would find his objections to those passages removed; read them to him exactly as they were at first: and his lordship was extremely pleased with them, and cried out, *Ay, now they are perfectly right: nothing can be better."*

It is seldom that the great or the wise suspect that they are despised or cheated. Halifax, thinking this a lucky opportunity of securing immortality, made some advances of favour and some overtures of advantage to Pope, which
20 he seems to have received wlth sullen coldness. All our knowledge of this transaction is derived from a single letter (Dec. 1, 1714), in which Pope says, "I am obliged to you, both for the favours you have done me, and those you intend me. I distrust neither your will nor your memory, when it is to do good; and if I ever become troublesome or solicitous, it must not be out of expectation, but out of gratitude. Your Lordship may cause me to live agreeably in the town, or contentedly in the country, which is really all the difference I set between an easy fortune and a small one. It is indeed
30 a high strain of generosity in you to think of making me easy all my life, only because I have been so happy as to divert you some few hours: but, if I may have leave to add it is because you think me no enemy to my native country, there will appear a better reason; for I must of consequence be very much (as I sincerely am) yours, &c."

These voluntary offers, and this faint acceptance, ended

without effect. The patron was not accustomed to such frigid gratitude; and the poet fed his own pride with the dignity of independence. They probably were suspicious of each other. Pope would not dedicate till he saw at what rate his praise was valued; he would be *troublesome out of gratitude, not expectation.* Halifax thought himself entitled to confidence; and would give nothing, unless he knew what he should receive. Their commerce had its beginning in hope of praise on one side, and of money on the other, and ended because Pope was less eager of money than Halifax of praise. It is not likely that Halifax had any personal benevolence to Pope; it is evident that Pope looked on Halifax with scorn and hatred.

The reputation of this great work failed of gaining him a patron; but it deprived him of a friend. [Addison and he were now at the head of poetry and criticism; and both in such a state of elevation, that, like the two rivals in the Roman state, one could no longer bear an equal, nor the other a superior.] Of the gradual abatement of kindness between friends, the beginning is often scarcely discernible by themselves, and the process is continued by petty provocations, and incivilities sometimes peevishly returned, and sometimes contemptuously neglected, which would escape all attention but that of pride, and drop from any memory but that of resentment. That the quarrel of those two wits should be minutely deduced, is not to be expected from a writer, to whom, as, Homer says, *nothing but rumour has reached, and who has no personal knowledge.*

Pope doubtless approached Addison, when the reputation of their wit first brought them together, with the respect due to a man whose abilities were acknowledged, and who, having attained that eminence to which he was himself aspiring, had in his hands the distribution of literary fame. He paid court with sufficient diligence by his Prologue to Cato, by his abuse of Dennis, and with praise yet more direct, by his poem on the Dialogues on Medals, of which

C

the immediate publication was then intended. In all this there was no hypocrisy; for he confessed that he found in Addison something more pleasing than in any other man. It may be supposed, that as Pope saw himself favoured by the world, and more frequently compared his own powers with those of others, his confidence increased, and his submission lessened; and that Addison felt no delight from the advances of a young wit, who might soon contend with him for the highest place. Every great man, of whatever
10 kind be his greatness, has among his friends those who officiously, or insidiously, quicken his attention to offences, heighten his disgust, and stimulate his resentment. Of such adherents Addison doubtless had many, and Pope was now too high to be without them. From the emission and reception of the Proposals for the Iliad, the kindness of Addison seems to have abated. Jervas, the painter, once pleased himself (Aug. 20, 1714) with imagining that he had re-established their friendship; and wrote to Pope that Addison once suspected him of too close a confederacy with
20 Swift, but was now satisfied with his conduct. To this Pope answered, a week after, that his engagements to Swift were such as his services in regard to the subscription demanded, and that the Tories never put him under the necessity of asking leave to be grateful. *But,* says he, *as Mr. Addison must be the judge in what regards himself, and seems to have no very just one in regard to me, so I must own to you I expect nothing but civility from him.* In the same letter he mentions Philips, as having been busy to kindle animosity between them; but, in a letter to Addison, he expresses some
30 consciousness of behaviour, inattentively deficient in respect.

Of Swift's industry in promoting the subscription there remains the testimony of Kennet, no friend to either him or Pope.

"Nov. 2, 1713, Dr. Swift came into the coffee-house, and had a bow from everybody but me, who, I confess, could not but despise him. When I came to the antechamber to wait, before prayers, Dr. Swift was the principal man of talk and business, and acted as master of requests.—Then he instructed a young nobleman that the *best Poet in England* was Mr. Pope (a papist) who had begun a translation of Homer into English verse, for which *he must have them all subscribe*; for, says he, the author *shall not* begin to print till *I have a thousand guineas for him.*"

About this time it is likely that Steele, who was, with all his political fury, good-natured and officious, procured an interview between these angry rivals, which ended in aggravated malevolence. On this occasion, if the reports be true, Pope made his complaint with frankness and spirit, as a man undeservedly neglected or opposed; and Addison affected a contemptuous unconcern, and, in a calm, even voice, reproached Pope with his vanity, and, telling him of the improvements which his early works had received from his own remarks and those of Steele, said, that he, being now engaged in public business, had no longer any care for his poetical reputation: nor had any other desire, with regard to Pope, than that he should not, by too much arrogance, alienate the public.

To this Pope is said to have replied with great keenness and severity, upbraiding Addison with perpetual dependence, and with the abuse of those qualifications which he had obtained at the public cost, and charging him with mean endeavours to obstruct the progress of rising merit. The contest rose so high, that they parted at last without any interchange of civility.

The first volume of Homer was (1715) in time published; and a rival version of the first Iliad, for rivals the time of their appearance inevitably made them, was immediately printed, with the name of Tickell. It was soon perceived that, among the followers of Addison, Tickell had the preference, and the critics and poets divided into factions. *I,* says Pope, *have the town, that is, the mob, on my side; but it is not uncommon for the smaller party to supply by industry what it wants in numbers.—I appeal to the people as my rightful judges, and, while they are not inclined to condemn me, shall not fear the high-flyers at Button's.* This opposition he immediately imputed to Addison, and complained of it in terms sufficiently resentful to Craggs, their common friend.

When Addison's opinion was asked, he declared the versions to be both good, but Tickell's the best that had ever been written; and sometimes said that they were both good, but that Tickell had more of Homer.

Pope was now sufficiently irritated; his reputation and his interest were at hazard. He once intended to print together the four versions of Dryden, Maynwaring, Pope, and Tickell, that they might be readily compared, and fairly estimated. This design seems to have been defeated by the refusal of Tonson, who was the proprietor of the other three versions.

Pope intended, at another time, a rigorous criticism of Tickell's translation, and had marked a copy, which I have seen, in all places that appeared defective. But while he was thus meditating defence or revenge, his adversary sunk before him without a blow; the voice of the public was not long divided, and the preference was universally given to Pope's performance. He was convinced, by adding one circumstance to another, that the other translation was the work of Addison himself; but, if he knew it in Addison's lifetime, it does not appear that he told it. He left his illustrious antagonist to be punished by what has been considered as the most painful of all reflections—the remembrance of a crime perpetrated in vain. The other circumstances of their quarrel were thus related by Pope.

"Philips seemed to have been encouraged to abuse me in coffee-houses, and conversations; and Gildon wrote a thing about Wycherley, in which he had abused both me and my relations very grossly. Lord Warwick himself told me one day, that it was in vain for me to endeavour to be well with Mr. Addison; that his jealous temper would never admit of a settled friendship between us: and, to convince me of what he had said, assured me, that Addison had encouraged Gildon to publish those scandals, and had given him ten guineas after they were published. The next day, while I was heated with what I had heard, I wrote a letter to Mr. Addison, to let him know that I was not unacquainted with this behaviour of his; that, if I was to speak severely of him in return for it, it should not be in such a dirty way, that I should rather tell him, himself, fairly of his faults, and allow his good qualities; and that it should be something in the following manner: I then adjoined the first sketch of what has since been called my satire on Addison. Mr. Addison used me very civilly ever after."

The verses on Addison, when they were sent to Atterbury were considered by him as the most excellent of Pope's performances; and the writer was advised, since he knew where his strength lay, not to suffer it to remain unemployed.

This year (1715) being, by the subscription, enabled to live more by choice, having persuaded his father to sell their estate at Binfield, he purchased, I think only for his life, that house at Twickenham to which his residence afterwards procured so much celebration, and removed thither with his father and mother. Here he planted the vines and the quincunx which his verses mention; and being under the necessity of making a subterraneous passage to a garden on the other side of the road, he adorned it with fossil bodies, and dignified it with the title of a grotto; a place of silence and retreat, from which he endeavoured to persuade his friends and himself that cares and passions could be excluded.

A grotto is not often the wish or pleasure of an Englishman, who has more frequent need to solicit than exclude the sun; but Pope's excavation was requisite as an entrance to his garden; and, as some men try to be proud of their defects, he extracted an ornament from an inconvenience, and vanity produced a grotto where necessity enforced a passage. It may be frequently remarked of the studious and speculative, that they are proud of trifles, and that their amusements seem frivolous and childish: whether it be that men conscious of great reputation think themselves above the reach of censure, and safe in the admission of negligent indulgences, or that mankind expect from elevated genius an uniformity of greatness, and watch its degradation with malicious wonder; like him who, having followed with his eye an eagle into the clouds, should lament that she ever descended to a perch.

10   While the volumes of his Homer were annually published, he collected his former works (1717) into one quarto volume, to which he prefixed a preface, written with great sprightliness and elegance, which was afterwards reprinted, with some passages subjoined that he at first omitted; other marginal additions of the same kind he made in the later editions of his poems. Waller remarks, that poets lose half their praise, because the reader knows not what they have blotted. Pope's voracity of fame taught him the art of obtaining the accumulated honour, both of what he had 20 published, and of what he had suppressed. In this year his father died suddenly, in his seventy-fifth year, having passed twenty-nine years in privacy. He is not known but by the character which his son has given him. If the money with which he retired was all gotten by himself, he had traded very successfully in times when sudden riches were rarely attainable.

The publication of the Iliad was at last completed in 1720. The splendour and success of this work raised Pope many enemies, that endeavoured to depreciate his abilities. 30 Burnet, who was afterwards a judge of no mean reputation, censured him in a piece called Homerides before it was published. Ducket likewise endeavoured to make him ridiculous. Dennis was the perpetual persecutor of all his studies. But, whoever his critics were, their writings are lost; and the names which are preserved, are preserved in the Dunciad.

In this disastrous year (1720) of national infatuation, when more riches than Peru can boast were expected from the South Sea, when the contagion of avarice tainted every mind, and even poets panted after wealth, Pope was seized with the universal passion, and ventured some of his money. The stock rose in its price; and he for a while thought himself *the Lord of thousands*. But this dream of happiness did not last long, and he seems to have waked soon enough to get clear with the loss only of what he once thought himself to have won, and perhaps not wholly of that.

Next year, he published some select poems of his friend Dr. Parnell, with a very elegant Dedication to the Earl of Oxford; who, after all his struggles and dangers, then lived in retirement, still under the frown of a victorious faction, who could take no pleasure in hearing his praise. [He gave the same year (1721) an edition of Shakespeare. His name was now of so much authority, that Tonson thought himself entitled, by annexing it, to demand a subscription of six guineas for Shakespeare's plays in six quarto volumes; nor did his expectation much deceive him; for of seven hundred and fifty which he printed, he dispersed a great number at the price proposed. The reputation of that edition, indeed, sunk afterwards so low, that one hundred and forty copies were sold at sixteen shillings each.] On this undertaking, to which Pope was induced by a reward of two hundred and seventeen pounds twelve shillings, he seems never to have reflected afterwards without vexation; for [Theobald, a man of heavy diligence, with very slender powers, first, in a book called Shakespeare Restored, and then in a formal edition, detected his deficiencies with all the insolence of victory; and, as he was now high enough to be feared and hated, Theobald had from others all the help that could be supplied by the desire of humbling a haughty character.

From this time Pope became an enemy to editors, collators, commentators, and verbal critics; and hoped to persuade the world, that he miscarried in this undertaking, only by having a mind too great for such minute employment.

Pope, in his edition, undoubtedly did many things wrong, and left many things undone; but let him not be defrauded of his due praise. He was the first that knew, at least the first that told, by what helps the text might be improved. If he inspected the early editions negligently, he taught others to be more accurate. In his Preface he expanded with great skill and elegance the character which had been
10 given of Shakspeare by Dryden; and he drew the public attention upon his works, which, though often mentioned, had been little read. Soon after the appearance of the Iliad, resolving not to let the general kindness cool, he published proposals for a translation of the Odyssey, in five volumes, for five guineas. He was willing, however, now to have associates in his labour, being either weary with toiling upon another's thoughts, or having heard, as Ruffhead relates, that Fenton and Broome had already begun the work, and liking better to have them con-
20 federates than rivals. In the patent, instead of saying that he had *translated* the Odyssey, as he had said of the Iliad, he says that he had *undertaken* a translation : and in the proposals, the subscription is said to be not solely for his own use, but for that of *two of his friends who have assisted him in this work.*

In 1723, while he was engaged in this new version, he appeared before the Lords at the memorable trial of Bishop Atterbury, with whom he had lived in great familiarity, and frequent correspondence. Atterbury had honestly re-
30 commended to him the study of the Popish controversy, in hope of his conversion; to which Pope answered in a manner that cannot much recommend his principles, or his judgement. In questions and projects of learning, they agreed better. He was called at the trial to give an account of Atterbury's domestic life, and private employment, that it might appear how little time he had left for plots. Pope

had but few words to utter, and in those few he made several blunders.

His Letters to Atterbury express the utmost esteem, tenderness, and gratitude: *perhaps,* says he, *it is not only in this world that I may have cause to remember the Bishop of Rochester.* At their last interview in the Tower Atterbury presented him with a Bible.

[Of the Odyssey, Pope translated only twelve books; the rest were the work of Broome and Fenton: the notes were written wholly by Broome, who was not over-liberally rewarded. The public was carefully kept ignorant of the several shares; and an acccount was subjoined at the conclusion, which is now known not to be true.] The first copy of Pope's books, with those of Fenton, are to be seen in the Museum. The parts of Pope are less interlined than the Iliad; and the latter books of the Iliad less than the former. He grew dexterous by practice, and every sheet enabled him to write the next with more facility. The books of Fenton have very few alterations by the hand of Pope. Those of Broome have not been found; but Pope complained, as it is reported, that he had much trouble in correcting them.

His contract with Lintot was the same as for the Iliad, except that only one hundred pounds were to be paid him for each volume. The number of subscribers was five hundred and seventy-four, and of copies, eight hundred and nineteen; so that his profit, when he had paid his assistants, was still very considerable. The work was finished in 1725, and from that time he resolved to make no more translations. The sale did not answer Lintot's expectation, and he then pretended to discover something of a fraud in Pope, and commenced or threatened a suit in Chancery.

On the English Odyssey, a criticism was published by Spence, at that time Prelector of Poetry at Oxford; a man whose learning was not very great, and whose mind was not very powerful. His criticism, however, was commonly just; what he thought, he thought rightly; and his remarks were recommended by his coolness and candour. In him, Pope had the first experience of a critic without malevolence, who thought it as much his duty to display beauties as expose faults; who censured with respect, and praised with alacrity.

With this criticism Pope was so little offended, that he sought the acquaintance of the writer, who lived with him from that time in great familiarity, attended him in his last
10 hours, and compiled memorials of his conversation. The regard of Pope recommended him to the great and powerful; and he obtained very valuable preferments in the Church. Not long after, Pope was returning home from a visit in a friend's coach, which, in passing a bridge, was overturned into the water; the windows were closed, and, being unable to force them open, he was in danger of immediate death, when the postilion snatched him out by breaking the glass, of which the fragments cut two of his fingers in such a manner, that he lost their use.
20 Voltaire, who was then in England, sent him a letter of consolation. He had been entertained by Pope at his table, where he talked with so much grossness that Mrs. Pope was driven from the room. Pope discovered, by a trick, that he was a spy for the Court, and never considered him as a man worthy of confidence. He soon afterwards (1727) joined with Swift, who was then in England, to publish three volumes of Miscellanies, in which, amongst other things, he inserted the Memoirs of a Parish Clerk, in ridicule of Burnet's importance in his own History, and a Debate
30 upon Black and White Horses, written in all the formalities of a legal process, by the assistance, as is said, of Mr. Fortescue, afterwards Master of the Rolls. Before these Miscellanies is a preface signed by Swift and Pope, but apparently written by Pope; in which he makes a ridiculous and romantic complaint of the robberies committed upon authors by the clandestine seizure and sale of their papers.

He tells, in tragic strains, how *the cabinets of the Sick and the closets of the Dead have been broken open and ransacked*; as if those violences were often committed for papers of uncertain and accidental value, which are rarely provoked by real treasures; as if epigrams and essays were in danger where gold and diamonds are safe. A cat hunted for his musk is, according to Pope's account, but the emblem of a wit winded by booksellers. His complaint, however, received some attestation ; for the same year the letters written by him to Mr. Cromwell, in his youth, were sold by 10 Mrs. Thomas to Curll, who printed them.

In these Miscellanies was first published the Art of Sinking in Poetry, which, by such a train of consequences as usually passes in literary quarrels, gave in a short time, according to Pope's account, occasion to the Dunciad.

In the following year (1728) he began to put Atterbury's advice in practice; and showed his satirical powers by publishing the Dunciad, one of his greatest and most elaborate performances, in which he endeavoured to sink into contempt all the writers by whom he had been 20 attacked, and some others whom he thought unable to defend themselves. At the head of the Dunces he placed poor Theobald, whom he accused of ingratitude ; but whose real crime was supposed to be that of having revised Shakspeare more happily than himself. This satire had the effect which he intended, by blasting the characters which it touched. Ralph, who, unnecessarily interposing in the quarrel, got a place in a subsequent edition, complained that for a time he was in danger of starving, as the booksellers had no longer any confidence in his capacity. 30

The prevalence of this poem was gradual and slow : the plan, if not wholly new, was little understood by common readers. Many of the allusions required illustration ; the names were often expressed only by the initial and final letters, and, if they had been printed at length, were such as few had known or recollected. The subject itself had nothing generally interesting, for whom did it concern to know that one or another scribbler was a dunce ? If therefore it had been possible for those who were attacked, to conceal their pain and their resentment, the Dunciad might have made its way very slowly in the world. This, however, was not to be expected : every man is of importance to himself, and therefore, in his own opinion, to others ; and, supposing the world already acquainted with all his pleasures and his pains, is perhaps the first to publish injuries or misfortunes, which 10 had never been known unless related by himself, and at which those that hear them will only laugh; for no man sympathises with the sorrows of vanity.

The history of the Dunciad is very minutely related by Pope himself, in a Dedication which he wrote to Lord Middlesex, in the name of Savage.

"I will relate the war of the Dunces (for so it has been commonly called), which began in the year 1727, and ended in 1730.

"When Dr. Swift and Mr. Pope thought it proper, for 20 reasons specified in the Preface to their Miscellanies, to publish such little pieces of theirs as had casually got abroad, there was added to them the Treatise of the Bathos, or the Art of Sinking in Poetry. It happened that in one chapter of this piece, the several species of bad poets were ranged in classes, to which were prefixed almost all the letters of the alphabet (the greatest part of them at random); but such was the number of poets eminent in that art, that some one or other took every letter to himself : all fell into so violent a fury, that, for half a year or more, the common newspapers 30 (in most of which they had some property, as being hired writers) were filled with the most abusive falsehoods and scurrilities they could possibly devise ; a liberty no way to be wondered at, in those people, and in those papers, that, for many years, during the uncontrolled licence of the press, had aspersed almost all the great characters of the age ; and this with impunity, their own persons and names being utterly secret and obscure. This gave Mr. Pope the thought that he had now some opportunity of doing good, by detecting and dragging into light these common enemies of mankind; since, to invalidate this universal slander, it sufficed to show what contemptible men were the authors of it. He was not without hopes, that, by manifesting the dulness of those who had only malice to recommend them, either the booksellers would not find their account in employing them, or the men themselves, when discovered, want courage to proceed in so unlawful an occupation. This it was that gave birth to the Dunciad; and he thought it a happiness that, by the late flood of slander on himself, he had acquired such a peculiar right over their names as was necessary to this design.

"On the 12th of March, 1729, at St. James's, that poem was presented to the king and queen (who had before been pleased to read it) by the right honourable Sir Robert Walpole; and, some days after, the whole impression was taken and dispersed by several noblemen and persons of the first distinction.

"It is certainly a true observation, that no people are so impatient of censure as those who are the greatest slanderers, which was wonderfully exemplified on this occasion. On the day the book was first vended, a crowd of authors besieged the shop; entreaties, advices, threats of law and battery, nay, cries of treason, were all employed to hinder the coming out of the Dunciad : on the other side, the booksellers and hawkers made as great efforts to procure it. What could a few poor authors do against so great a majority as the public? There was no stopping a torrent with a finger, so out it came.

"Many ludicrous circumstances attended it. [The *Dunces* (for by this name they were called) held weekly clubs, to consult of hostilities against the author : one wrote a letter to a great minister, assuring him Mr. Pope was the greatest enemy the government had ; and another bought his image in clay, to execute him in effigy ; with which sad sort of satisfaction the gentlemen were a little comforted.]

Some false editions of the book having an owl in their frontispiece, the true one, to distinguish it, fixed in its stead an ass laden with authors. Then another surreptitious one being printed with the same ass, the new edition in octavo returned for distinction to the owl again. Hence arose a great contest of booksellers against booksellers, and advertisements against advertisements; [some recommending the edition of the owl, and others the edition of the ass; by which names they came to be distinguished, to the great
10 honour also of the gentlemen of the Dunciad."]

Pope appears by this narrative to have contemplated his victory over the Dunces with great exultation; and such was his delight in the tumult which he had raised, that for a while his natural sensibility was suspended, and he read reproaches and invectives without emotion, considering them only as the necessary effects of that pain which he rejoiced in having given. It cannot however be concealed that, by his own confession, he was the aggressor: for nobody believes that the letters in the Bathos were placed at random; and
20 it may be discovered that, when he thinks himself concealed, he indulges the common vanity of common men, and triumphs in those distinctions which he had affected to despise. He is proud that his book was presented to the King and Queen by the right honourable Sir Robert Walpole; he is proud that they had read it before; he is proud that the edition was taken off by the nobility and persons of the first distinction.

The edition of which he speaks was, I believe, that which, by telling in the text the names, and in the notes the characters of those whom he had satirised, was made intelligible and
30 diverting. The critics had now declared their approbation of the plan, and the common reader began to like it without fear; those who were strangers to petty literature, and therefore unable to decipher initials and blanks, had now names and persons brought within their view; and delighted in the visible effect of those shafts of malice, which they had hitherto contemplated as shot into the air.

Dennis, upon the fresh provocation now given him, renewed the enmity which had for a time been appeased by mutual civilities; and published remarks, which he had till then suppressed, upon the Rape of the Lock. Many more grumbled in secret, or vented their resentment in the newspapers by epigrams or invectives. Ducket, indeed, being mentioned as loving Burnet with *pious passion*, pretended that his moral character was injured, and for some time declared his resolution to take vengeance with a cudgel. But Pope appeased him, by changing *pious passion* to *cordial friendship*; and by a note, in which he vehemently disclaims the malignity of the meaning imputed to the first expression.

Aaron Hill, who was represented as diving for the prize, expostulated with Pope in a manner so much superior to all mean solicitation, that Pope was reduced to sneak and shuffle, sometimes to deny, and sometimes to apologize; he first endeavours to wound, and is then afraid to own that he meant a blow.

The Dunciad, in the complete edition, is addressed to Dr. Swift: of the notes, part was written by Dr. Arbuthnot, and an apologetical Letter was prefixed, signed by Cleland, but supposed to have been written by Pope.

After this general war upon dulness, he seems to have indulged himself a while in tranquillity; but his subsequent productions prove that he was not idle. He published (1731) a poem on Taste, in which he very particularly and severely criticises the house, the furniture, the gardens, and the entertainments of Timon, a man of great wealth and little taste. By Timon he was universally supposed, and by the Earl of Burlington, to whom the poem is addressed, was privately said, to mean the Duke of Chandos; a man perhaps too much delighted with pomp and show, but of a temper kind and beneficent, and who had consequently the voice of the public in his favour. A violent outcry was therefore raised against the ingratitude and treachery of Pope, who was said to have been indebted to the patronage of Chandos

48   JOHNSON'S LIFE OF POPE.

for a present of a thousand pounds, and who gained the opportunity of insulting him by the kindness of his invitation.
The receipt of the thousand pounds Pope publicly denied; but, from the reproach which the attack on a character so amiable brought upon him, he tried all means of escaping. The name of Cleland was again employed in an apology, by which no man was satisfied; and he was at last reduced to shelter his temerity behind dissimulation, and endeavour to make that disbelieved which he never had
10 confidence openly to deny. He wrote an exculpatory letter to the Duke, which was answered with great magnanimity, as by a man who accepted his excuse without believing his professions. He said, that to have ridiculed his taste, or his buildings, had been an indifferent action in another man; but that in Pope, after the reciprocal kindness that had been exchanged between them, it had been less easily excused.
Pope, in one of his Letters, complaining of the treatment which his poem had found, *owns that such critics can intimidate him, nay almost persuade him to write no more,*
20 *which is a compliment this age deserves.* The man who threatens the world is always ridiculous; for the world can easily go on without him, and in a short time will cease to miss him. I have heard of an idiot, who used to revenge his vexations by lying all night upon the bridge. *There is nothing,* says Juvenal, *that a man will not believe in his own favour.* Pope had been flattered till he thought himself one of the moving powers in the system of life. When he talked of laying down his pen, those who sat round him entreated and implored, and self-love did not suffer him to
30 suspect that they went away and laughed.
The following year deprived him of Gay, a man whom he had known early, and whom he seemed to love with more tenderness than any other of his literary friends. Pope was now forty-four years old; an age at which the mind begins less easily to admit new confidence, and the will to grow less flexible, and when therefore the departure of an old

friend is very acutely felt. In the next year (1733) he lost his mother, not by an unexpected death, for she had lasted to the age of ninety-three: but she did not die unlamented. The filial piety of Pope was in the highest degree amiable and exemplary; his parents had the happiness of living till he was at the summit of poetical reputation, till he was at ease in his fortune, and without a rival in his fame, and found no diminution of his respect or tenderness. Whatever was his pride, to them he was obedient; and whatever was his irritability, to them he was gentle. Life has, among its soothing and quiet comforts, few things better to give than such a son.

One of the passages of Pope's life, which seems to deserve some enquiry, was a publication of Letters between him and many of his friends, which falling into the hands of Curll, a rapacious bookseller of no good fame, were by him printed and sold. This volume containing some Letters from noblemen, Pope incited a prosecution against him in the House of Lords for breach of privilege, and attended himself to stimulate the resentment of his friends. Curll appeared at the bar, and, knowing himself in no great danger, spoke of Pope with very little reverence. *He has*, said Curll, *a knack at versifying, but in prose I think myself a match for him.* When the orders of the House were examined, none of them appeared to have been infringed; Curll went away triumphant, and Pope was left to seek some other remedy.

Curll's account was, that one evening a man in a clergyman's gown, but with a lawyer's band, brought and offered to sale a number of printed volumes, which he found to be Pope's epistolary correspondence; that he asked no name, and was told none, but gave the price demanded, and thought himself authorised to use his purchase to his own advantage.

That Curll gave a true account of the transaction, it is reasonable to believe, because no falsehood was ever detected; and when, some years afterwards, I mentioned it to Lintot, the son of Bernard, he declared his opinion to be, that Pope knew better than anybody else how Curll obtained the copies, because another parcel was at the same time sent to himself, for which no price had ever been demanded, as he made known his resolution not to pay a porter, and consequently not to deal with a nameless agent.

Such care had been taken to make them public, that they were sent at once to two booksellers; to Curll, who was likely to seize them as a prey; and to Lintot, who might be
10 expected to give Pope information of the seeming injury. Lintot, I believe, did nothing; and Curll did what was expected. That to make them public was the only purpose, may be reasonably supposed, because the numbers, offered to sale by the private messengers, showed that hope of gain could not have been the motive of the impression. It seems that Pope, being desirous of printing his Letters, and not knowing how to do, without imputation of vanity, what has in this country been done very rarely, contrived an appearance of compulsion; that, when he could complain that his
20 Letters were surreptitiously published, he might decently and defensively publish them himself.

Pope's private correspondence, thus promulgated, filled the nation with praises of his candour, tenderness, and benevolence, the purity of his purposes, and the fidelity of his friendship. There were some Letters which a very good or a very wise man would wish suppressed; but, as they had been already exposed, it was impracticable now to retract them.

From the perusal of those Letters, Mr. Allen first con-
30 ceived the desire of knowing him; and with so much zeal did he cultivate the friendship which he had newly formed, that, when Pope told his purpose of vindicating his own property by a genuine edition, he offered to pay the cost.

This, however, Pope did not accept; but in time solicited a subscription for a Quarto volume, which appeared

JOHNSON'S LIFE OF POPE.

(1737), I believe, with sufficient profit. In the Preface he tells that his Letters were reposited in a friend's library, said to be the Earl of Oxford's, and that the copy thence stolen was sent to the press. The story was doubtless received with different degrees of credit. It may be suspected that the Preface to the Miscellanies was written to prepare the public for such an incident; and, to strengthen this opinion, James Worsdale, a painter, who was employed in clandestine negotiations, but whose veracity was very doubtful, declared that he was the messenger who carried, by Pope's direction, the books to Curll. When they were thus published and avowed, as they had relation to recent facts, and persons either then living or not yet forgotten, they may be supposed to have found readers; but as the facts were minute, and the characters being either private or literary, were little known, or little regarded, they awaked no popular kindness or resentment; the book never became much the subject of conversation; some read it as contemporary history, and some perhaps as a model of epistolary language; but those who read it did not talk of it. Not much therefore was added by it to fame or envy; nor do I remember that it produced either public praise or public censure.

It had, however, in some degree, the recommendation of novelty. Our language has few Letters, except those of statesmen. Howel, indeed, about a century ago, published his Letters, which are commended by Morhoff, and which alone of his hundred volumes continue his memory. Loveday's Letters were printed only once; those of Herbert and Suckling are hardly known. Mrs. Phillip's [Orinda's] are equally neglected; and those of Walsh seem written as exercises, and were never sent to any living mistress or friend. Pope's epistolary excellence had an open field; he had no English rival, living or dead.

Pope is seen in this collection as connected with the other contemporary wits, and certainly suffers no disgrace in the comparison; but it must be remembered, that he had the power of favouring himself: he might have originally had publication in his mind, and have written with care, or have afterwards selected those which he had most happily conceived, or most diligently laboured; and I know not whether there does not appear something more studied and artificial in his productions than the rest, except one long Letter by Bolingbroke, composed with all the skill and industry of a professed author. It is indeed not easy to distinguish affectation from habit; he that has once studiously formed a style, rarely writes afterwards with complete ease. Pope may be said to write always with his reputation in his head; Swift perhaps like a man who remembered that he was writing to Pope; but Arbuthnot, like one who lets thoughts drop from his pen as they rise into his mind.

Before these Letters appeared, he published the first part of what he persuaded himself to think a system of Ethics, under the title of an Essay on Man; which, if his letter to Swift (of September 14, 1725) be rightly explained by the commentator, had been eight years under his consideration, and of which he seems to have desired the success with great solicitude. He had now many open and doubtless many secret, enemies. The Dunces were yet smarting with the war; and the superiority which he publicly arrogated disposed the world to wish his humiliation. All this he knew, and against all this he provided. His own name and that of his friend to whom the work is inscribed were in the first editions carefully suppressed; and the poem, being of a new kind, was ascribed to one or another, as favour determined, or conjecture wandered; it was given, says Warburton, to every man, except him only who could write it. Those who like only when they like the author, and who are under the dominion of a name, condemned it; and those admired it who are willing to scatter praise at random, which while it is unappropriated excites no envy. Those friends of Pope that were trusted with the secret went about lavishing honours

on the new-born poet, and hinting that Pope was never
so much in danger from any former rival. To those authors
whom he had personally offended, and to those whose
opinion the world considered as decisive, and whom he
suspected of envy or malevolence, he sent his essay as a
present before publication, that they might defeat their own
enmity by praises which they could not afterwards decently
retract.

With these precautions, in 1733, was published the first
part of the Essay on Man. There had been for some 10
time a report that Pope was busy upon a System of
Morality; but this design was not discovered in the new
poem, which had a form and a title with which its readers
were unacquainted. Its reception was not uniform; some
thought it a very imperfect piece, though not without good
lines. While the author was unknown, some, as will always
happen, favoured him as an adventurer, and some censured
him as an intruder; but all thought him above neglect ; the
sale increased, and editions were multiplied. The subsequent editions of the first Epistle exhibited two memorable 20
corrections. At first, the poet and his friend

> Expatiate freely o'er this scene of man,
> A mighty maze *of walks without a plan;*

for which he wrote afterwards,

> A mighty maze, *but not without a plan;*

for if there were no plan, it was in vain to describe or to trace
the maze.

The other alteration was of these lines:

> And spite of pride, *and in thy reason's spite*,
> One truth is clear, whatever is, is right: 30

but having afterwards discovered, or been shown, that the
truth which subsisted *in spite of reason* could not be very
clear, he substituted

> And spite of pride, *in erring reason's spite.*

To such oversights will the most vigorous mind be liable, when it is employed at once upon argument and poetry.

The second and third Epistles were published, and Pope was, I believe, more and more suspected of writing them: at last, in 1734, he avowed the fourth, and claimed the honour of a moral poet.

In the conclusion it is sufficiently acknowledged, that the doctrine of the Essay on Man was received from Bolingbroke, who is said to have ridiculed Pope, among 10 those who enjoyed his confidence, as having adopted and advanced principles of which he did not perceive the consequence, and as blindly propagating opinions contrary to his own. That those communications had been consolidated into a scheme regularly drawn, and delivered to Pope, from whom it returned only transformed from prose to verse, has been reported, but hardly can be true. The Essay plainly appears the fabric of a poet: what Bolingbroke supplied could be only the first principles; the order, illustration, and embellishments, must all be Pope's.

20 These principles it is not my business to clear from obscurity, dogmatism, or falsehood; but they were not immediately examined; philosophy and poetry have not often the same readers; and the Essay abounded in splendid amplifications and sparkling sentences, which were read and admired with no great attention to their ultimate purpose; its flowers caught the eye, which did not see what the gay foliage concealed, and for a time flourished in the sunshine of universal approbation. So little was any evil tendency discovered, that, as innocence is unsuspicious, many read it 30 for a manual of piety. Its reputation soon invited a translator. It was first turned into French prose, and afterwards by Resnel into verse. Both translations fell into the hands of Crousaz, who first, when he had the version in prose, wrote a general censure, and afterwards reprinted Resnel's version, with particular remarks upon every paragraph.

Crousaz was a professor of Switzerland, eminent for his treatise of Logic, and his Examen de Pyrrhonisme ; and, however little known or regarded here, was no mean antagonist. His mind was one of those in which philosophy and piety are happily united. He was accustomed to argument and disquisition, and perhaps was grown too desirous of detecting faults ; but his intentions were always right, his opinions were solid, and his religion pure. His incessant vigilance for the promotion of piety disposed him to look with distrust upon all metaphysical systems of Theology, and all schemes of virtue and happiness purely rational ; and therefore it was not long before he was persuaded that the positions of Pope, as they terminated for the most part in natural religion, were intended to draw mankind away from revelation, and to represent the whole course of things as a necessary concatenation of indissoluble fatality ; and it is undeniable that in many passages a religious eye may easily discover expressions not very favourable to morals, or to liberty.

About this time Warburton began to make his appearance in the first ranks of learning. He was a man of vigorous faculties, a mind fervid and vehement, supplied by incessant and unlimited enquiry, with wonderful extent and variety of knowledge, which yet had not oppressed his imagination, nor clouded his perspicacity. To every work he brought a memory full fraught, together with a fancy fertile of original combinations, and at once exerted the powers of the scholar, the reasoner, and the wit. But his knowledge was too multifarious to be always exact, and his pursuits were too eager to be always cautious. His abilities gave him an haughty confidence, which he disdained to conceal or mollify; and his impatience of opposition disposed him to treat his adversaries with such contemptuous superiority as made his readers commonly his enemies, and excited against the advocate the wishes of some who favoured the cause. He seems to have adopted the Roman Emperor's determination, *oderint dum metuant;* he used no allurements of gentle language, but wished to compel rather than persuade.

His style is copious without selection, and forcible without neatness; he took the words that presented themselves: his diction is coarse and impure, and his sentences are unmeasured. He had, in the early part of his life, pleased himself with the notice of inferior wits, and corresponded with the enemies of Pope. A Letter was produced, when he had perhaps himself forgotten it, in which he tells Concanen, *Dryden, I observe, borrows for want of leisure, and Pope for want of genius;* Milton *out of pride, and Addison out of modesty.* And when Theobald published Shakespeare, in opposition to Pope, the best notes were supplied by Warburton. But the time was now come when Warburton was to change his opinion; and Pope was to find a defender in him who had contributed so much to the exaltation of his rival.

The arrogance of Warburton excited against him every artifice of offence, and therefore it may be supposed that his union with Pope was censured as hypocritical inconstancy; but surely to think differently at different times of poetical merit may be easily allowed. Such opinions are often admitted, and dismissed, without nice examination. Who is there that has not found reason for changing his mind about questions of greater importance?

Warburton, whatever was his motive, undertook, without solicitation, to rescue Pope from the talons of Crousaz, by freeing him from the imputation of favouring fatality, or rejecting revelation; and from month to month continued a vindication of the Essay on Man, in the literary journal of that time called The Republic of Letters.

Pope, who probably began to doubt the tendency of his own work, was glad that the positions, of which he perceived himself not to know the full meaning, could by any mode of interpretation be made to mean well. How much he was pleased with his gratuitous defender, the following Letter evidently shows:

"March 24, 1743.

"SIR,—I have just received from Mr. R. two more of your Letters. It is in the greatest hurry imaginable that I write this; but I cannot help thanking you in particular for your third Letter, which is so extremely clear, short, and full, that I think Mr. Crousaz ought never to have another answer, and deserved not so good an one. I can only say, you do him too much honour, and me too much right, so odd as the expression seems; for you have made my system as clear as I ought to have done, and could not. It is indeed the same system as mine, but illustrated with a ray of your own, as they say our natural body is the same still when it is glorified. I am sure I like it better than I did before, and so will every man else. I know I meant just what you explain; but I did not explain my own meaning so well as you. You understand me as well as I do myself; but you express me better than I could express myself. Pray accept the sincerest acknowledgments. I cannot but wish these Letters were put together in one Book; and intend (with your leave) to procure a translation of part at least of all of them, into French; but I shall not proceed a step without your consent and opinion," &c.

By this fond and eager acceptance of an exculpatory comment, Pope testified that, whatever might be the seeming or real import of the principles which he had received from Bolingbroke, he had not intentionally attacked religion; and Bolingbroke, if he meant to make him, without his own consent, an instrument of mischief, found him now engaged with his eyes open on the side of truth. It is known that Bolingbroke concealed from Pope his real opinions. He once discovered them to Mr. Hooke, who related them again to Pope, and was told by him that he must have mistaken the meaning of what he heard; and Bolingbroke, when

Pope's uneasiness incited him to desire an explanation, declared that Hooke had misunderstood him.

Bolingbroke hated Warburton, who had drawn his pupil from him; and a little before Pope's death they had a dispute, from which they parted with mutual aversion. From this time, Pope lived in the closest intimacy with his commentator, and amply rewarded his kindness and his zeal; for he introduced him to Mr. Murray, by whose interest he became preacher at Lincoln's Inn; and to Mr. Allen, who
10 gave him his niece and his estate, and by consequence a bishopric. When he died, he left him the property of his works; a legacy which may be reasonably estimated at four thousand pounds.

Pope's fondness for the Essay on Man appeared by his desire of its propagation. Dobson, who had gained reputation by his version of Prior's Solomon, was employed by him to translate it into Latin verse, and was for that purpose some time at Twickenham; but he left his work, whatever was the reason, unfinished; and, by Benson's
20 invitation, undertook the longer task of Paradise Lost. Pope then desired his friend to find a scholar who should turn his Essay into Latin prose; but no such performance has ever appeared.

Pope lived at this time *among the great*, with that reception and respect to which his works entitled him, and which he had not impaired by any private misconduct or factious partiality. Though Bolingbroke was his friend, Walpole was not his enemy; but treated him with so much consideration as, at his request, to solicit and obtain from the French
30 Minister an abbey for Mr. Southcot, whom he considered himself as obliged to reward, by this exertion of his interest, for the benefit which he had received from his attendance in a long illness.

It was said, that when the Court was at Richmond, Queen Caroline had declared her intention to visit him. This may have been only a careless effusion, thought on no more: the report of such notice, however, was soon in many mouths; and, if I do not forget or misapprehend Savage's account, Pope, pretending to decline what was not yet offered, left his house for a time, not, I suppose, for any other reason than lest he should be thought to stay at home in expectation of an honour which would not be conferred. He was therefore angry at Swift, who represents him as *refusing the visits of a Queen*, because he knew that what had never been offered, had never been refused. 10

Beside the general system of morality, supposed to be contained in the Essay on Man, it was his intention to write distinct poems upon the different duties or conditions of life; one of which is the Epistle to Lord Bathurst (1733) on the Use of Riches, a piece on which he declared great labour to have been bestowed. Into this poem some incidents are historically thrown, and some known characters are introduced, with others of which it is difficult to say how far they are real or fictitious; but the praise of Kyrl, the Man of Ross, deserves particular examination, who, after a long and 20 pompous enumeration of his public works and private charities, is said to have diffused all those blessings from *five hundred a year*. Wonders are willingly told, and willingly heard. The truth is, that Kyrl was a man of known integrity and active benevolence, by whose solicitation the wealthy were persuaded to pay contributions to his charitable schemes; this influence he obtained by an example of liberality exerted to the utmost extent of his power, and was thus enabled to give more than he had. This account Mr. Victor received from the minister of the place; and I have preserved it, that 30 the praise of a good man, being made more credible, may be more solid. Narrations of romantic and impracticable virtue will be read with wonder, but that which is unattainable is recommended in vain; that good may be endeavoured, it must be shown to be possible. This is the only piece in which the author has given a hint of his religion, by ridiculing the ceremony of burning the pope, and by mentioning with some indignation the inscription on the Monument.

When this poem was first published, the dialogue, having no letters of direction, was perplexed and obscure. Pope seems to have written with no very distinct idea; for he calls that an Epistle to Bathurst in which Bathurst is introduced as speaking. He afterwards (1734) inscribed to Lord Cobham his Characters of Men, written with close attention to the operations of the mind and modifications of life. In this poem he has endeavoured to establish and exemplify his favourite theory of the *ruling Passion*, by which he means an original direction of desire to some particular object, an innate affection which gives all action a determinate and invariable tendency, and operates upon the whole system of life, either openly, or more secretly by the intervention of some accidental or subordinate propension. Of any passion, thus innate and irresistible, the existence may reasonably be doubted. Human characters are by no means constant; men change by change of place, of fortune, of acquaintance; he who is at one time a lover of pleasure, is at another a lover of money. Those indeed who attain any excellence, commonly spend life in one pursuit; for excellence is not often gained upon easier terms. But to the particular species of excellence men are directed, not by an ascendant planet or predominating humour, but by the first book which they read, some early conversation which they heard, or some accident which excited ardour and emulation.

It must be at least allowed, that this *ruling Passion*, antecedent to reason and observation, must have an object independent on human contrivance; for there can be no natural desire of artificial good. No man therefore can be born, in the strict acceptation, a lover of money; for he may be born where money does not exist: nor can he be born, in a moral sense, a lover of his country; for society, politically regulated, is a state contradistinguished from a state of nature; and any attention to that coalition of

JOHNSON'S LIFE OF POPE. 6?

interests which makes the happiness of a country, is possible only to those whom enquiry and reflection have enabled to comprehend it. This doctrine is in itself pernicious as well as false : its tendency is to produce the belief of a kind of moral predestination, or over-ruling principle which cannot be resisted ; he that admits it is prepared to comply with every desire that caprice or opportunity shall excite, and to flatter himself that he submits only to the lawful dominion of Nature, in obeying the resistless authority of his *ruling Passion*. 10

Pope has formed his theory with so little skill that, in the examples by which he illustrates and confirms it, he has confounded passions, appetites, and habits. To the Characters of Men, he added soon after, in an epistle supposed to have been addressed to Martha Blount, but which the last edition has taken from her, the Characters of Women. This poem, which was laboured with great diligence, and in the author's opinion with great success, was neglected at its first publication, as the commentator supposes, because the public was informed, by an advertisement, that it contained 20 *no Character drawn from the life;* an assertion which Pope probably did not expect nor wish to have been believed, and which he soon gave his readers sufficient reason to distrust, by telling them in a note that the work was imperfect, because part of his subject was *Vice too high* to be yet exposed.

The time, however, soon came in which it was safe to display the Duchess of Marlborough under the name of Atossa; and her character was inserted with no great honour to the writer's gratitude.

He published from time to time (between 1730 and 1740) 30 Imitations of different poems of Horace, generally with his name, and once, as was suspected, without it. What he was upon moral principles ashamed to own, he ought to have suppressed. Of these pieces it is useless to settle the dates, as they had seldom much relation to the times, and perhaps had been long in his hands. This mode of imitation, in which

the ancients are familiarised, by adapting their sentiments to
modern topics, by making Horace say of Shakspeare what he
originally said of Ennius, and accommodating his satires on
Pantolabus and Nomentanus to the flatterers and prodigals
of our own time, was first practised in the reign of Charles
the Second, by Oldham and Rochester, at least I remember
no instances more ancient. It is a kind of middle composition
between translation and original design, which pleases when
the thoughts are unexpectedly applicable, and the parallels
10 lucky. It seems to have been Pope's favourite amusement;
for he has carried it further than any former poet.

He published likewise a revival, in smoother numbers, of Dr.
Donne's Satires, which was recommended to him by the Duke
of Shrewsbury and the Earl of Oxford. They made no great
impression on the public. Pope seems to have known their
imbecility, and therefore suppressed them while he was yet
contending to rise in reputation, but ventured them when
he thought their deficiencies more likely to be imputed to
Donne than to himself.

20 [The Epistle to Dr. Arbuthnot, which seems to be derived
in its first design from Boileau's Address *à son Esprit*, was
published in January, 1735, about a month before the death of
him to whom it is inscribed.] It is to be regretted, that either
honour or pleasure should have been missed by Arbuthnot;
a man estimable for his learning, amiable for his life, and
venerable for his piety. Arbuthnot was a man of great
comprehension, skilful in his profession, versed in the
sciences, acquainted with ancient literature, and able to
animate his mass of knowledge by a bright and active
30 imagination; a scholar with great brilliance of wit; a wit
who, in the crowd of life, retained and discovered a noble
ardour of religious zeal. In this poem Pope seems to reckon
with the public. He vindicates himself from censures; and
with dignity, rather than arrogance, enforces his own claims
to kindness and respect. [Into this poem are interwoven
several paragraphs which had been before printed as a frag-

ment, and among them the satirical lines upon Addison, of which the last couplet has been twice corrected. It was at first,

> Who would not smile if such a man there be?.
> Who would not laugh if Addison were he?

Then,

> Who would not grieve if such a man there be?
> Who would not laugh if Addison were he?

At last it is,

> Who but must laugh if such a man there be?
> Who would not weep if Atticus were he?

He was at this time at open war with Lord Hervey, who had distinguished himself as a steady adherent to the Ministry; and, being offended with a contemptuous answer to one of his pamphlets, had summoned Pulteney to a duel. Whether he or Pope made the first attack, perhaps cannot now be easily known: he had written an invective against Pope, whom he calls, *Hard as thy heart, and as thy birth obscure;* and hints that his father was a *hatter.* To this Pope wrote a reply in verse and prose; the verses are in this poem; and the prose, though it was never sent, is printed among his Letters; but to a cool reader of the present time exhibits nothing but tedious malignity.

His last Satires, of the general kind, were two Dialogues, named, from the year in which they were published, Seventeen hundred and thirty-eight. In these poems many are praised and many are reproached. Pope was then entangled in the Opposition; a follower of the Prince of Wales, who dined at his house, and the friend of many who obstructed and censured the conduct of the ministers. His political partiality was too plainly shown: he forgot the prudence with which he passed, in his earlier years, uninjured and unoffending through much more violent conflicts of faction.

In the first Dialogue, having an opportunity of praising Allen of Bath, he asked his leave to mention him as a man not illustrious by any merit of his ancestors, and called him in his verses *low-born Allen*. Men are seldom satisfied with praise introduced or followed by any mention of defect. Allen seems not to have taken any pleasure in his epithet, which was afterwards softened into *humble Allen*.

In the second Dialogue he took some liberty with one of the Foxes, among others; which Fox, in a reply to Lyttelton, took an opportunity of repaying, by reproaching him with the friendship of a lampooner, who scattered his ink without fear
10 or decency, and against whom he hoped the resentment of the Legislature would quickly be discharged.

About this time, Paul Whitehead, a small poet, was summoned before the Lords for a poem called Manners, together with Dodsley, his publisher. Whitehead, who hung loose upon society, skulked and escaped ; but Dodsley's shop and family made his appearance necessary. He was, however, soon dismissed ; and the whole process was probably intended rather to intimidate Pope than to punish Whitehead.

20 Pope never afterwards attempted to join the patriot with the poet, nor drew his pen upon statesmen. That he desisted from his attempts of reformation is imputed, by his commentator, to his despair of prevailing over the corruption of the time. He was not likely to have been ever of opinion that the dread of his satire would countervail the love of power or of money; he pleased himself with being important and formidable, and gratified sometimes his pride, and sometimes his resentment ; till at last he began to think he should be more safe, if he were less busy.

30 The Memoirs of Scriblerus, published about this time, extend only to the first book of a work projected in concert by Pope, Swift, and Arbuthnot, who used to meet in the time of Queen Anne, and denominated themselves the Scriblerus Club. Their purpose was to censure the abuses of learning, by a fictitious Life of an infatuated Scholar. They were dispersed ; the design was never completed ; and

Warburton laments its miscarriage, as an event very disastrous to polite letters. If the whole may be estimated by this specimen, which seems to be the production of Arbuthnot, with a few touches perhaps by Pope, the want of more will not be much lamented; for the follies which the writer ridicules are so little practised, that they are not known; nor can the satire be understood but by the learned: he raises phantoms of absurdity, and then drives them away. He cures diseases that were never felt. For this reason this joint production of three great writers has never obtained any notice from mankind; it has been little read, or when read has been forgotten, as no man could be wiser, better, or merrier, by remembering it. The design cannot boast of much originality; for, besides its general resemblance to Don Quixote, there will be found in it particular imitations of the History of Mr. Ouffle.

Swift carried so much of it into Ireland as supplied him with hints for his Travels; and with those the world might have been contented, though the rest had been suppressed.

Pope had sought for images and sentiments in a region not known to have been explored by many other of the English writers; he had consulted the modern writers of Latin poetry, a class of authors whom Boileau endeavoured to bring into contempt, and who are too generally neglected. Pope, however, was not ashamed of their acquaintance, nor ungrateful for the advantages which he might have derived from it. A small selection from the Italians who wrote in Latin had been published at London, about the latter end of the last century, by a man who concealed his name, but whom his Preface shows to have been well qualified for his undertaking. This collection Pope amplified by more than half, and (1740) published it in two volumes, but injuriously omitted his predecessor's preface. To these books, which had nothing but the mere text, no regard was paid, the authors were still neglected, and the editor was neither praised nor censured. He did not sink into idleness; he

E

had planned a work, which he considered as subsequent to his Essay on Man, of which he has given this account to Dr. Swift.

"March 25, 1736.

"If ever I write any more Epistles in verse, one of them shall be addressed to you. I have long concerted it, and begun it; but I would make what bears your name as finished as my last work ought to be, that is to say, more finished than any of the rest. The subject is large, and will
10 divide into four Epistles, which naturally follow the Essay on Man, viz. 1. Of the Extent and Limits of Human Reason and Science. 2. A view of the useful and therefore attainable, and of the unuseful and therefore unattainable Arts. 3. Of the Nature, Ends, Application, and Use, of different Capacities. 4. Of the Use of Learning, of the Science, of the World, and of Wit.' It will conclude with a satire against the Misapplication of all these, exemplified by Pictures, Characters, and Examples."

This work in its full extent, being now afflicted with an
20 asthma, and finding the powers of life gradually declining, he had no longer courage to undertake; but, from the materials which he had provided, he added, at Warburton's request, another book to the Dunciad, of which the design is to ridicule such studies as are either hopeless or useless, as either pursue what is unattainable, or what, if it be attained, is of no use.

When this book was printed (1742) the laurel had been for some time upon the head of Cibber; a man whom it cannot be supposed that Pope could regard with much
30 kindness or esteem, though in one of the Imitations of Horace he has liberally enough praised the Careless Husband. In the Dunciad, among other worthless scribblers, he had mentioned Cibber : who, in his Apology, complains of the great Poet's unkindness as more injurious, *because*, says he, *I never have offended him.*

It might have been expected that Pope should have been, in some degree, mollified by this submissive gentleness, but no such consequence appeared. Though he condescended to commend Cibber once, he mentioned him afterwards contemptuously in one of his Satires, and again in his Epistle to Arbuthnot; and in the fourth book of the Dunciad attacked him with acrimony, to which the provocation is not easily discoverable. Perhaps he imagined that, in ridiculing the Laureat, he satirised those by whom the laurel had been given, and gratified that ambitious petulance with which he 10 affected to insult the great. The severity of this satire left Cibber no longer any patience. He had confidence enough in his own powers to believe that he could disturb the quiet of his adversary, and doubtless did not want instigators, who, without any care about the victory, desired to amuse themselves by looking on the contest. He therefore gave the town a pamphlet, in which he declares his resolution from that time never to bear another blow without returning it, and to tire out his adversary by perseverance, if he cannot conquer him by strength. 20

The incessant and unappeasable malignity of Pope he imputes to a very distant cause. After the Three Hours after Marriage had been driven off the stage, by the offence which the mummy and crocodile gave the audience, while the exploded scene was yet fresh in memory, it happened that Cibber played Bayes in the Rehearsal; and, as it had been usual to enliven the part by the mention of any recent theatrical transactions, he said, that he once thought to have introduced his lovers disguised in a Mummy and a Crocodile. "This," says he, "was received with loud claps, which in- 30 dicated contempt of the play." Pope, who was behind the scenes, meeting him as he left the stage, attacked him, as he says, with all the virulence of a *Wit out of his senses*; to which he replied, " that he would take no other notice of what was said by so particular a man, than to declare, that, as often as he played that part, he would repeat the same provocation." He shows his opinion to be, that Pope was one of the authors of the play which he so zealously defended; and adds an idle story of Pope's behaviour at a tavern.

The pamphlet was written with little power of thought or language, and, if suffered to remain without notice, would have been very soon forgotten. [Pope had now been enough acquainted with human life to know, if his passion had not been too powerful for his understanding, that, from a contention like his with Cibber, the world seeks nothing but diversion, which is given at the expense of the higher character.] When Cibber lampooned Pope, curiosity was excited; what Pope would say of Cibber nobody enquired, but in hope that Pope's asperity might betray his pain and lessen his dignity.

He should therefore have suffered the pamphlet to flutter and die, without confessing that it stung him. The dishonour of being shown as Cibber's antagonist could never be compensated by the victory. Cibber had nothing to lose; when Pope had exhausted all his malignity upon him, he would rise in the esteem both of his friends and his enemies. Silence only could have made him despicable; the blow which did not appear to be felt would have been struck in vain. But Pope's irascibility prevailed, and he resolved to tell the whole English world that he was at war with Cibber; [and, to show that he thought him no common adversary, he prepared no common vengeance; he published a new edition of the Dunciad, in which he degraded Theobald from his painful pre-eminence, and enthroned Cibber in his stead. Unhappily the two heroes were of opposite characters, and Pope was unwilling to lose what he had already written; he has therefore depraved his poem by giving to Cibber the old books, the cold pedantry and sluggish pertinacity of Theobald.]

Pope was ignorant enough of his own interest to make another change, and introduced Osborne contending for the prize among the booksellers. Osborne was a man entirely destitute of shame, without sense of any disgrace but that of poverty. He told me, when he was doing that which raised Pope's resentment, that he should be put into the Dunciad; but he had the fate of Cassandra; I gave no credit to his prediction, till in time I saw it accomplished. The shafts of satire were directed equally in vain against Cibber and Osborne; being repelled by the impenetrable impudence of one, and deadened by the impassive dulness of the other. Pope confessed his own pain by his anger; but he gave no pain to those who had provoked him. He was able to hurt none but himself; by transferring the same ridicule from one to another he destroyed its efficacy, for by showing that what he had said of one he was ready to say of another he reduced himself to the insignificance of his own magpye, who from his cage calls cuckold at a venture.

Cibber, according to his engagement, repaid the Dunciad with another pamphlet, which, Pope said, *would be as good as a dose of hartshorn to him*; but his tongue and his heart were at variance. I have heard Mr. Richardson relate that he attended his father the painter on a visit; when one of Cibber's pamphlets came into the hands of Pope, who said, *These things are my diversion.* They sat by him while he perused it, and saw his features writhen with anguish; and young Richardson said to his father, when they returned, that he hoped to be preserved from such diversion as had been that day the lot of Pope.

From this time, finding his diseases more oppressive, and his vital powers gradually declining, he no longer strained his faculties with any original composition, nor proposed any other employment for his remaining life than the revisal and correction of his former works; in which he received advice and assistance from Warburton, whom he appears to have trusted and honoured in the highest degree. He laid aside his Epic Poem, perhaps without much loss to mankind; for his hero was Brutus the Trojan, who, according to a

ridiculous fiction, established a colony in Britain. The subject therefore was of the fabulous age; the actors were a race upon whom imagination has been exhausted, and attention wearied, and to whom the mind will not easily be recalled, when it is invited in blank verse, which Pope had adopted with great imprudence, and, I think, without due consideration of the nature of our language. The sketch is, at least in part, preserved by Ruffhead; by which it appears that Pope was thoughtless enough to model the names of his
10 heroes with terminations not consistent with the time or country in which he places them. He lingered through the next year; but perceived himself, as he expresses it, *going down the hill*. He had for at least five years been afflicted with an asthma, and other disorders, which his physicians were unable to relieve. Towards the end of his life he consulted Dr. Thomson, a man who had, by large promises, and free censures of the common practice of physic, forced himself up into sudden reputation. Thomson declared his distemper to be a dropsy, and evacuated part of the water by
20 tincture of jalap; but confessed that his belly did not subside. Thomson had many enemies, and Pope was persuaded to dismiss him.

While he was yet capable of amusement and conversation, as he was one day sitting in the air with Lord Bolingbroke and Lord Marchmont, he saw his favourite Martha Blount at the bottom of the terrace, and asked Lord Bolingbroke to go and hand her up. Bolingbroke, not liking his errand, crossed his legs and sat still; but Lord Marchmont, who was younger and less captious, waited on the lady, who, when he
30 came to her, asked, *What, is he not dead yet?* She is said to have neglected him, with shameful unkindness, in the latter time of his decay; yet, of the little which he had to leave she had a very great part. Their acquaintance began early; the life of each was pictured on the other's mind; their conversation therefore was endearing, for when they met, there was an immediate coalition of congenial notions.

Perhaps he considered her unwillingness to approach the chamber of sickness as female weakness, or human frailty; perhaps he was conscious to himself of peevishness and impatience, or, though he was offended by her inattention, might yet consider her merit as overbalancing her fault; and, if he had suffered his heart to be alienated from her, he could have found nothing that might fill her place; he could have only shrunk within himself; it was too late to transfer his confidence or fondness.

In May, 1744, his death was approaching; on the 6th he was all day delirious, which he mentioned four days afterwards as a sufficient humiliation of the vanity of man; he afterwards complained of seeing things as through a curtain, and in false colours, and one day, in the presence of Dodsley, asked what arm it was that came out from the wall. He said that his greatest inconvenience was inability to think. Bolingbroke sometimes wept over him in this state of helpless decay; and being told by Spence, that Pope, at the intermission of his deliriousness, was always saying something kind either of his present or absent friends, and that his humanity seemed to have survived his understanding, answered, *It has so.* And added, *I never in my life knew a man that had so tender a heart for his particular friends, or more general friendship for mankind.* At another time he said, *I have known Pope these thirty years, and value myself more in his friendship than* —— his grief then suppressed his voice.

Pope expressed undoubting confidence of a future state. Being asked by his friend Mr. Hooke, a papist, whether he would not die like his father and mother, and whether a priest should not be called, he answered, *I do not think it essential, but it will be very right; and I thank you for putting me in mind of it.* In the morning, after the priest had given him the last sacraments, he said, "There is nothing that is meritorious but virtue and friendship; and indeed friendship itself is only a part of virtue." He died in the evening of the thirtieth day of May, 1744, so placidly, that the attendants did not discern the exact time of his expiration. He was buried at Twickenham, near his father and mother, where a monument has been erected to him by his commentator, the Bishop of Gloucester.

He left the care of his papers to his executors; first to Lord Bolingbroke; and, if he should not be living, to the Earl of Marchmont; undoubtedly expecting them to be proud of the trust, and eager to extend his fame. But let no man dream of influence beyond his life. After a decent time Dodsley the bookseller went to solicit preference as the publisher, and was told that the parcel had not been yet inspected; and, whatever was the reason, the world has been disappointed of what was *reserved for the next age.*

He lost, indeed, the favour of Bolingbroke by a kind of posthumous offence. The political pamphlet called The Patriot King had been put into his hands that he might procure the impression of a very few copies, to be distributed, according to the author's directions among his friends, and Pope assured him that no more had been printed than were allowed; but, soon after his death, the printer brought and resigned a complete edition of fifteen hundred copies, which Pope had ordered him to print, and to retain in secret. He kept, as was observed, his engagement to Pope better than Pope had kept it to his friend; and nothing was known of the transaction, till, upon the death of his employer, he thought himself obliged to deliver the books to the right owner, who, with great indignation, made a fire in his yard, and delivered the whole impression to the flames.

Hitherto nothing had been done which was not naturally dictated by resentment of violated faith; resentment more acrimonious, as the violator had been more loved or more trusted. But here the anger might have stopped; the injury was private, and there was little danger from the example.

Bolingbroke, however, was not yet satisfied; his thirst of vengeance excited him to blast the memory of the man over whom he had wept in his last struggles; and he employed Mallet, another friend of Pope, to tell the tale to the public, with all its aggravations. Warburton, whose heart was warm with his legacy, and tender by the recent separation, thought it proper for him to interpose; and undertook, not indeed to vindicate the action, for breach of trust has always something criminal, but to extenuate it by an apology. Having advanced what cannot be denied, that moral obliquity is made more or less excusable by the motives that produce it, he enquires what evil purpose could have induced Pope to break his promise. He could not delight his vanity by usurping the work, which, though not sold in shops, had been shown to a number more than sufficient to preserve the author's claim; he could not gratify his avarice, for he could not sell his plunder till Bolingbroke was dead; and even then, if the copy was left to another, his fraud would be defeated, and if left to himself would be useless. Warburton therefore supposes, with great appearance of reason, that the irregularity of his conduct proceeded wholly from his zeal for Bolingbroke, who might perhaps have destroyed the pamphlet, which Pope thought it his duty to preserve, even without its author's approbation. To this apology an answer was written in A Letter to the most Impudent Man living.

He brought some reproach upon his own memory by the petulant and contemptuous mention made in his will of Mr. Allen, and an affected repayment of his benefactions. Mrs. Blount, as the known friend and favourite of Pope, had been invited to the house of Allen, where she comported herself with such indecent arrogance, that she parted from Mrs. Allen in a state of irreconcilable dislike, and the door was for ever barred against her. This exclusion she resented with so much bitterness as to refuse any legacy from Pope, unless he left the world with a disavowal of obligation to Allen. Having been long under her dominion, now tottering in the decline of life, and unable to resist the violence of her temper or, perhaps with the prejudice of a lover, persuaded that she had suffered improper treatment, he complied with her demand, and polluted his will with female resentment. Allen accepted the legacy, which he gave to the Hospital at Bath; observing that Pope was always a bad accomptant, and that, if to 150*l*. he had put a cipher more, he had come nearer to the truth.

The person of Pope is well known not to have been formed by the nicest model. He has, in his account of the Little Club, compared himself to a spider, and by another is described as protuberant behind and before. He is said to have been beautiful in his infancy; but he was of a constitution originally feeble and weak: and, as bodies of a tender frame are easily distorted, his deformity was probably in part the effect of his application. His stature was so low that, to bring him to a level with common tables, it was necessary to raise his seat. But his face was not displeasing, and his eyes were animated and vivid. By natural deformity, or accidental distortion, his vital functions were so much disordered, that his life was *a long disease.* His most frequent assailant was the headache, which he used to relieve by inhaling the steam of coffee, which he very frequently required.

Most of what can be told concerning his petty peculiarities was communicated by a female domestic of the Earl of Oxford, who knew him perhaps after the middle of life. He was then so weak as to stand in perpetual need of female attendance; extremely sensible of cold, so that he wore a kind of fur doublet, under a shirt of very coarse warm linen with fine sleeves. When he rose, he was invested in boddice made of stiff canvas, being scarce able to hold himself erect till they were laced, and he then put on a flannel waistcoat. One side was contracted. His legs were so slender, that he enlarged their bulk with three pair of stockings, which were drawn on and off by the maid; for he was not able to dress or undress himself, and neither went to bed nor rose without help. His weakness made it very difficult for him to be clean.

His hair had fallen almost all away; and he used to dine sometimes with Lord Oxford, privately, in a velvet cap. His dress of ceremony was black, with a tye-wig, and a little sword. The indulgence and accommodation which his sickness required, had taught him all the unpleasing and unsocial qualities of a valetudinary man. He expected that everything should give way to his ease or humour, as a child, whose parents will not hear her cry, has an unresisted dominion in the nursery.

> C'est que l'enfant toûjours est homme,
> C'est que l'homme est toûjours enfant.

When he wanted to sleep he *nodded in company*; and once slumbered at his own table while the Prince of Wales was talking of poetry.

The reputation which his friendship gave procured him many invitations; but he was a very troublesome inmate. He brought no servant, and had so many wants, that a numerous attendance was scarcely able to supply them. Wherever he was, he left no room for another, because he exacted the attention, and employed the activity of the whole family. His errands were so frequent and frivolous, that the footmen in time avoided and neglected him; and the Earl of Oxford discharged some of his servants for their resolute refusal of his messages. The maids, when they had neglected their business, alleged that they had been employed by Mr. Pope. One of his constant demands was of coffee in the night, and to the woman that waited on him in his chamber he was very burthensome: but he was careful to recompense her want of sleep; and Lord Oxford's servant declared, that in a house where her business was to answer his call, she would not ask for wages. He had another fault, easily incident to those who, suffering much pain, think themselves entitled to whatever pleasures they can snatch. He was too

indulgent to his appetite: he loved meat highly seasoned and of strong taste; and, at the intervals of the table, amused himself with biscuits and dry conserves. If he sat down to a variety of dishes, he would oppress his stomach with repletion; and though he seemed angry when a dram was offered him, did not forbear to drink it. His friends, who knew the avenues to his heart, pampered him with presents of luxury, which he did not suffer to stand neglected. The death of great men is not always proportioned to the lustre of
10 their lives. Hannibal, says Juvenal, did not perish by a javelin or a sword; the slaughters of Cannæ were revenged by a ring. The death of Pope was imputed by some of his friends, to a silver saucepan, in which it was his delight to heat potted lampreys.

That he loved too well to eat, is certain; but that his sensuality shortened his life will not be hastily concluded, when it is remembered that a conformation so irregular lasted six and fifty years, notwithstanding such pertinacious diligence of study and meditation. In all his
20 intercourse with mankind, he had great delight in artifice, and endeavoured to attain all his purposes by indirect and unsuspected methods. *He hardly drank tea without a stratagem.* If, at the house of friends, he wanted any accommodation, he was not willing to ask for it in plain terms, but would mention it remotely as something convenient; though, when it was procured, he soon made it appear for whose sake it had been recommended. Thus he teazed Lord Orrery till he obtained a screen. He practised his arts on such small occasions, that Lady Bolingbroke used
30 to say, in a French phrase, that *he played the politician about cabbages and turnips.* His unjustifiable impression of the Patriot King, as it can be imputed to no particular motive, must have proceeded from his general habit of secrecy and cunning; he caught an opportunity of a sly trick, and pleased himself with the thought of outwitting Bolingbroke.

In familiar or convivial conversation, it does not appear that he excelled. He may be said to have resembled Dryden, as being not one that was distinguished by vivacity in company. It is remarkable that, so near his time, so much should be known of what he has written, and so little of what he has said; traditional memory retains no sallies of raillery, nor sentences of observation; nothing either pointed or solid, either wise or merry. One apophthegm only stands upon record. When an objection raised against his inscription for Shakespeare, was defended by the authority of Patrick, he replied, *horresco referens*, that he *would allow the publisher of a Dictionary to know the meaning of a single word, but not of two words put together.*

He was fretful and easily displeased, and allowed himself to be capriciously resentful. He would sometimes leave Lord Oxford silently, no one could tell why, and was to be courted back by more letters and messages than the footmen were willing to carry. The table was indeed infested by Lady Mary Wortley, who was the friend of Lady Oxford, and who, knowing his peevishness, could by no entreaties be restrained from contradicting him, till their disputes were sharpened to such asperity, that one or the other quitted the house. He sometimes condescended to be jocular with servants or inferiors; but by no merriment, either of others or his own, was he ever seen excited to laughter.

Of his domestic character, frugality was a part eminently remarkable. Having determined not to be dependent, he determined not to be in want, and therefore wisely and magnanimously rejected all temptations to expense unsuitable to his fortune. This general care must be universally approved; but it sometimes appeared in petty artifices of parsimony, such as the practice of writing his compositions on the back of letters, as may be seen in the remaining copy of the Iliad, by which perhaps in five years five shillings were saved; or in a niggardly reception of his friends, and scantiness of entertainment, as, when he had two guests in his house, he would set at supper a single pint upon the table; and having himself taken two small glasses, would retire, and say, *Gentlemen, I leave you to your wine.* Yet he tells his friends, that *he has a heart for all, a house for all, and, whatever they may think, a fortune for all.*

He sometimes, however, made a splendid dinner, and is said to have wanted no part of the skill or elegance which such performances require. That this magnificence should be often displayed, that obstinate prudence with which he conducted his affairs would not permit; for his revenue, certain and casual, amounted only to about eight hundred pounds a year, of which however he declares himself able to assign one hundred to charity. Of this fortune, which, as it arose from public approbation, was very honourably obtained, his imagination seems to have been too full: it would be hard to find a man, so well entitled to notice by his wit, that ever delighted so much in talking of his money. In his Letters, and in his poems, his garden and his grotto, his quincunx and his vines, or some hints of his opulence, are always to be found.

The great topic of his ridicule is poverty; the crimes with which he reproaches his antagonists are their debts, their habitation in the Mint, and their want of a dinner. He seems to be of an opinion not very uncommon in the world, that to want money is to want everything. Next to the pleasure of contemplating his possessions, seems to be that of enumerating the men of high rank with whom he was acquainted, and whose notice he loudly proclaims not to have been obtained by any practices of meanness or servility; a boast which was never denied to be true, and to which very few poets have ever aspired. Pope never set genius to sale; he never flattered those whom he did not love, or praised those whom he did not esteem. Savage, however, remarked, that he began a little to relax his dignity when he wrote a distich for *his Highness's dog.*

His admiration of the Great seems to have increased in the

advance of life. He passed over peers and statesmen to inscribe his Iliad to Congreve, with a magnanimity of which the praise had been complete, had his friend's virtue been equal to his wit. Why he was chosen for so great an honour, it is not now possible to know; there is no trace in literary history of any particular intimacy between them. The name of Congreve appears in the Letters among those of his other friends, but without any observable distinction or consequence. To his latter works, however, he took care to annex names dignified with titles, but was not very happy in his choice; for, except Lord Bathurst, none of his noble friends were such as that a good man would wish to have his intimacy with them known to posterity ; he can derive little honour from the notice of Cobham, Burlington, or Bolingbroke.

Of his social qualities, if an estimate be made from his Letters, an opinion too favourable cannot easily be formed; they exhibit a perpetual and unclouded effulgence of general benevolence, and particular fondness. There is nothing but liberality, gratitude, constancy, and tenderness. It has been so long said as to be commonly believed, that the true characters of men may be found in their Letters, and that he who writes to his friend lays his heart open before him. But the truth is, that such were the simple friendships of the Golden Age, and are now the friendships only of children. Very few can boast of hearts which they dare lay open to themselves, and of which, by whatever accident exposed, they do not shun a distinct and continued view ; and, certainly, what we hide from ourselves we do not show to our friends. There is, indeed, no transaction which offers stronger temptations to fallacy and sophistication than epistolary intercourse. In the eagerness of conversation the first emotions of the mind often burst out before they are considered; in the tumult of business interest and passion have their genuine effect ; but a friendly Letter is a calm and deliberate performance in the cool of leisure, in the stillness of solitude, and surely no man sits down to depreciate by design his own character.)

Friendship has no tendency to secure veracity; for by whom can a man so much wish to be thought better than he is, as by him whose kindness he desires to gain or keep? Even in writing to the world there is less constraint; the author is not confronted with his reader, and takes his chance of approbation among the different dispositions of mankind; but a Letter is addressed to a single mind, of which the prejudices and partialities are known; and must therefore please, if not by favouring them, by forbearing to oppose them.

To charge those favourable representations, which men give of their own minds, with the guilt of hypocritical falsehood, would show more severity than knowledge. [The writer commonly believes himself. Almost every man's thoughts, while they are general, are right; and most hearts are pure, while temptation is away.] It is easy to awaken generous sentiments in privacy; to despise death when there is no danger; to glow with benevolence when there is nothing to be given. While such ideas are formed they are felt; and self-love does not suspect the gleam of virtue to be the meteor of fancy.

If the Letters of Pope are considered merely as compositions, they seem to be premeditated and artificial. It is one thing to write because there is something which the mind wishes to discharge; and another, to solicit the imagination because ceremony or vanity requires something to be written. Pope confesses his early letters to be vitiated with *affectation and ambition:* to know whether he disentangled himself from these perverters of epistolary integrity, his book and his life must be set in comparison. One of his favourite topics is contempt of his own poetry. For this, if it had been real, he would deserve no commendation; and in this he was certainly not sincere, for his high value of himself was sufficiently observed; and of what could he be proud but of his poetry? [He writes, he says, when *he has just nothing else to do*; yet Swift complains that he was never at leisure for conversation, because he *had always some poetical scheme in his head.*] It was punctually required that his writing-box should be set upon his bed before he rose; and Lord Oxford's domestic related, that, in the dreadful winter of Forty, she was called from her bed by him four times in one night, to supply him with paper, lest he should lose a thought.

[He pretends insensibility to censure and criticism, though it was observed by all who knew him that every pamphlet disturbed his quiet, and that his extreme irritability laid him open to perpetual vexation;] but he wished to despise his critics, and therefore hoped that he did despise them. As he happened to live in two reigns when the Court paid little attention to poetry, he nursed in his mind a foolish disesteem of kings, and proclaims that *he never sees Courts*. Yet a little regard shown him by the Prince of Wales melted his obduracy; and he had not much to say when he was asked by His Royal Highness *how he could love a Prince while he disliked Kings?*

He very frequently professes contempt of the world, and represents himself as looking on mankind, sometimes with gay indifference, as on emmets of a hillock, below his serious attention; and sometimes with gloomy indignation, as on monsters more worthy of hatred than of pity. These were dispositions apparently counterfeited. How could he despise those whom he lived by pleasing, and on whose approbation his esteem of himself was superstructed? Why should he hate those to whose favour he owed his honour and his ease? Of things that terminate in human life, the world is the proper judge: to despise its sentence, if it were possible, is not just; and if it were just, is not possible. Pope was far enough from this unreasonable temper; he was sufficiently *a fool to Fame*, and his fault was that he pretended to neglect it. His levity and his sullenness were only in his Letters;

F

he passed through common life, sometimes vexed, and sometimes pleased, with the natural emotions of common men. His scorn of the Great is repeated too often to be real; no man thinks much of that which he despises; and as falsehood is always in danger of inconsistency, he makes it his boast at another time that he lives among them. It is evident that his own importance swells often in his mind. He is afraid of writing lest the clerks of the Post-office should know his secrets; he has many enemies; he considers himself as surrounded by universal jealousy: *after many deaths, and many dispersions, two or three of us*, says he, *may still be brought together, not to plot, but to divert ourselves, and the world too, if it pleases*; and they can live together, and *shew what friends wits may be, in spite of all the fools in the world.* All this while it was likely that the clerks did not know his hand; he certainly had no more enemies than a public character like his inevitably excites; and with what degree of friendship the wits might live, very few were so much fools as ever to enquire.

Some part of this pretended discontent he learned from Swift, and expresses it, I think, most frequently in his correspondence with him. Swift's resentment was unreasonable, but it was sincere; Pope's was the mere mimicry of his friend, a fictitious part which he began to play before it became him. When he was only twenty-five years old, he related that "a glut of study and retirement had thrown him on the world," and that there was danger lest "a glut of the world should throw him back upon study and retirement." To this Swift answered with great propriety, that Pope had not yet either acted or suffered enough in the world to have become weary of it. [And, indeed, it must be some very powerful reason that can drive back to solitude him who has once enjoyed the pleasures of society.]

In the Letters both of Swift and Pope there appears such narrowness of mind, as makes them insensible of any excellence that has not some affinity with their own, and confines their esteem and approbation to so small a number, that whoever should form his opinion of the age from their representation, would suppose them to have lived amidst ignorance and barbarity, unable to find among their contemporaries either virtue or intelligence, and persecuted by those that could not understand them.

When Pope murmurs at the world, when he professes contempt of fame, when he speaks of riches and poverty, of success and disappointment, with negligent indifference, he certainly does not express his habitual and settled sentiments, but either wilfully disguises his own character, or, what is more likely, invests himself with temporary qualities, and sallies out in the colours of the present moment. His hopes and fears, his joys and sorrows, acted strongly upon his mind; and, if he differed from others, it was not by carelessness; he was irritable and resentful; his malignity to Philips, whom he had first made ridiculous, and then hated for being angry, continued too long. Of his vain desire to make Bentley contemptible, I never heard any adequate reason. He was sometimes wanton in his attacks; and, before Chandos, Lady Wortley, and Hill, was mean in his retreat.

The virtues which seem to have had most of his affection were liberality and fidelity of friendship, in which it does not appear that he was other than he describes himself. His fortune did not suffer his charity to be splendid and conspicuous; but he assisted Dodsley with a hundred pounds, that he might open a shop; and, of the subscription of forty pounds a year that he raised for Savage, twenty were paid by himself. He was accused of loving money; but his love was eagerness to gain, not solicitude to keep it.

In the duties of friendship he was zealous and constant; his early maturity of mind commonly united him with men older than himself; and therefore, without attaining any considerable length of life, he saw many companions of his youth sink into the grave; but it does not appear that he lost a single friend by coldness or by injury; those who loved him once, continued their kindness. His ungrateful mention of Allen in his will, was the effect of his adherence to one whom he had known much longer, and whom he naturally loved with greater fondness. His violation of the trust reposed in him by Bolingbroke could have no motive inconsistent with the warmest affection; he either thought the action so near to indifferent that he forgot it, or so laudable that he expected his friend to approve it.

10 It was reported, with such confidence as almost to enforce belief, that in the papers entrusted to his executors, was found a defamatory Life of Swift, which he had prepared as an instrument of vengeance, to be used if any provocation should be ever given. About this I inquired of the Earl of Marchmont, who assured me that no such piece was among his remains.

The religion in which he lived and died was that of the Church of Rome, to which in his correspondence with Racine he professes himself a sincere adherent. That he was not
20 scrupulously pious in some part of his life, is known by many idle and indecent applications of sentences taken from the Scriptures; a mode of merriment which a good man dreads for its profaneness, and a witty man disdains for its easiness and vulgarity. But to whatever levities he has been betrayed, it does not appear that his principles were ever corrupted, or that he ever lost his belief of Revelation. The positions which he transmitted from Bolingbroke he seems not to have understood, and was pleased with an interpretation that made them orthodox.

30 A man of such exalted superiority, and so little moderation, would naturally have all his delinquencies observed and aggravated; those who could not deny that he was excellent, would rejoice to find that he was not perfect. Perhaps it may be imputed to the unwillingness with which the same man is allowed to possess many advantages, that his learning has been depreciated. He certainly was in his early life a

man of great literary curiosity; and, when he wrote his Essay on Criticism, had, for his age, a very wide acquaintance with books. When he entered into the living world it seems to have happened to him as to many others, that he was less attentive to dead masters; he studied in the academy of Paracelsus, and made the universe his favourite volume. He gathered his notions fresh from reality, not from the copies of authors, but the originals of Nature. Yet there is no reason to believe that literature ever lost his esteem; he always professed to love reading; and Dobson, who spent some time at his house translating his Essay on Man, when I asked him what learning he found him to possess, answered, *More than I expected.* His frequent references to history, his allusions to various kinds of knowledge, and his images selected from art and nature, with his observations on the operations of the mind and the modes of life, show an intelligence perpetually on the wing, excursive, vigorous, and diligent, eager to pursue knowledge, and attentive to retain it.

From this curiosity arose the desire of travelling, to which he alludes in his verses to Jervas, and which, though he never found an opportunity to gratify it, did not leave him till his life declined.

Of his intellectual character the constituent and fundamental principle was Good Sense, a prompt and intuitive perception of consonance and propriety. He saw immediately, of his own conceptions, what was to be chosen, and what to be rejected; and, in the works of others, what was to be shunned, and what was to be copied. But good sense alone is a sedate and quiescent quality, which manages its possessions well, but does not increase them; it collects few materials for its own operations, and preserves safety, but never gains supremacy. Pope had likewise genius; a mind active, ambitious, and adventurous, always investigating, always aspiring; in its widest searches still longing to go forward, in its highest flights still wishing to be higher;

always imagining something greater than it knows, always endeavouring more than it can do. To assist these powers, he is said to have had great strength and exactness of memory. That which he had heard or read was not easily lost; and he had before him not only what his own meditations suggested, but what he had found in other writers that might be accommodated to his present purpose. These benefits of nature he improved by incessant and unwearied diligence; he had recourse to every source of intelligence, and lost no opportunity of information; he consulted the living as well as the dead; he read his compositions to his friends, and was never content with mediocrity when excellence could be attained. He considered poetry as the business of his life; and however he might seem to lament his occupation, he followed it with constancy; to make verses was his first labour, and to mend them was his last.

From his attention to poetry he was never diverted. If conversation offered anything that could be improved, he committed it to paper; if a thought, or perhaps an expression more happy than was common, rose to his mind, he was careful to write it; an independent distich was preserved for an opportunity of insertion; and some little fragments have been found containing lines, or parts of lines, to be wrought upon at some other time. He was one of those few whose labour is their pleasure: he was never elevated to negligence, nor wearied to impatience; he never passed a fault unamended by indifference, nor quitted it by despair. He laboured his works first to gain reputation, and afterwards to keep it.

Of composition there are different methods. Some employ at once memory and invention, and, with little intermediate use of the pen, form and polish large masses by continued meditation, and write their productions only when, in their own opinion, they have completed them. It is related of Virgil that his custom was to pour out a great number of verses in the morning, and pass the day in retrenching exuberances and correcting inaccuracies. The method of Pope, as may be collected from his translation, was to write his first thoughts in his first words, and gradually to amplify, decorate, rectify, and refine them. With such faculties and such dispositions he excelled every other writer in *poetical prudence*: he wrote in such a manner as might expose him to few hazards. He used almost always the same fabric of verse; and, indeed, by those few essays which he made of any other, he did not enlarge his reputation. Of this uniformity the certain consequence was readiness and 10 dexterity. By perpetual practice, language had in his mind a systematical arrangement; having always the same use for words, he had words so selected and combined as to be ready at his call. This increase of facility he confessed himself to have perceived in the progress of his translation.

But what was yet of more importance, his effusions were always voluntary, and his subjects chosen by himself. His independence secured him from drudging at a task, and labouring upon a barren topic: he never exchanged praise for money, nor opened a shop of condolence or congratu- 20 lation. His poems, therefore, were scarcely ever temporary. He suffered coronations and royal marriages to pass without a song; and derived no opportunities from recent events, nor any popularity from the accidental disposition of his readers. He was never reduced to the necessity of soliciting the sun to shine upon a birthday, of calling the Graces and Virtues to a wedding, or of saying what multitudes have said before him. When he could produce nothing new, he was at liberty to be silent.

His publications were for the same reason never hasty. 30 He is said to have sent nothing to the press till it had lain two years under his inspection: it is at least certain, that he ventured nothing without nice examination. He suffered the tumult of imagination to subside, and the novelties of invention to grow familiar. He knew that the mind is always enamoured of its own productions, and did not trust his first fondness. He consulted his friends, and listened with great willingness to criticism; and, what was of more importance, he consulted himself, and let nothing pass against his own judgement. He professed to have learned his poetry from Dryden, whom, whenever an opportunity was presented, he praised through his whole life with unvaried liberality; and perhaps his character may receive some illustration, if he be compared with his master.

Integrity of understanding and nicety of discernment were not allotted in a less proportion to Dryden than to Pope. The rectitude of Dryden's mind was sufficiently shown by the dismission of his poetical prejudices, and the rejection of unnatural thoughts and rugged numbers. But Dryden never desired to apply all the judgement that he had. He wrote, and professed to write, merely for the people; and when he pleased others, he contented himself. He spent no time in struggles to rouse latent powers; he never attempted to make that better which was already good, nor often to mend what he must have known to be faulty. He wrote, as he tells us, with very little consideration; when occasion or necessity called upon him, he poured out what the present moment happened to supply, and, when once it had passed the press, ejected it from his mind; for when he had no pecuniary interest, he had no further solicitude.

Pope was not content to satisfy; he desired to excel, and therefore always endeavoured to do his best; he did not court the candour, but dared the judgement of his reader, and, expecting no indulgence from others, he showed none to himself. He examined lines and words with minute and punctilious observation, and retouched every part with indefatigable diligence, till he had left nothing to be forgiven.

For this reason he kept his pieces very long in his hands, while he considered and reconsidered them. The only poems which can be supposed to have been written with such regard to the times as might hasten their publication, were the two satires of *Thirty-eight*; of which Dodsley told me, that they were brought to him by the author, that they might be fairly copied. "Almost every line," he said, "was then written twice over; I gave him a clean transcript, which he sent some time afterwards to me for the press, with almost every line written twice over a second time." His declaration, that his care for his works ceased at their publication, was not strictly true. His parental attention never abandoned them; what he found amiss in the first edition, he silently corrected in those that followed. He appears to have revised the Iliad, and freed it from some of its imperfections; and the Essay on Criticism received many improvements after its first appearance. It will seldom be found that he altered without adding clearness, elegance, or vigour. Pope had perhaps the judgement of Dryden; but Dryden certainly wanted the diligence of Pope.

In acquired knowledge, the superiority must be allowed to Dryden, whose education was more scholastic, and who before he became an author had been allowed more time for study, with better means of information. His mind has a larger range, and he collects his images and illustrations from a more extensive circumference of science. Dryden knew more of man in his general nature, and Pope in his local manners. The notions of Dryden were formed by comprehensive speculation; and those of Pope by minute attention. There is more dignity in the knowledge of Dryden, and more certainty in that of Pope. Poetry was not the sole praise of either; for both excelled likewise in prose; but Pope did not borrow his prose from his predecessor. The style of Dryden is capricious and varied; that of Pope is cautious and uniform; Dryden obeys the motions of his own mind, Pope constrains his mind to his own rules of composition. Dryden is sometimes vehement and rapid; Pope is always smooth, uniform, and gentle. Dryden's page is a natural field, rising into inequalities, and diversified by the varied exuberance of abundant vegetation; Pope's is a velvet lawn, shaven by the scythe, and levelled by the roller.

Of genius, that power which constitutes a poet; that quality without which judgement is cold and knowledge is inert; that energy which collects, combines, amplifies, and animates; the superiority must, with some hesitation, be allowed to Dryden. It is not to be inferred that of this poetical vigour Pope had only a little, because Dryden had more; for every other writer since Milton must give place to
10 Pope; and even of Dryden it must be said, that, if he has brighter paragraphs, he has not better poems. Dryden's performances were always hasty, either excited by some external occasion, or extorted by domestic necessity; he composed without consideration, and published without correction. What his mind could supply at call, or gather in one excursion, was all that he sought, and all that he gave. The dilatory caution of Pope enabled him to condense his sentiments, to multiply his images, and to accumulate all that study might produce, or chance might supply. If the
20 flights of Dryden therefore are higher, Pope continues longer on the wing. If of Dryden's fire the blaze is brighter, of Pope's the heat is more regular and constant. Dryden often surpasses expectation, and Pope never falls below it. Dryden is read with frequent astonishment, and Pope with perpetual delight.

This parallel will, I hope, when it is well considered, be found just; and if the reader should suspect me, as I suspect myself, of some partial fondness for the memory of Dryden, let him not too hastily condemn me; for meditation
30 and enquiry may, perhaps, show him the reasonableness of my determination.

The Works of Pope are now to be distinctly examined, not so much with attention to slight faults or petty beauties, as to the general character and effect of each performance.

It seems natural for a young poet to initiate himself by Pastorals, which, not professing to imitate real life, require no experience; and, exhibiting only the simple operation of unmingled passions, admit no subtle reasoning or deep enquiry. Pope's Pastorals are not however composed but with close thought; they have reference to the times of the day, the seasons of the year, and the periods of human life. The last, that which turns the attention upon age and death, was the author's favourite. To tell of disappointment and misery, to thicken the darkness of futurity, and perplex the labyrinth of uncertainty, has been always a delicious employment of the poets. His preference was probably just. I wish, however, that his fondness had not overlooked a line in which the *Zephyrs* are made to *lament in silence*.

To charge these Pastorals with want of invention, is to require what never was intended. The imitations are so ambitiously frequent, that the writer evidently means rather to show his literature than his wit. It is surely sufficient for an author of sixteen not only to be able to copy the poems of antiquity with judicious selection, but to have obtained sufficient power of language, and skill in metre, to exhibit a series of versification, which had in English poetry no precedent, nor has since had an imitation.

The design of Windsor Forest is evidently derived from Cooper's Hill, with some attention to Waller's poem on The Park; but Pope cannot be denied to excel his masters in variety and elegance, and the art of interchanging description, narrative, and morality. The objection made by Dennis is the want of plan, of a regular subordination of parts terminating in the principal and original design. There is this want in most descriptive poems, because as the scenes, which they must exhibit successively, are all subsisting at the same time, the order in which they are shown must by necessity be arbitrary, and more is not to be expected from the last part than from the first. The attention, therefore, which cannot be detained by suspense, must be excited by diversity, such as his poem offers to its reader.

But the desire of diversity may be too much indulged; the parts of Windsor Forest which deserve least praise are those which were added to enliven the stillness of the scene, the appearance of Father Thames, and the transformation of Lodona. Addison had in his Campaign derided the rivers that *rise from their oozy beds* to tell stories of heroes; and it is therefore strange that Pope should adopt a fiction not only unnatural but lately censured. The story of Lodona is told with sweetness; but a new metamorphosis is
10 a ready and puerile expedient; nothing is easier than to tell how a flower was once a blooming virgin, or a rock an obdurate tyrant.

The Temple of Fame has, as Steele warmly declared, *a thousand beauties*. Every part is splendid; there is great luxuriance of ornaments; the original vision of Chaucer was never denied to be much improved; the allegory is very skilfully continued, the imagery is properly selected, and learnedly displayed: yet, with all this comprehension of excellence, as its scene is laid in remote ages, and its senti-
20 ments, if the concluding paragraph be excepted, have little relation to general manners or common life, it never obtained much notice, but is turned silently over, and seldom quoted or mentioned with either praise or blame.

That the Messiah excels the Pollio is no great praise, if it be considered from what original the improvements are derived.

The Verses on the Unfortunate Lady have drawn much attention by the illaudable singularity of treating suicide with respect; and they must be allowed to be written in
30 some parts with vigorous animation, and in others with gentle tenderness; nor has Pope produced any poem in which the sense predominates more over the diction. But the tale is not skilfully told; it is not easy to discover the character of either the Lady or her Guardian. History relates that she was about to disparage herself by a marriage with an inferior; Pope praises her for the dignity of ambition, and

yet condemns the uncle to detestation for his pride; the ambitious love of a niece may be opposed by the interest, malice, or envy of an uncle, but never by his pride. On such an occasion a poet may be allowed to be obscure, but inconsistency never can be right.

The Ode for St. Cecilia's Day was undertaken at the desire of Steele: in this the author is generally confessed to have miscarried, yet he has miscarried only as compared with Dryden; for he has far outgone other competitors. Dryden's plan is better chosen; history will always take 10 stronger hold of the attention than fable: the passions excited by Dryden are the pleasures and pains of real life, the scene of Pope is laid in imaginary existence; Pope is read with calm acquiescence, Dryden with turbulent delight; Pope hangs upon the ear, and Dryden finds the passes of the mind.

Both the odes want the essential constituent of metrical compositions, the stated recurrence of settled numbers. It may be alleged, that Pindar is said by Horace to have written *numeris lege solutis:* but as no such lax per- 20 formances have been transmitted to us, the meaning of that expression cannot be fixed; and perhaps the like return might properly be made to a modern Pindarist, as Mr. Cobb received from Bentley, who, when he found his criticisms upon a Greek Exercise, which Cobb had presented, refuted one after another by Pindar's authority, cried out at last, *Pindar was a bold fellow, but thou art an impudent one.*

If Pope's ode be particularly inspected, it will be found that the first stanza consists of sounds well chosen indeed, 30 but only sounds. The second consists of hyperbolical common-places, easily to be found, and perhaps without much difficulty to be as well expressed. In the third, however, there are numbers, images, harmony, and vigour, not unworthy the antagonist of Dryden. Had all been like this— but every part cannot be the best. The next stanzas place

and detain us in the dark and dismal regions of mythology, where neither hope nor fear, neither joy nor sorrow, can be found: the poet however faithfully attends us; we have all that can be performed by elegance of diction, or sweetness of versification; but what can form avail without better matter? The last stanza recurs again to common-places. The conclusion is too evidently modelled by that of Dryden; and it may be remarked that both end with the same fault; the comparison of each is literal on one side, and meta-
10 phorical on the other. Poets do not always express their own thoughts: Pope, with all this labour in the praise of Music, was ignorant of its principles, and insensible of its effects.

One of his greatest, though of his earliest works, is the Essay on Criticism which, if he had written nothing else, would have placed him among the first critics and the first poets, as it exhibits every mode of excellence that can embellish or dignify didactic composition, selection of matter, novelty of arrangement, justness of precept, splendour of
20 illustration, and propriety of digression. I know not whether it be pleasing to consider that he produced this piece at twenty, and never afterwards excelled it: he that delights himself with observing that such powers may be soon attained, cannot but grieve to think that life was ever after at a stand.

To mention the particular beauties of the Essay would be unprofitably tedious: but I cannot forbear to observe, that the comparison of a student's progress in the sciences with the journey of a traveller in the Alps, is perhaps the best
30 that English poetry can show. A simile, to be perfect, must both illustrate and ennoble the subject; must show it to the understanding in a clearer view, and display it to the fancy with greater dignity; but either of these qualities may be sufficient to recommend it. In didactic poetry, of which the great purpose is instruction, a simile may be praised which illustrates, though it do s not ennoble; in heroics, that may

be admitted which ennobles, though it does not illustrate.
That it may be complete, it is required to exhibit, in-
dependently of its references, a pleasing image; for a simile
is said to be a short episode. To this antiquity was so
attentive, that circumstances were sometimes added, which,
having no parallels, served only to fill the imagination, and
produced what Perrault ludicrously called *comparisons with
a long tail*. In their similes the greatest writers have
sometimes failed; the ship-race, compared with the chariot-
race, is neither illustrated nor aggrandised, land and water
make all the difference; when Apollo, running after Daphne,
is likened to a greyhound chasing a hare, there is nothing
gained; the ideas of pursuit and flight are too plain to be
made plainer; and a god and the daughter of a god, are not
represented much to their advantage by a hare and dog.
The simile of the Alps has no useless parts, yet affords a
striking picture by itself; it makes the foregoing position
better understood, and enables it to take faster hold on the
attention; it assists the apprehension, and elevates the fancy.
Let me likewise dwell a little on the celebrated paragraph,
in which it is directed that *the sound should seem an echo
to the sense*; a precept which Pope is allowed to have
observed beyond any other English poet.

This notion of representative metre, and the desire of
discovering frequent adaptations of the sound to the sense,
have produced, in my opinion, many wild conceits and
imaginary beauties. All that can furnish this representation
are the sounds of the words considered singly, and the time
in which they are pronounced. Every language has some
words framed to exhibit the noises which they express, as
thump, rattle, growl, hiss. These, however, are but few, and
the poet cannot make them more, nor can they be of any use
but when sound is to be mentioned. The time of pronuncia-
tion was in the dactylic measures of the learned languages
capable of considerable variety; but that variety could be
accommodated only to motion or duration, and different

degrees of motion were perhaps expressed by verses rapid or slow, without much attention of the writer, when the image had full possession of his fancy : but our language having little flexibility, our verses can differ very little in their cadence. The fancied resemblances, I fear, arise sometimes merely from the ambiguity of words; there is supposed to be some relation between a *soft* line and a *soft* couch, or between *hard* syllables and *hard* fortune. Motion, however, may be in some sort exemplified ; and yet it may be sus-
10 pected that even in such resemblances the mind often governs the ear, and the sounds are estimated by their meaning. One of the most successful attempts has been to describe the labour of Sisyphus :

>With many a weary step, and many a groan,
>Up a high hill he heaves a huge round stone,
>The huge round stone, resulting with a bound,
>Thunders impetuous down, and smokes along the ground.

Who does not perceive the stone to move slowly upward, ano roll violently back ? But set the same numbers to another
20 sense :

>While many a merry tale, and many a song,
>Cheer'd the rough road, we wish'd the rough road long.
>The rough road then, returning in a round,
>Mock'd our impatient steps, for all was fairy ground.

We have now surely lost much of the delay, and much of the rapidity. But, to show how little the greatest master of numbers can fix the principles of representative harmony, it will be sufficient to remark that the poet who tells us that
30   When Ajax strives—the words move slow.
    Not so, when swift Camilla scours the plain,
    Flies o'er th' unbending corn, and skims along the main ;

when he had enjoyed for about thirty years the praise of

Camilla's lightness of foot, he tried another experiment upon *sound* and *time*, and produced this memorable triplet:

> Waller was smooth; but Dryden taught to join
> The varying verse, the full resounding line,
> The long majestic march, and energy divine.

Here are the swiftness of the rapid race, and the march of slow-paced majesty, exhibited by the same poet in the same sequence of syllables, except that the exact prosodist will find the line of *swiftness* by one time longer than that of *tardiness*. Beauties of this kind are commonly fancied; and, when real, are technical and nugatory, not to be rejected, and not to be solicited.

To the praises which have been accumulated on the Rape of the Lock by readers of every class, from the critic to the waiting-maid, it is difficult to make any addition. Of that which is universally allowed to be the most attractive of all ludicrous compositions, let it rather be now enquired from what sources the power of pleasing is derived.

Mr. Warburton, who excelled in critical perspicacity, has remarked that the preternatural agents are very happily adapted to the purposes of the poem. The heathen deities can no longer gain attention; we should have turned away from a contest between Venus and Diana. The employment of allegorical persons always excites conviction of its own absurdity; they may produce effects, but cannot conduct actions; when the phantom is put in motion, it dissolves: thus Discord may raise a mutiny; but Discord cannot conduct a march, nor besiege a town. Pope brought into view a new race of Beings, with powers and passions proportionate to their operation. The Sylphs and Gnomes act, at the toilet and the tea-table, what more terrific and more powerful phantoms perform on the stormy ocean, or the field of battle; they give their proper help, and do their proper mischief.

Pope is said, by an objector, not to have been the inventor of this petty nation; a charge which might with more justice

G

have been brought against the author of the Iliad, who doubtless adopted the religious system of his country; for what is there, but the names of his agents, which Pope has not invented? Has he not assigned them characters and operations never heard of before? Has he not, at least, given them their first poetical existence? If this is not sufficient to denominate his work original, nothing original ever can be written.

In this work are exhibited, in a very high degree, the two most engaging powers of an author. New things are made familiar, and familiar things are made new. A race of aërial people, never heard of before, is presented to us in a manner so clear and easy, that the reader seeks for no further information, but immediately mingles with his new acquaintance, adopts their interests, and attends their pursuits, loves a Sylph, and detests a Gnome. That familiar things are made new, every paragraph will prove. The subject of the poem is an event below the common incidents of common life; nothing real is introduced that is not seen so often as to be no longer regarded: yet the whole detail of a female day is here brought before us, invested with so much art of decoration, that, though nothing is disguised, everything is striking, and we feel all the appetite of curiosity for that from which we have a thousand times turned fastidiously away.

The purpose of the Poet is, as he tells us, to laugh at *the little unguarded follies of the female sex.* It is therefore without justice that Dennis charges the Rape of the Lock with the want of a moral, and for that reason sets it below the Lutrin, which exposes the pride and discord of the clergy. Perhaps neither Pope nor Boileau has made the world much better than he found it; but, if they had both succeeded, it were easy to tell who would have deserved most from public gratitude. The freaks, and humours, and spleen, and vanity of women, as they embroil families in discord, and fill houses with disquiet, do more to obstruct the happiness of life in a year than the ambition of the clergy in many

centuries. It has been well observed, that the misery of man proceeds not from any single crush of overwhelming evil, but from small vexations continually repeated. It is remarked by Dennis, likewise, that the machinery is superfluous; that by all the bustle of preternatural operation the main event is neither hastened nor retarded. To this charge an efficacious answer is not easily made. The Sylphs cannot be said to help or to oppose; and it must be allowed to imply some want of art, that their power. ¹
mingled -.,..   tr i
ance which no age or nation can   .   - ins
10 Greeks translation was almost unknown; it was unknown to the inhabitants of Greece. They had no recourse to the barbarians for poetical beauties, but sought for everything in Homer, where, indeed, there is but little which they might not find. The Italians have been very diligent translators; but I can hear of no version, unless perhaps Anguillara's Ovid may be excepted, which is read with
- eagerness. The Iliad of Salvini every reader may discover to be punctiliously exact; but it seems to be the work of a linguist skilfully pedantic; and his countrymen, the proper
20 judges of its power to please, reject it with disgust.

Their predecessors, the Romans, have left some specimens of translation behind them, and that employment must have had some credit in which Tully and Germanicus engaged; but unless we suppose, what is perhaps true, that the plays of Terence were versions of Menander, nothing translated seems ever to have risen to high reputation. The French, in the meridian hour of their learning, were very laudably industrious to enrich their own language with the wisdom of the ancients; but found themselves reduced, by
30 whatever necessity, to turn the Greek and Roman poetry into prose. Whoever could read an author could translate him. From such rivals little can be feared.

The chief help of Pope in this arduous undertaking was drawn from the versions of Dryden. Virgil had borrowed much of his imagery from Homer; and part of the debt was now paid by his translator. Pope searched the pages of sentiments, which have so much vigour and efficacy, have been drawn, are shown to be the mystic writers by the learned author of the Essay on the Life and Writings of Pope; a book which teaches how the brow of Criticism may be smoothed, and how she may be enabled, with all her severity, to attract and to delight.

The train of my disquisition has now conducted me to that poetical wonder, the translation of the Iliad; a performpretend to equal. To the
totally
has not been sufficiently interwith the action. Other parts may likewise be 10 charged with want of connection; the game at *ombre* might be spared; but, if the Lady had lost her hair while she was intent upon her cards, it might have been inferred that those who are too fond of play will be in danger of neglecting more important interests. Those perhaps are faults; but what are such faults to so much excellence!

The Epistle of Eloise to Abelard is one of the most happy productions of human wit: the subject is so judiciously chosen, that it would be difficult, in turning over the annals of the world, to find another which so many circumstances 20 concur to recommend. We regularly interest ourselves most in the fortune of those who most deserve our notice. Abelard and Eloise were conspicuous in their days for eminence of merit. The heart naturally loves truth. The adventures and misfortunes of this illustrious pair are known from undisputed history. Their fate does not leave the mind in hopeless dejection; for they both found quiet and consolation in retirement and piety. So new and so affecting is their story, that it supersedes invention; and imagination ranges at full liberty without straggling into scenes of fable. 30

The story, thus skilfully adopted, has been diligently improved. Pope has left nothing behind him, which seems more the effect of studious perseverance and laborious revisal. Here is particularly observable the *curiosa felicitas*, a fruitful soil and careful cultivation. Here is no crudeness of sense, nor asperity of language. The sources from which

Dryden for happy combinations of heroic diction; but it will not be denied that he added much to what he found. He cultivated our language with so much diligence and art, that he has left in his Homer a treasure of poetical elegances to posterity. His version may be said to have tuned the English tongue; for since its appearance no writer, however deficient in other powers, has wanted melody. Such a series of lines, so elaborately corrected, and so sweetly modulated, took possession of the public ear; the vulgar was enamoured of the poem, and the learned wondered at the translation.

But in the most general applause discordant voices will always be heard. It has been objected by some, who wish to be numbered among the sons of learning, that Pope's version of Homer is not Homerical; that it exhibits no resemblance of the original and characteristic manner of the Father of Poetry, as it wants his awful simplicity, his artless grandeur, his unaffected majesty. This cannot be totally denied; but it must be remembered that *necessitas quod cogit defendit;* that may be lawfully done which cannot be forborne. Time and place will always enforce regard. In estimating this translation, consideration must be had of the nature of our language, the form of our metre, and, above all, of the change which two thousand years have made in the modes of life and the habits of thought. Virgil wrote in a language of the same general fabric with that of Homer, in verses of the same measure, and in an age nearer to Homer's time by eighteen hundred years; yet he found, even then, the state of the world so much altered, and the demand for elegance so much increased, that mere nature would be endured no longer; and perhaps, in the multitude of borrowed passages, very few can be shown which he has not embellished.

There is a time when nations, emerging from barbarity, and falling into regular subordination, gain leisure to grow wise, and feel the shame of ignorance, and the craving pain

of unsatisfied curiosity. To this hunger of the mind plain sense is grateful; that which fills the void removes uneasiness, and to be free from pain for a while is pleasure; but repletion generates fastidiousness; a saturated intellect soon becomes luxurious, and knowledge finds no willing reception till it is recommended by artificial diction. Thus it will be found, in the progress of learning, that in all nations the first writers are simple, and that every age improves in elegance. One refinement always makes way for another;
10 and what was expedient to Virgil was necessary to Pope.

I suppose many readers of the English Iliad when they have been touched with some unexpected beauty of the lighter kind, have tried to enjoy it in the original, where, alas! it was not to be found. Homer doubtless owes to his translator many Ovidian graces not exactly suitable to his character; but to have added can be no great crime, if nothing be taken away. Elegance is surely to be desired, if it be not gained at the expense of dignity. A hero would wish to be loved, as well as to be reverenced. To a thousand
20 cavils one answer is sufficient; the purpose of a writer is to be read, and the criticism which would destroy the power of pleasing must be blown aside. Pope wrote for his own age and his own nation: he knew that it was necessary to colour the images and point the sentiments of his author; he therefore made him graceful, but lost him some of his sublimity.

The copious notes with which the version is accompanied, and by which it is recommended to many readers, though they were undoubtedly written to swell the
30 volumes, ought not to pass without praise: commentaries which attract the reader by the pleasure of perusal have not often appeared; the notes of others are read to clear difficulties, those of Pope to vary entertainment. It has however been objected, with sufficient reason, that there is in the commentary too much of unseasonable levity and affected gaiety; that too many appeals are made to the Ladies,

and the ease which is so carefully preserved is sometimes the ease of a trifler. Every art has its terms, and every kind of instruction its proper style; the gravity of common critics may be tedious, but is less despicable than childish merriment.

Of the Odyssey nothing remains to be observed: the same general praise may be given to both translations, and a particular examination of either would require a large volume. The notes were written by Broome, who endeavoured, not unsuccessfully, to imitate his master. 10

Of the Dunciad the hint is confessedly taken from Dryden's Mac Flecknoe; but the plan is so enlarged and diversified as justly to claim the praise of an original, and affords perhaps the best specimen that has yet appeared of personal satire ludicrously pompous. That the design was moral, whatever the author might tell either his readers or himself, I am not convinced. The first motive was the desire of revenging the contempt with which Theobald had treated his Shakespeare, and regaining the honour which he had lost, by crushing his opponent. Theobald was not of bulk 20 enough to fill a poem, and therefore it was necessary to find other enemies with other names, at whose expence he might divert the public.

In this design there was petulance and malignity enough; but I cannot think it very criminal. An author places himself uncalled before the tribunal of Criticism, and solicits fame at the hazard of disgrace. Dulness or deformity are not culpable in themselves, but may be very justly reproached when they pretend to the honour of wit or the influence of beauty. If bad writers were to pass without 30 reprehension, what should restrain them? *impune diem consumpserit ingens Telephus;* and upon bad writers only will censure have much effect. The satire which brought Theobald and Moore into contempt, dropped impotently from Bentley, like the javelin of Priam. All truth is valuable, and satirical criticism may be considered as useful when it rectifies error and improves judgement; he that refines the public taste is a public benefactor. The beauties of this poem are well known; its chief fault is the grossness of its images. Pope and Swift had an unnatural delight in ideas physically impure, such as every other tongue utters with unwillingness, and of which every ear shrinks from the mention.

But even this fault, offensive as it is, may be forgiven for the excellence of other passages; such as the formation and dissolution of Moore, the account of the Traveller, the misfortune of the Florist, and the crowded thoughts and stately numbers which dignify the concluding paragraph. The alterations which have been made in the Dunciad, not always for the better, require that it should be published, as in the last collection, with all its variations.

The Essay on Man was a work of great labour and long consideration, but certainly not the happiest of Pope's performances. The subject is perhaps not very proper for poetry; and the poet was not sufficiently master of his subject; metaphysical morality was to him a new study, he was proud of his acquisitions, and, supposing himself master of great secrets, was in haste to teach what he had not learned. Thus he tells us, in the first Epistle, that from the nature of the Supreme Being may be deduced an order of beings such as mankind, because Infinite Excellence can do only what is best. He finds out that these beings must be *somewhere;* and that *all the question is whether man be in a wrong place.* Surely if, according to the poet's Leibnitian reasoning, we may infer that man ought to be, only because he is, we may allow that his place is the right place, because he has it. Supreme Wisdom is not less infallible in disposing than in creating. But what is meant by *somewhere,* and *place,* and *wrong place,* it had been vain to ask Pope, who probably had never asked himself.

Having exalted himself into the chair of wisdom, he tells us much that every man knows, and much that he does not know himself; that we see but little, and that the order of the universe is beyond our comprehension; an opinion not very uncommon; and that there is a chain of subordinate beings *from infinite to nothing*, of which himself and his readers are equally ignorant. But he gives us one comfort, which without his help he supposes unattainable, in the position *that though we are fools, yet God is wise.*

This Essay affords an egregious instance of the predominance of genius, the dazzling splendour of imagery, and the seductive powers of eloquence. Never were penury of knowledge and vulgarity of sentiment so happily disguised. The reader feels his mind full, though he learns nothing; and when he meets it in its new array, no longer knows the talk of his mother and his nurse. When these wonder-working sounds sink into sense, and the doctrine of the Essay, disrobed of its ornaments, is left to the powers of its naked excellence, what shall we discover? That we are, in comparison with our Creator, very weak and ignorant; that we do not uphold the chain of existence; and that we could not make one another with more skill than we are made. We may learn yet more: that the arts of human life were copied from the instinctive operations of other animals; that, if the world be made for man, it may be said that man was made for geese. To these profound principles of natural knowledge are added some moral instructions equally new; that self-interest, well understood, will produce social concord; that men are mutual gainers by mutual benefits; that evil is sometimes balanced by good; that human advantages are unstable and fallacious, of uncertain duration and doubtful effect; that our true honour is, not to have a great part, but to act it well; that virtue only is our own; and that happiness is always in our power. Surely a man of no very comprehensive search may venture to say that he has heard all this before; but it was never till now recommended by such a blaze of embellishments, or such sweetness of melody. The vigorous contraction of some thoughts, the luxuriant amplification of others, the incidental illustrations, and sometimes the dignity, sometimes the softness of the verses, enchain philosophy, suspend criticism, and oppress judgement by overpowering pleasure. This is true of many paragraphs; yet, if I had undertaken to exemplify Pope's felicity of composition before a rigid critic, I should not select the Essay on Man; for it contains more lines unsuccessfully laboured, more harshness of diction, and more thoughts imperfectly expressed, more levity without elegance, and more heaviness without strength, than will easily be found in all his other works.

The Characters of Men and Women are the product of diligent speculation upon human life; much labour has been bestowed upon them, and Pope very seldom laboured in vain. That his excellence may be properly estimated, I recommend a comparison of his Characters of Women with Boileau's Satire; it will then be seen with how much more perspicacity female nature is investigated, and female excellence selected; and he surely is no mean writer to whom Boileau should be found inferior. The Characters of Men however are written with more, if not with deeper, thought, and exhibit many passages exquisitely beautiful. The Gem and the Flower will not easily be equalled. In the women's part are some defects; the character of Atossa is not so neatly finished as that of Clodio; and some of the female characters may be found perhaps more frequently among men; what is said of Philomede was true of Prior.

In the Epistles to Lord Bathurst and Lord Burlington, Dr. Warburton has endeavoured to find a train of thought which was never in the writer's head, and to support his hypothesis, has printed that first which was published last. In one the most valuable passage is perhaps the Eulogy on Good Sense; and the other the End of the Duke of Buckingham.

The Epistle to Arbuthnot, now arbitrarily called the Prologue to the Satires, is a performance consisting, as it seems, of many fragments wrought into one design, which by this union of scattered beauties contains more striking paragraphs than could probably have been brought together into an occasional work. As there is no stronger motive to exertion than self-defence, no part has more elegance, spirit, or dignity, than the poet's vindication of his own character. The meanest passage is the satire upon Sporus.

Of the two poems which derived their names from the year, and which are called the Epilogue to the Satires, it was very justly remarked by Savage, that the second was in the whole more strongly conceived, and more equally supported, but that it had no single passages equal to the contention in the first for the dignity of Vice, and the celebration of the triumph of Corruption.

The Imitations of Horace seem to have been written as relaxations of his genius. This employment became his favourite by its facility; the plan was ready to his hand, and nothing was required but to accommodate as he could the sentiments of an old author to recent facts or familiar images; but what is easy is seldom excellent; such imitations cannot give pleasure to common readers; the man of learning may be sometimes surprised and delighted by an unexpected parallel; but the comparison requires knowledge of the original, which will likewise often detect strained applications. Between Roman images and English manners there will be an irreconcilable dissimilitude, and the work will be generally uncouth and party-coloured; neither original nor translated, neither ancient nor modern.

Pope had, in proportions very nicely adjusted to each other, all the qualities that constitute genius. He had *Invention*, by which new trains of events are formed, and new scenes of imagery displayed, as in the Rape of the Lock; and by which extrinsic and adventitious embellishments and illustrations are connected with a known subject, as in the Essay on Criticism. He had *Imagination*, which strongly impresses on the writer's mind, and enables him to convey to

the reader, the various forms of nature, incidents of life, and energies of passion, as in his Eloisa, Windsor Forest, and Ethic Epistles. He had *Judgement*, which selects from life or nature what the present purpose requires, and, by separating the essence of things from its concomitants, often makes the representation more powerful than the reality: and he had colours of language always before him, ready to decorate his matter with every grace of elegant expression, as when he accommodates his diction to the wonderful multiplicity
10 of Homer's sentiments and descriptions.

Poetical expression includes sound as well as meaning: *Music*, says Dryden, *is inarticulate poetry;* among the excellences of Pope, therefore, must be mentioned the melody of his metre. By perusing the works of Dryden, he discovered the most perfect fabric of English verse, and habituated himself to that only which he found the best; in consequence of which restraint, his poetry has been censured as too uniformly musical, and as glutting the ear with unvaried sweetness. I suspect this objection to be the
20 cant of those who judge by principles rather than perception; and who would even themselves have less pleasure in his works, if he had tried to relieve attention by studied discords, or affected to break his lines and vary his pauses.

But though he was thus careful of his versification, he did not oppress his powers with superfluous rigour. He seems to have thought with Boileau, that the practice of writing might be refined till the difficulty should overbalance the advantage. The construction of his language is not always strictly grammatical; with those rhymes which prescription
30 had conjoined he contented himself, without regard to Swift's remonstrances, though there was no striking consonance; nor was he very careful to vary his terminations, or to refuse admission at a small distance to the same rhymes. To Swift's edict for the exclusion of alexandrines and triplets he paid little regard; he admitted them, but, in the opinion of Fenton, too rarely; he uses them more

liberally in his translation than his poems. He has a few double rhymes; and always, I think, unsuccessfully, except once in the Rape of the Lock. Expletives he very early ejected from his verses; but he now and then admits an epithet rather commodious than important. Each of the six first lines of the Iliad might lose two syllables with very little diminution of the meaning; and sometimes, after all his art and labour, one verse seems to be made for the sake of another. In his latter productions the diction is sometimes vitiated by French idioms, with which Bolingbroke had perhaps infected him.

I have been told that the couplet by which he declared his own ear to be most gratified was this:

> Lo, where Mœotis sleeps, and hardly flows
> The freezing Tanais through a waste of snows.

But the reason of this preference I cannot discover.

It is remarked by Watts, that there is scarcely a happy combination of words, or a phrase poetically elegant in the English language, which Pope has not inserted into his version of Homer. How he obtained possession of so many beauties of speech, it were desirable to know. That he gleaned from authors, obscure as well as eminent, what he thought brilliant or useful, and preserved it all in a regular collection, is not unlikely. When, in his last years, Hall's Satires were shown him, he wished that he had seen them sooner.

New sentiments and new images others may produce; but to attempt any further improvement of versification will be dangerous. Art and diligence have now done their best, and what shall be added will be the effort of tedious toil and needless curiosity. After all this, it is surely superfluous to answer the question that has once been asked, Whether Pope was a poet, otherwise than by asking in return, If Pope be not a poet, where is poetry to be found? To circumscribe poetry by a definition will only shew the narrowness of the definer, though a definition which shall exclude Pope will not easily be made. Let us look round upon the present time, and back upon the past; let us enquire to whom the voice of mankind has decreed the wreath of poetry; let their productions be examined, and their claims stated, and the pretensions of Pope will be no more disputed. Had he given the world only his version, the name of poet must have been allowed him: if the writer of the Iliad were to class his successors, he would assign a very high place to his translator, without requiring any other evidence of Genius.

The following letter, of which the original is in the hands of Lord Hardwicke, was communicated to me by the kindness of Mr. Jodrell:—

"To MR. BRIDGES, at the Bishop of London's at Fulham.

"SIR,—The favour of your Letter, with your Remarks, can never be enough acknowledged; and the speed with which you discharged so troublesome a task doubles the obligation.

"I must own you have pleased me very much by the commendations so ill bestowed upon me; but I assure you, much more by the frankness of your censure, which I ought to take the more kindly of the two, as it is more advantage to a scribbler to be improved in his judgement than to be soothed in his vanity. The greater part of those deviations from the Greek, which you have observed, I was led into by Chapman and Hobbes; who are (it seems) as much celebrated for their knowledge of the original, as they are decryed for the badness of their translations. Chapman pretends to have restored the genuine sense of the author, from the mistakes of all former explainers, in several hundred places: and the Cambridge editors of the large Homer, in Greek and Latin, attributed so much to Hobbes, that they confess they have corrected the old Latin interpretation very often by his version. For my part I generally took the author's meaning to be as you have explained it; yet their authority,

joined to the knowledge of my own imperfectness in the
language, over-ruled me. However, sir, you may be confident I think you in the right, because you happen to be
of my opinion : for men (let them say what they will) never
approve any other's sense, but as it squares with their own.
But you have made me much more proud of, and positive in
my judgement, since it is strengthened by yours. I think
your criticisms, which regard the expression, very just, and
shall make my profit of them ; to give you some proof that
I am in earnest I will alter three verses on your bare 10
objection, though I have Mr. Dryden's example for each of
them. And this, I hope, you will account no small piece of
obedience, from one who values the authority of one true
poet above that of twenty critics or commentators. But,
though I speak thus of commentators, I will continue to
read carefully all I can procure, to make up, that way, for
my own want of critical understanding in the original
beauties of Homer. Though the greatest of them are certainly those of the Invention and Design, which are not at all
confined to the language : for the distinguishing excellences 20
of Homer are (by the consent of the best critics of all
nations) first in the manners, (which include all the speeches,
as being no other than the representations of each person's
manners by his words :) and then in that rapture and fire,
which carries you away with him, with that wonderful force,
that no man who has a true poetical spirit is master of himself,
while he reads him. Homer makes you interested and concerned before you are aware, all at once, whereas Virgil does
it by soft degrees. This, I believe, is what a translator of
Homer ought principally to imitate ; and it is very hard for 30
any translator to come up to it, because the chief reason
why all translations fall short of their originals is, that the
very constraint they are obliged to, renders them heavy and
dispirited.

"The great beauty of Homer's language, as I take it,
consists in that noble simplicity which runs through all his

works; (and yet his diction, contrary to what one would imagine consistent with simplicity, is at the same time very copious). I don't know how I have run into this pedantry in a letter, but I find I have said too much, as well as spoken too inconsiderately; what farther thoughts I have upon this subject, I shall be glad to communicate to you (for my own improvement) when we meet; which is a happiness I very earnestly desire, as I do likewise some opportunity of proving how much I think myself obliged to your friendship,
10 and how truly I am, sir,
"Your most faithful humble servant,
"A. POPE."

The criticism upon Pope's Epitaphs, which was printed in The Visitor, is placed here, being too minute and particular to be inserted in the Life.

Every Art is best taught by example. Nothing contributes more to the cultivation of propriety than remarks on the works of those who have most excelled. I shall therefore endeavour, at this *visit*, to entertain the young students in
20 poetry with an examination of Pope's Epitaphs.

To define an epitaph is useless; every one knows that it is an inscription on a tomb. An epitaph, therefore, implies no particular character of writing, but may be composed in verse or prose. It is indeed commonly panegyrical, because we are seldom distinguished with a stone but by our friends; but it has no rule to restrain or mollify it, except this, that it ought not to be longer than common beholders may be expected to have leisure and patience to peruse.

I.

On CHARLES, *Earl of* DORSET, *in the Church of Wythyham*
30 *in Sussex.*

Dorset, the grace of courts, the Muse's pride,
Patron of arts, and judge of nature, dy'd.

JOHNSON'S LIFE OF POPE. 113

> The scourge of pride, though sanctify'd or great,
> Of fops in learning, and of knaves in state;
> Yet soft in nature, though severe his lay,
> His anger moral, and his wisdom gay.
> Blest satyrist! who touch'd the mean so true,
> As show'd Vice had his hate and pity too.
> Blest courtier! who could king and country please,
> Yet sacred kept his friendship, and his ease.
> Blest peer! his great forefathers' every grace
> Reflecting, and reflected on his race; 10
> Where other Buckhursts, other Dorsets shine,
> And patriots still, or poets, deck the line.

The first distich of this epitaph contains a kind of information which few would want, that the man for whom the tomb was erected *died*. There are indeed some qualities worthy of praise ascribed to the dead, but none that were likely to exempt him from the lot of man, or incline us much to wonder that he should die. What is meant by *judge of nature*, is not easy to say. Nature is not the object of human judgement; for it is vain to judge where 20 we cannot alter. If by nature is meant, what is commonly called *nature* by the critics, a just representation of things really existing, and actions really performed, nature cannot be properly opposed to *art;* nature being, in this sense, only the best effect of *art*.

> The scourge of pride—

Of this couplet, the second line is not, what is intended, an illustration of the former. *Pride*, in the *Great*, is indeed well enough connected with knaves in state, though *knaves* is a word rather too ludicrous and light; but the 30 mention of *sanctified* pride will not lead the thoughts to *fops in learning*, but rather to some species of tyranny or oppression, something more gloomy and more formidable than foppery.

> Yet soft his nature—

H

This is a high compliment, but was not first bestowed on Dorset by Pope. The next verse is extremely beautiful.

Blest satyrist!—

In this distich is another line of which Pope was not the author. I do not mean to blame these imitations with much harshness; in long performances they are scarcely to be avoided, and in shorter they may be indulged, because the train of the composition may naturally involve them, or the scantiness of the subject allow little choice. However, what is borrowed is not to be enjoyed as our own; and it is the business of critical justice to give every bird of the Muses his proper feather.

Blest courtier!—

Whether a courtier can properly be commended for keeping his *ease sacred*, may perhaps be disputable. To please king and country, without sacrificing friendship to any change of times, was a very uncommon instance of prudence or felicity, and deserved to be kept separate from so poor a commendation as care of his ease. I wish our poets would attend a little more accurately to the use of the word *sacred*, which surely should never be applied in a serious composition but where some reference may be made to a higher Being, or where some duty is exacted or implied. A man may keep his friendship sacred, because promises of friendship are very awful ties; but methinks he cannot, but in a burlesque sense, be said to keep his ease *sacred*.

Blest peer!

The blessing ascribed to the *peer* has no connection with his peerage: they might happen to any other man whose ancestors were remembered or whose posterity were likely to be regarded.

I know not whether this epitaph be worthy either of the writer or the man entombed.

II.

On Sir WILLIAM TRUMBAL, *one of the Principal Secretaries of State to King* WILLIAM III., *who, having resigned his place, died in his retirement at Easthamsted in Berkshire,* 1716.

> A pleasing form, a firm, yet cautious mind,
> Sincere, though prudent; constant, yet resign'd;
> Honour unchanged, a principle profest,
> Fix'd to one side, but moderate to the rest;
> An honest courtier, yet a patriot too,
> Just to his prince, and to his country too;   10
> Fill'd with the sense of age, the fire of youth,
> A scorn of wrangling, yet a zeal for truth;
> A generous faith, from superstition free;
> A love to peace, and hate of tyranny;
> Such this man was; who now, from earth remov'd,
> At length enjoys that liberty he lov'd.

In this epitaph, as in many others, there appears, at the first view, a fault which I think scarcely any beauty can compensate. The name is omitted. The end of an epitaph is to convey some account of the dead; and to what pur- 20 pose is anything told of him whose name is concealed? An epitaph, and a history, of a nameless hero, are equally absurd, since the virtues and qualities so recounted in either are scattered at the mercy of fortune to be appropriated by guess. The name, it is true, may be read upon the stone; but what obligation has it to the poet, whose verses wander over the earth, and leave their subject behind them, and who is forced, like an unskilful painter, to make his purpose known by adventitious help? This epitaph is wholly without elevation, and contains nothing striking or particular; 30 but the poet is not to be blamed for the defects of his subject. He said perhaps the best that could be said. There are, however, some defects which were not made necessary by the character in which he was employed. There is no opposition between an *honest courtier* and a *patriot;* for an *honest courtier* cannot but be a *patriot*. It was unsuitable to the nicety required in short compositions to close his verse with the word *too;* every rhyme should be a word of emphasis; nor can this rule be safely neglected, except where the length of the poem makes slight inaccuracies excusable, or allows room for beauties sufficient to overpower the effects of petty faults.

At the beginning of the seventh line the word *filled* is weak and prosaic, having no particular adaptation to any of the words that follow it. The thought in the last line is impertinent, having no connexion with the foregoing character, nor with the condition of the man described. Had the epitaph been written on the poor conspirator, who died lately in prison, after a confinement of more than forty years, without any crime proved against him, the sentiment had been just and pathetical; but why should Trumbal be congratulated upon his liberty who had never known restraint?

III.

On the Hon. SIMON HARCOURT, *only son of the Lord Chancellor* HARCOURT, *at the Church of Stanton-Harcourt in Oxfordshire,* 1720.

> To this sad shrine, whoe'er thou art, draw near,
> Here lies the friend most lov'd, the son most dear;
> Who ne'er knew joy, but friendship might divide,
> Or gave his father grief but when he died.
>
> How vain is reason, eloquence how weak!
> If Pope must tell what Harcourt cannot speak.
> Oh let thy once loved friend inscribe thy stone,
> And with a father's sorrows mix his own!

This epitaph is principally remarkable for the artful introduction of the name, which is inserted with a peculiar felicity, to which chance must concur with genius, which no man can hope to attain twice, and which cannot be copied but with servile imitation. I cannot but wish that, of this inscription, the two last lines had been omitted, as they take away from the energy what they do not add to the sense.

iv.

On JAMES CRAGGS, *Esq., in Westminster Abbey.*

JACOBVS CRAGGS,
REGI MAGNAE BRITANNIAE A SECRETIS
ET CONCILIIS SANCTIORIBVS,
PRINCIPIS PARITER AC POPVLI AMOR ET DELICIAE:
VIXIT TITVLIS ET INVIDIA MAJOR
ANNOS HEV PAVCOS, XXXV.
OB. FEB. XVI. MDCCXX.

Statesman, yet friend to truth! of soul sincere,
In action faithful, and in honour clear!
Who broke no promise, serv'd no private end,
Who gain'd no title, and who lost no friend;
Ennobled by himself, by all approv'd,
Praised, wept, and honour'd by the Muse he lov'd.

The lines on Craggs were not originally intended for an epitaph; and therefore some faults are to be imputed to the violence with which they are torn from the poem that first contained them. We may, however, observe some defects. There is a redundancy of words in the first couplet: it is superfluous to tell of him, who was *sincere, true,* and *faithful* that he was *in honour clear.* There seems to be an opposition intended in the fourth line, which is not very obvious: where is the relation between the two positions, that he *gained no title* and *lost no friend?*

It may be proper here to remark the absurdity of joining, in the same inscription, Latin and English, or verse and prose. If either language be preferable to the other, let that only be used; for no reason can be given why part of the information should be given in one tongue, and part in another, on a tomb, more than in any other place, or any other occasion; and to tell all that can be conveniently told in verse, and then to call in the help of prose, has always the appearance of a very artless expedient, or of an attempt unaccomplished. Such an epitaph resembles the conversation of a foreigner, who tells part of his meaning by words, and conveys part by signs.

V.

Intended for Mr. ROWE, *in Westminster Abbey.*

Thy reliques, Rowe, to this fair urn we trust,
And sacred, place by Dryden's awful dust:
Beneath a rude and nameless stone he lies,
To which thy tomb shall guide inquiring eyes.
10   Peace to thy gentle shade, and endless rest!
Blest in thy genius, in thy love too blest;
One grateful woman to thy fame supplies
What a whole thankless land to his denies.

Of this inscription the chief fault is, that it belongs less to Rowe, for whom it was written, than to Dryden, who was buried near him; and indeed gives very little information concerning either.

To wish *Peace to thy shade* is too mythological to be admitted into a christian temple: the ancient worship has
20 infected almost all our other compositions, and might therefore be contented to spare our epitaphs. Let fiction, at least, cease with life, and let us be serious over the grave.

VI.

On Mrs. CORBET, *who died of a Cancer in her Breast.*

Here rests a woman, good without pretence,
Blest with plain reason, and with sober sense;
No conquest she, but o'er herself, desir'd;
No arts essay'd, but not to be admir'd.
Passion and pride were to her soul unknown,
Convinced that Virtue only is our own.
30   So unaffected, so compos'd a mind,
So firm, yet soft, so strong, yet so refin'd,
Heaven, as its purest gold, by tortures try'd;
The saint sustained, but the woman dy'd.

I have always considered this as the most valuable of all Pope's epitaphs; the subject of it is a character not discriminated by any shining or eminent peculiarities; yet that which really makes, though not the splendour, the felicity of life, and that which every wise man will choose for his final and lasting companion in the languor of age, in the quiet of privacy, when he departs weary and disgusted from the ostentatious, the volatile, and the vain. Of such a character, which the dull overlook, and the gay despise, it was fit that the value should be made known, and the dignity established. Domestic virtue, as it is exerted without great occasions, or conspicuous consequences, in an even unnoted tenor, required the genius of Pope to display it in such a manner as might attract regard, and enforce reverence. Who can forbear to lament that this amiable woman has no name in the verses? If the particular lines of this inscription be examined, it will appear less faulty than the rest. There is scarce one line taken from common-places, unless it be that in which *only Virtue* is said to be *our own*. I once heard a Lady of great beauty and excellence object to the fourth line, that it contained an unnatural and incredible panegyric. Of this let the Ladies judge.

VII.

On the Monument of the Hon. ROBERT DIGBY, *and of his Sister* MARY, *erected by their Father the Lord* DIGBY, *in the Church of Sherborne in Dorsetshire,* 1727.

Go! fair example of untainted youth,
Of modest wisdom, and pacific truth:
Compos'd in sufferings, and in joy sedate,
Good without noise, without pretension great.
Just of thy word, in every thought sincere,
Who knew no wish but what the world might hear:
Of softest manners, unaffected mind,
Lover of peace, and friend of human kind:
Go, live! for heaven's eternal year is thine,
Go, and exalt thy mortal to divine.

>   And thou, blest maid! attendant on his doom,
>   Pensive hast follow'd to the silent tomb,
>   Steer'd the same course to the same quiet shore.
>   Not parted long, and now to part no more!
>   Go, then, where only bliss sincere is known!
>   Go, where to love and to enjoy are one!
>   Yet take these tears, Mortality's relief,
>   And, till we share your joys, forgive our grief:
>   These little rites, a stone, a verse receive,
> 10 'Tis all a father, all a friend can give!

This epitaph contains of the brother only a general indiscriminate character, and of the sister tells nothing but that she died. The difficulty in writing epitaphs is to give a particular and appropriate praise. This, however, is not always to be performed, whatever be the diligence or ability of the writer; for, the greater part of mankind *have no character at all*, have little that distinguishes them from others equally good or bad, and therefore nothing can be said of them which may not be applied with equal propriety to a thousand more. It is indeed no great panegyric, that there is inclosed in this tomb one who was born in one year, and died in another; yet many useful and amiable lives have been spent, which yet leave little materials for any other memorial. These are however not the proper subjects of poetry; and whenever friendship, or any other motive, obliges a poet to write on such subjects, he must be forgiven if he sometimes wanders in generalities, and utters the same praises over different tombs.

The scantiness of human praises can scarcely be made more apparent, than by remarking how often Pope has, in the few epitaphs which he composed, found it necessary to borrow from himself. The fourteen epitaphs, which he has written, comprise about an hundred and forty lines, in which there are more repetitions than will easily be found in all the rest of his works. In the eight lines which make the character of Digby, there is scarce any thought, or word,

which may not be found in the other epitaphs. The ninth
line, which is far the strongest and most elegant, is borrowed
from Dryden. The conclusion is the same with that on
Harcourt, but is here more elegant and better connected.

VIII.

On Sir GODFREY KNELLER, *in Westminster Abbey*, 1723.

Kneller, by heaven, and not a master, taught,
Whose art was nature, and whose pictures thought;
Now for two ages, having snatch'd from fate
Whate'er was beauteous, or whate'er was great,
Lies crown'd with Princes honours, Poets lays,   10
Due to his merit, and brave thirst of praise.
Living, great Nature fear'd he might outvie
Her works; and dying, fears herself may die.

Of this epitaph the first couplet is good, the second not
bad, the third is deformed with a broken metaphor, the word
crowned not being applicable to the *honours* or the *lays*, and
the fourth is not only borrowed from the epitaph on Raphael,
but of very harsh construction.

IX.

On General HENRY WITHERS, *in Westminster Abbey*, 1729.

Here, Withers, rest! thou bravest, gentlest mind,   20
Thy country's friend, but more of human kind.
O! born to arms! O! worth in youth approved!
O! soft humanity in age belov'd!
For thee the hardy veteran drops a tear,
And the gay courtier feels the sigh sincere.
Withers, adieu! yet not with thee remove
Thy martial spirit, or thy social love!
Amidst corruption, luxury, and rage,
Still leave some ancient virtues to our age!
Nor let us say (those English glories gone)   30
The last true Briton lies beneath this stone.

The epitaph on Withers affords another instance of common-places, though somewhat diversified by mingled qualities, and the peculiarity of a profession. The second couplet is abrupt, general, and unpleasing; exclamation seldom succeeds in our language; and, I think, it may be observed that the particle O! used at the beginning of a sentence, always offends. The third couplet is more happy; the value expressed for him, by different sorts of men, raises him to esteem; there is yet something of the common cant of superficial satirists, who suppose that the insincerity of a courtier destroys all his sensations, and that he is equally a dissembler to the living and the dead. At the third couplet I should wish the epitaph to close, but that I should be unwilling to lose the two next lines, which yet are dearly bought if they cannot be retained without the four that follow them.

X.

On Mr. ELIJAH FENTON, *at Easthamsted in Berkshire*, 1730.

> This modest stone, what few vain marbles can,
> May truly say, Here lies an honest man:
> A poet, blest beyond the poet's fate,
> Whom Heaven kept sacred from the Proud and Great:
> Foe to loud praise, and friend to learned ease,
> Content with science in the vale of peace.
> Calmly he look'd on either life, and here
> Saw nothing to regret, or there to fear;
> From nature's temperate feast rose satisfy'd,
> Thank'd Heaven that he had liv'd, and that he dy'd.

The first couplet of this epitaph is borrowed from Crashaw. The four next lines contain a species of praise peculiar, original, and just. Here, therefore, the inscription should have ended, the latter part containing nothing but what is common to every man who is wise and good. The character of Fenton was so amiable, that I cannot forbear to wish for some poet or biographer to display it more fully for the advantage of posterity. If he did not stand in the first rank of genius, he may claim a place in the second; and, whatever

criticism may object to his writings, censure could find very
little to blame in his life.

XI.

On Mr. GAY, *in Westminster Abbey,* 1732.

Of manners gentle, of affections mild;
In wit, a man; simplicity, a child:
With native humour tempering virtuous rage,
Form'd to delight at once and lash the age:
Above temptation in a low estate,
And uncorrupted, ev'n among the Great:
A safe companion and an easy friend,   10
Unblam'd through life, lamented in thy end,
These are thy honours! not that here thy bust
Is mix'd with heroes, or with kings thy dust;
But that the Worthy and the Good shall say,
Striking their pensive bosoms—Here lies GAY.

As Gay was the favourite of our author, this epitaph was
probably written with an uncommon degree of attention; yet
it is not more successfully executed than the rest, for it will
not always happen that the success of a poet is proportionate
to his labour. The same observation may be extended to all 20
works of imagination, which are often influenced by causes
wholly out of the performer's power, by hints of which he
perceives not the origin, by sudden elevations of mind which
he cannot produce in himself, and which sometimes rise when
he expects them least. The two parts of the first line are
only echoes of each other; *gentle manners* and *mild affections*,
if they mean anything, must mean the same.

That Gay was a *man in wit* is a very frigid commendation;
to have the wit of a man is not much for a poet. The *wit of
man,* and the *simplicity of a child,* make a poor and vulgar 30
contrast, and raise no ideas of excellence, either intellectual
or moral.

In the next couplet *rage* is less properly introduced after
the mention of *mildness* and *gentleness,* which are made the
constituents of his character : for a man so *mild* and *gentle* to

temper his *rage* was not difficult. The next line is inharmonious in its sound, and mean in its conception; the opposition is obvious, and the word *lash* used absolutely, and without any modification, is gross and improper. To be *above temptation* in poverty, and *free from corruption among the Great*, is indeed such a peculiarity as deserved notice. But to be a *safe companion* is a praise merely negative, arising not from possession of virtue, but the absence of vice, and that one of the most odious.

10   As little can be added to his character, by asserting that he was *lamented in his end.* Every man that dies is, at least by the writer of his epitaph, supposed to be lamented, and therefore this general lamentation does no honour to Gay.

The first eight lines have no grammar; the adjectives are without any substantive, and the epithets without a subject. The thought in the last line, that Gay is buried in the bosoms of the *worthy* and *good*, who are distinguished only to lengthen the line, is so dark that few understand it; and so harsh, when it is explained, that still fewer approve.

XII.

20   *Intended for Sir* ISAAC NEWTON, *in Westminster Abbey.*

ISAACUS NEWTONIUS:
Quem Immortalem
Testantur, *Tempus, Natura, Cœlum :*
Mortalem hoc marmor fatetur.
Nature, and Nature's laws, lay hid in night,
God said, *Let Newton be!* And all was light.

Of this epitaph, short as it is, the faults seem not to be very few. Why part should be Latin, and part English, it is not easy to discover. In the Latin the opposition of
30 *Immortalis* and *Mortalis*, is a mere sound, or a mere quibble; he is not *immortal* in any sense contrary to that in which he is *mortal.* In the verses the thought is obvious, and the words *night* and *light* are too nearly allied.

XIII.

On EDMUND *Duke of* BUCKINGHAM, *who died in the* 19*th Year of his Age*, 1735.

> If modest youth, with cool reflection crown'd,
> And every opening virtue blooming round,
> Could save a parent's justest pride from fate,
> Or add one patriot to a sinking state;
> This weeping marble had not ask'd thy tear,
> Or sadly told how many hopes lie here!
> The living virtue now had shone approv'd,
> The senate heard him, and his country lov'd.   10
> Yet softer honours, and less noisy fame,
> Attend the shade of gentle Buckingham:
> In whom a race, for courage fam'd and art,
> Ends in the milder merit of the heart:
> And chiefs or sages long to Britain given,
> Pays the last tribute of a saint to heaven.

This epitaph Mr. Warburton prefers to the rest, but I know not for what reason. To *crown* with *reflection* is surely a mode of speech approaching to nonsense. *Opening virtues blooming round* is something like tautology; the six following lines are poor and prosaic. *Art* is in another couplet used for *arts*, that a rhyme may be had to *heart*. The six last lines are the best, but not excellent.

The rest of his sepulchral performances hardly deserve the notice of criticism. The contemptible Dialogue between He and She should have been suppressed for the author's sake.

In his last epitaph on himself, in which he attempts to be jocular upon one of the few things that make wise men serious, he confounds the living man with the dead:

> Under this stone, or under this sill,   30
> Or under this turf, etc.

When a man is once buried, the question, under what he is buried, is easily decided. He forgot that though he wrote the epitaph in a state of uncertainty, yet it could not be laid over him till his grave was made. Such is the folly of wit when it is ill employed.

The world has but little new; even this wretchedness seems to have been borrowed from the following tuneless lines:

>   Ludovici Areosti humantur ossa
>   Sub hoc marmore, vel sub hac humo, seu
>   Sub quicquid voluit benignus hæres
>   Sive hærede benignior comes, seu
>   Opportunius incidens Viator:
>   Nam scire haud potuit futura, sed nec
>   Tanti erat vacuum sibi cadaver
>   Ut utnam cuperet parare vivens,
>   Vivens ista tamen sibi paravit.
>   Quæ inscribi voluit suo sepulchro
>   Olim si quod haberet is sepulchrum.

Surely Ariosto did not venture to expect that his trifle would have ever had such an illustrious imitator.

NOTES.

Page 1, l. 9. [**general officer in Spain.** In common with many Royalists who left England at the end of the Civil War. Property changed hands in consequence of the death or absence of Royalists, and in subsequent disputes as to ownership estates were often "sequestered" by government, that is, taken from both disputants. Other estates were "forfeited" by Royalists and given to supporters of the Parliament. C. D. P.]

l. 11. **This, and this only, is told by Pope.** Johnson is relying here (a) on a passage in Pope's *Epistle to Arbuthnot*, (b) on one of Pope's own notes to that Epistle, and (c) on a communication made by Pope to Spence. But he has misquoted this last authority, and so given a wrong date for the birth of the poet. "Mr. Pope was born on the 21st day of May, 1688" (Spence, p. 196).

"Of gentle blood (part shed in Honour's cause,
While yet in Britain Honour had applause)
Each parent sprung."
Pope, *Epistle to Arbuthnot* (Globe edition, p. 283).

Johnson has reproduced the note almost textually, except that he has suppressed the fact that the son of Mr. Turner mentioned third was the eldest. Compare the note below, on p. 3, l. 26.

l. 14. **whether in a shop or on the Exchange,** whether as a tradesman or a merchant. [The Exchange, in Cornhill, first built in 1566-1567, was a market with shops of all descriptions. Later it became a meeting-place for merchants of all nations, and contained the offices of various important trading companies. C. D. P.]

l. 15. **till Mr. Tyers told, on the authority of Mrs. Racket.** This Mrs. Racket was the poet's half-sister, but it is not certain whether she was the daughter by a previous marriage of Pope's father or of his mother. Mr. Thomas Tyers was a friend of

Johnson's, who published biographical sketches of Addison, Pope, and Johnson himself. See Boswell's *Life of Johnson* (Globe edition, p. 475).

Page 2, l. 1. Being not sent early to school, etc. "His first education was extremely loose and disconcerted. He began to learn Latin and Greek together (as is customary in the schools of the Jesuits, and which he seemed to think a good way) under Banister, their family priest, who, he said, was living about two years ago at Sir Harry Tichborne's. He then learned his accidence at Twiford, where he wrote a satire on some faults of his master. He was then, a little while, at Mr. Dean's seminary at Marylebone, and some time under the same, after he removed to Hyde Park Corner. After this he taught himself both Greek and Latin. 'I did not follow the grammar; but rather hunted in the authors for a syntax of my own, and then began translating any parts that pleased me particularly in the best Greek and Latin poets; and by that means formed my taste, which, I think, verily, about sixteen, was very near as good as it is now.'"— Spence, writing from information supplied by Pope in 1742 (p. 196). Johnson takes the name Taverner, for the priest who was Pope's tutor, from Ruffhead, who published a *Life of Pope* in 1769. There may, of course, have been two priests.

l. 7. [a Romish·priest. In consequence of the laws against Roman Catholics, Pope was excluded from the ordinary schools. C. D. P.]

l. 10. [John Ogilby (1600-1676) translated both Virgil and Homer. C. D. P.]

l. 11. [Sandys (1577-1644), besides books on travel, published a translation of Ovid's *Metamorphoses* (1626). C. D. P.]

l. 24. [Ajax, one of the heroes who fought against Troy. He is represented as second only to Achilles in bravery. C. D. P.]

l. 28. [lampoon, a scurrilous satire in writing. C. D. P.]

l. 32. that he "lisp'd in numbers."

"Why did I write? what sin to me unknown
Dipt me in ink, my parents', or my own?
As yet a child, nor yet a fool to Fame,
I lisp'd in numbers, for the numbers came.
I left no calling for this idle trade,
No duty broke, no father disobey'd.
The Muse but serv'd to ease some friend, not Wife,
To help me thro' this long disease, my Life,
To second, Arbuthnot! thy Art and Care,
And teach the Being you preserv'd, to bear.'
Epistle to Arbuthnot.

l. 35. [**Pindar** (B.C. 522-442), the greatest lyric poet of Greece, commenced his career as a poet at a very early age. C. D. P.]

Page 3, l. 2. the sudden blast, the ruin that suddenly overtook the prosperity which the Papists had enjoyed under James II. [The effect of the Revolution on the hopes of the Catholics is shown in the terms of the Declaration of Rights, accepted by William of Orange before his accession (1689). C. D. P.]

l. 3. [**Binfield**, a village about nine miles from Windsor, and near the south-west border of the Forest. C. D. P.]

l. 6. **he found no better use than that of locking it up in a chest.** This statement is taken from Ruffhead. Carruthers has shown that it must be pure fiction. "Besides Binfield, the elder Pope possessed property at Windsham, or Windlesham, in the county of Surrey, and a yearly rent-charge upon the manor of Ruston in Yorkshire. He had also money invested for himself on French securities, to all which father and son devoted prudent and zealous attention" (Carruthers' *Life of Pope*, p. 15).

l. 13. **Tully's Offices**, Cicero's *De Officiis*.

l. 26. **obliging him to correct his performances**, etc. "Mr. Pope's father (who was an honest merchant, and dealt in Holland's wholesale) was no poet, but he used to set him to make English verses when very young. He was pretty difficult in being pleased; and used often to send him back to new turn them. 'These are not good rhimes'; for that was my husband's word for verses" (Spence, from Mr. Pope's mother, p. 6). Johnson is quoting Warburton, who, in a note on the passage from the *Epistle to Arbuthnot* given above, tells this story, but makes the last part of it read, "when they were to his mind, he took great pleasure in them, and would say, '*These are good rhymes.*'"

l. 29. **he soon distinguished the versification of Dryden.** "I learned versification wholly from Dryden's works; who had improved it much beyond any of our former poets; and would, probably, have brought it to its perfection, had not he been unhappily obliged to write so often in haste" (Pope, in Spence, p. 212).

Page 4, l. 7. [**Cowley** (1618-1667), a poet and writer of essays. He wrote much in support of the Restoration. His *Poetical Blossoms* was published when he was in his fifteenth year. C. D. P.]

l. 17. [**more fashionable appearance.** The language of Chaucer (1328-1400) contained many words and expressions which had become obsolete, and consequently unintelligible. The two works here mentioned are taken from the *Canterbury Tales* of

Chaucer, and related by two pilgrims, a merchant, and a wife of Bath respectively. C. D. P.]

l. 17. **January and May, and the Prologue of the Wife of Bath.** The first of these adaptations from Chaucer appeared in a volume of *Tonson's Miscellany* in 1709. The other was published in the same way in 1714.

l. 24. [**Rochester.** John Wilmot, Earl of Rochester, a dissolute member of the Court of Charles II., trifled in verse, his best piece being the one here mentioned, on *Nothing*. C. D. P.]

Page 5, l. 12. **Alcander, the epic poem**, etc. "We have it on Pope's own authority, as related by Spence, that some of the couplets in an epic poem on the subject of Alcander, Prince of Rhodes, which he begun soon after his twelfth birthday, were afterwards inserted by him without alteration, not only in the *Essay on Criticism*, but in the *Dunciad*. Alcander, after having progressed to the number of 4000 lines, and though uniting in itself specimens of every style admired by its author—Milton and Cowley and Spenser, Homer and Virgil, Ovid and Claudian and Statius—was left uncompleted, and ultimately perished in the flames, to which this juvenile *magnum opus* seems to have been sentenced by the author himself, and not, as has been stated, by Bishop Atterbury" (Ward, in the Introductory Memoir to the Globe edition of Pope, with a reference to Roscoe's *Life*, pp. 19, 20).

l. 14. [**St. Genevieve** (A.D. 422-512), the sainted patroness of the city of Paris. C. D. P.]

l. 16. [**Tully on Old Age.** *De Senectute* (concerning old age), written by Cicero, who is frequently called Tully from Tullius, one of his names. C. D. P.]

l. 17. [**Temple, Sir William,** a famous statesman and diplomatist of the reign of Charles II. C. D. P.]

l. 18. [**Locke,** a philosopher and politician of the same period as Temple. His *Essay on the Human Understanding* was published in 1687. C. D. P.]

l. 24. [**Sir William Trumbal.** See Epitaph on page 115. C. D. P.]

Page 6, l. 2. **He now wrote his Pastorals.** See text, p. 90, l. 36 fg.; also note on page 7, l. 12.

l. 14. **Wycherley,** the author of *The Plain Dealer* and other comedies. "Unsurpassed in brutal vigour" (Ward). He was at this time an old man of nearly seventy.

l. 19. For Dennis, see below, on p. 8, l. 17.

l. 20. **It is pleasant to remark.** By "pleasant" Johnson means what we should now call "amusing."

l. 32. **Mr. Cromwell.** "Another friend with whom Pope at this time became intimate, and to whom he addressed many letters (published surreptitiously in 1727 by the mistress of his correspondent), was Henry Cromwell. Of the latter personally little is known; except that he was slovenly in his person, and rode a-hunting in a tye-wig; but his letters to Pope show him to have been an amateur critic as well as student, and he seems to have largely contributed to introduce Pope and his writings to the knowledge of society in town, where Cromwell was a resident" (Ward, Memoir, p. xxi.). A tye-wig was a wig with its curls or tail tied with a ribbon. Most men who wore such a thing left it at home when going a-hunting. Compare below, p. 75, l. 5.

Page 7, l. 2. [**version**, translation from Latin to English. C. D. P.]

[**Statius**, born about A.D. 61, son of a Roman grammarian. His chief work was an Epic poem, *Thebais*, descriptive of the expedition of the Seven against Thebes. C. D. P.]

l. 12. **Walsh.** "To Trumbal, in the first instance, and then to Wycherley, Pope had communicated a copy of his first completed effort, the *Pastorals*. Wycherley in his turn sent them to Walsh, who was himself not unknown as a poet, but enjoyed a still higher reputation as a critic. He received the juvenile poems favourably, and returned a gratifying verdict upon them: 'It is not flattery at all to say that Virgil had written nothing so good at his age.' He then extended his personal patronage to the young aspirant after poetic fame, and invited him to his seat of Abberley in Worcestershire. Walsh died in 1708, a year before the *Pastorals* were actually published; but he lived to point out to his young friend the path from which the latter never swerved during his literary career; he bade him be a 'correct poet,' or, in other words, desired to limit the excursions of Pope's muse to regions already meted out by trustworthy predecessors, 'prescribed her heights and pruned her tender wing.' 'The best of the modern poets in all languages,' wrote Walsh to Pope in 1706, 'are those that have the nearest copied the ancients,' a maxim sufficiently characteristic of his critical standpoints" (Ward, p. xxi.). The quotation is from Pope's tribute to Walsh in the *Essay on Criticism*:

"Such late was Walsh—the Muse's judge and friend,
Who justly knew to blame or to commend;
To failings mild, but zealous for desert;
The clearest head, and the sincerest heart.
This humble praise, lamented shade! receive,
This praise at least a grateful Muse may give:
The Muse, whose early voice you taught to sing,
Prescrib'd her heights, and prun'd her tender wing
(Her guide now lost) no more attempts to rise," etc.

l. 21. [**Will's**. This would be in 1715. Steele in his first *Tatler* (April, 1709) says, "This place (Will's coffee-house) is very much altered since Mr. Dryden frequented it, where you used to see Songs, Epigrams, and Satires in the hands of every man, you have now only a pack of cards." C. D. P.]

l. 22. [**Convent Garden** (now Covent Garden) was so called from the tradition that the garden belonged to the abbots and monks of Westminster, who used it partly as their kitchen garden. C. D. P.]

Page 8, l. 8. [**Tonson**, Jacob, commenced business as a bookseller in 1678. He was Dryden's publisher, and for several years published an annual *Miscellany* containing various translations and originals. C. D. P.]

l. 9. [**Philips**, Ambrose (born 1671), was a great friend of Addison, who praised his works in the *Spectator*. C. D. P.]

l. 15. **being praised by Addison in the Spectator**. In No. 253, 20th December, 1711.

l. 17. **enraged Dennis**, "**who**," he says, "**found himself attacked**," etc. The attack is in ll. 585-8 of the poem:

"'Twere well might critics still this freedom take,
But Appius reddens at each word you speak,
And stares, tremendous, with a threat'ning eye,
Like some fierce Tyrant in old tapestry."

"This picture was taken to himself by John Dennis, a furious old critic by profession, who, upon no other provocation, wrote against this Essay and its author in a manner perfectly lunatic; for, as to the mention made of him in v. 270:

['Discours'd in terms as just, with looks as sage,
As e'er could Dennis of the Grecian stage.']

he took it as a compliment, and said it was treacherously meant to overlook this *abuse* of his *person*" (Pope's note on the passage).

l. 31. **an appetite to talk too frequently of his own virtues**. Compare the passage below at p. 50, l. 22.

Page 9, l. 3. **a sufficiency**. What we now call self-sufficiency, an overweening estimate of one's own abilities.

l. 6. **he is under the rod**. He is a pupil, not a master, in the art of criticism.

l. 23. [**bulls**, blunders, accidental contradiction of terms, for which the Irish are proverbial. See l. 28 below. C. D. P.]

Page 10, l. 7. as a double foil to his person and capacity. As fitted by the force of contrast to emphasize his own graces of person and of mind. "The very bow of the God of Love," two lines below, is a spiteful reference to Pope's physical deformity.

[**foil**, that which is used as a contrast in order to show something else to advantage. C. D. P.]

l. 8. [**Sunninghill** is a few miles east of Binfield, and **Oakingham** (now Wokingham) a few miles to the west. Both are well-known villages on the road from London to Bath. C. D. F.]

[**squab.** See Johnson's description of Pope's figure on p. 74. C. D. P.]

l. 9. [**the very bow.** This refers to his curved back, and is an example of Dennis's "delicacy." C. D. P.]

l. 12. **had he been born of Grecian parents**, etc. Among some Greek communities the new-born child was, in accordance with the law, laid at the feet of the father, whose right it was to decide whether it should be allowed to live or not.

l. 27. **he did not expect the sale to be quick, because**, etc. The quotation is from a letter to Caryll, July 19, 1711. "Old Mr. Lewis, the bookseller in Russell Street, who printed the first edition of this Essay in quarto, without Pope's name, informed me that it lay many days in his shop unnoticed and unread; and that, piqued with this neglect, the author came one day and packed up and directed twenty copies to several great men; among whom he could recollect none but Lord Lansdown and the Duke of Buckingham; and that in consequence of these presents, and his name being known, the book began to be called for." Warton's *Life of Pope,* quoted by Cunningham on this passage.

l. 33. **the zealous papists thought the monks**, etc. In ll. 684–696 of the poem.

> "Learning and Rome alike in empire grew;
> And Arts still follow'd where her eagles flew;
> From the same foes, at last, both felt their doom,
> And the same age saw Learning fall, and Rome.
> With Tyranny, then Superstition join'd,
> As that the body, this enslav'd the mind;
> Much was believ'd, but little understood,
> And to be dull was constru'd to be good;
> A second deluge Learning thus o'errun,
> And the Monks finished what the Goths begun.

> At length Erasmus, that great injur'd name,
> (The glory of the Priesthood, and the shame!)
> Stemm'd the wild torrent of a barb'rous age,
> And drove those holy Vandals off the stage."

Erasmus (born at Rotterdam, 1467; died at Basle, 1536) was the greatest scholar of his age. He incurred much obloquy by his attempts to induce the authorities of the Roman Church to accept some of the reforms, the refusal of which drove Luther out of the Church.

Page 11, l. 4. commented by Dr. Warburton. Warburton (1698-1779), who was afterwards Bishop of Gloucester, was Pope's literary executor. "Comment" is here used as a transitive verb, a construction which is not permissible now.

l. 15. [**Hooker**, Richard, a clergyman of Elizabeth's reign. His chief work was on the *Laws of Ecclesiastical Polity*. C. D. P.]

l. 19. [**concatenation**, a series of ideas joined together like the links of a chain (Lat. *catena*, a chain). C. D. P.]

l. 21. [**equally specious**, just as plausible, and apparently natural and accurate. C. D. P.]

l. 31. **In the Spectator.** Of May 14, 1712, No. 378.

[**The Messiah.** This poem was based partly on the prophecies in Isaiah of the coming of Christ, and partly on a very similar prediction in Virgil. C. D. P.]

l. 36. **The lady's name and adventures I have sought with fruitless enquiry.** Johnson took the story he proceeds to give, and which he evidently does not believe to be genuine, from Ruffhead, who found it in the *Life of Pope*, written by William Ayre a year after the poet's death. There is no reason to believe a word of it. But it is still uncertain who the lady was, and how far what is said about her in the poem is to be taken as historical. Compare Ward's note. "This Elegy was first published in 1717, but doubtless written earlier. After endless enquiries and conjectures as to the 'Unfortunate Lady' had failed in fixing her identity, it was pointed out that in certain letters of Pope, described by him in the table of contents as relating to an 'Unfortunate Lady,' we are introduced to a Mrs. W. who had endured a series of hardships and misfortunes. This Mrs. W. has been proved to have been a Mrs. Weston, who was soon after her marriage separated from her husband. Her case was warmly taken up by Pope, by whose aid the quarrel was adjusted, though with small thanks to him for interposing. 'Buckingham's lines,' says Carruthers, 'suggested the outline of the picture. Mrs. Weston's misfortunes and the poet's admiration of her gave it life and warmth, and *imagination did the rest* ...." In Warburton's edition of Pope there is a note signed

"P." to the following effect: "See the Duke of Buckingham's verses to a Lady designing to retire into a Monastery compared with Mr. Pope's letters to several Ladies, p. 206. She seems to be the same person whose unfortunate death is the subject of this poem." But Warburton is suspected, with some reason, of having written this note himself. "If this note was written by Pope (of which we have strong doubts) it must have been written purely for mystification and deception. The Duke's verses were first published in Tonson's *Miscellany* for 1709, when he was in his sixtieth year and married to his third wife! They were, most likely, a much earlier production, and this renders it in the highest degree improbable that the same lady should have also been commemorated by Pope, who was thirty-seven years younger than his friend" (Carruthers).

Page 13, l. 2. **Mrs. Arabella Fermor.** The title does not mean, as it would now, that the lady was married. Miss Arabella Fermor was, in 1714, married to Francis Perkins, Esq., of Ufton Court, Berks.

l. 6. [This King James was James II. He sent his Queen to France shortly before his own escape from England. C. D. P.]

l. 7. **being the author.** In the edition of 1781 I find "as the author."

l. 17. [**a surreptitious edition,** one published by others without the writer's permission. C. D. P.]

l. 18. [**event,** result (Lat. *eventus*). C. D. P.]

l. 23. **a niece of Mrs. Fermor,** etc. "Miss Arabella Fermor's niece, Prioress of the English Austin Nuns at the Fossée at Paris, told Mrs. Piozzi 'that she believed there was but little comfort to be found in a house that harboured *poets*; for that she remembered Mr. Pope's praise made her aunt very troublesome and conceited, while his numberless caprices would have employed ten servants to wait upon him'" (*Life of Mrs. Piozzi*, quoted by Ward).

l. 28. "**merum sal.**" Pure salt, pure wit.

l. 30. **to borrow his machinery from the Rosicrucians.** "Machinery" is here used in the technical sense of the supernatural 'business' of a poem. It was made matter of reproach to some of the Greek dramatists that, when they had got their plot so inextricably mixed up that no human action could unweave it, they brought in a god to put matters right. On the stage such a god was represented by an actor let down from above the stage in some sort of machine, and hence Horace's expression about the "*deus ex machina*," the 'god from a car,' who arrives so opportunely to put an end to the confusion into which the plot has fallen. For this use of the word, and for the reference to the Rosicrucians, compare Pope's own explanation to Miss Fermor in his dedication of the poem. "The Machinery, Madam, is a term invented by the Critics, to signify that part which the Deities, Angels, or Dæmons are made to act in a Poem: For the ancient Poets are in one respect like many modern Ladies: let an action be never so trivial in itself, they always make it appear of the utmost importance. These Machines I determined to raise on a very new and odd foundation, the Rosicrucian doctrine of Spirits.... The Rosicrucians are a people I must bring you acquainted with. ... According to these Gentlemen, the four Elements are inhabited by Spirits, which they call Sylphs, Gnomes, Nymphs, and Salamanders. The Gnomes or Dæmons of Earth delight in mischief; but the Sylphs, whose habitation is in the Air, are the best-condition'd creatures imaginable. For they say, any mortals may enjoy the most intimate familiarities with these gentle Spirits, upon a condition very easy to all true Adepts, an inviolate preservation of chastity." The Rosicrucians were "a celebrated but entirely fabulous secret society," who were supposed to possess "many secret gifts of knowledge, of which goldmaking was one of the least" (*Enc. Brit.*). They were gravely described as an existing sect in an anonymous pamphlet which was published in 1614, and which gave rise to great controversy. But it is generally believed now that the pamphlet was a squib, and that there never were any Rosicrucians.

l. 35. **This has been too hastily considered.** By Warburton, who professes to have taken the idea from Pope himself. He says that when Pope got the advice referred to from Addison, "he was shocked for his friend; and then first began to open his eyes to his character." It is possible that Pope was quite innocent of this absurdity.

Page 14, l. 13. **Berkeley.** The famous author of the *Principles of Human Knowledge* and other philosophical works. He was Dean of Derry, and afterwards Bishop of Cloyne. He died in 1753.

l. 17. **He always considered,** etc. "The things that I have written fastest have always pleased me most. I wrote the Essay on Criticism fast; for I had digested all the matter on prose before I began upon it in verse. The Rape of the Lock was written fast: all the machinery was added afterwards; and the making that, and what was published before, hit so well together, is, I think, one of the greatest proofs of judgment of anything I ever did. I wrote most of the Iliad fast; a great deal of it on journeys, from the little pocket Homer on that shelf there; and often forty or fifty verses in a morning in bed. The Dunciad cost me as much pains as anything I ever wrote" (Pope, in Spence, p. 107).

l. 22. [**casualty**, chance, accident. The word "felicity" in the next line has a similar meaning of "good luck"; hence Johnson attributes Pope's success as much to luck as to skill. C. D. P.]

l. 26. **Many years afterwards Dennis**, etc. See below, p. 98, l. 27 fg.

l. 31. **The Temple of Fame.** See below, p. 92, l. 13 fg. This poem was written in 1711, and appeared in 1715, with the following advertisement by the author: "The hint of the following piece was taken from Chaucer's *House of Fame*. The design is in a manner entirely altered, the descriptions and most of the particular thoughts my own: yet I would not suffer it to be printed without this acknowledgment. The reader who would compare this with Chaucer, may begin with his third Book of *Fame*, there being nothing in the two first books that answers to their title: wherever any hint is taken from him, the passage itself is set down in the marginal notes." Richard Steele, the famous critic and essayist, saw the *Temple of Fame* in manuscript, and was greatly charmed with it. Writing to Pope on the 12th Nov., 1712, he said, "I have read over your *Temple of Fame* twice, and cannot find anything amiss, of weight enough to call a fault, but see in it a thousand thousand beauties. Mr. Addison shall see it to-morrow."

l. 36. **Dennis afterwards published some remarks.** In the publication to which Johnson refers below, p. 38, l. 33, "Dennis was the perpetual persecutor of all his studies." See note on that passage.

Page 15, l. 1. **some of the lines represent motion as exhibited by sculpture.** "Dennis idly objected to these lines, because motion cannot be represented in sculpture. But Virgil, in his shield, uses such; but in one instance perhaps he carries it too far: 'Mulcere alternos.' Motion may be represented, but not change of motion" (Warton, quoted by Cunningham).

l. 3. **Of the Epistle from Eloisa to Abelard**, etc. It was first published in the collected edition of 1717. The following is Pope's argument of this poem: "Abelard and Eloisa flourished in the twelfth century; they were two of the most distinguished persons of their age in learning and beauty, but for nothing more famous than for their unfortunate passion. After a long course of calamities, they retired each to a several convent, and consecrated the remainder of their days to religion. It was many years after this separation, that a letter of Abelard's to a friend, which contained the history of his misfortune, fell into the hands of Eloisa. This, awakening all her tenderness, occasioned those celebrated letters (out of which the following is partly extracted) which give so lively a picture of the struggles of grace and nature, virtue and passion."

l. 6. **Prior's Nut-Brown Maid.** This is really the title of an old ballad, on the model of which the poet Prior wrote his *Henry and Emma*. [Matthew Prior (1664-1721) was a poet and politician of the reigns of William III. and Anne. C. D. P.]

l. 17. "**Windsor Forest.**" See below, p. 91, l. 22 fg. "This poem was written at two different times: the first part of it, which relates to the country, in the year 1704, at the same time with the *Pastorals*; the latter part was not added till the year 1713, in which it was published" (Pope). The peace referred to is the Peace of Utrecht.

l. 23. [**Tories.** This party had been in office since 1710. Addison had been a prominent minister in the previous Whig government, hence his pain at the support given by Pope to the Tories. C. D. P.]

l. 35. **Cato**, Addison's famous tragedy of that name. Compare with this passage that at p. 33, l. 35.

l. 36. **when Dennis published his Remarks.** *Remarks on Cato*, published in 1713.

Page 16, l. 1. Narrative of the Frenzy of John Dennis. "In 1713 was published a pamphlet entitled, *The Narrative of Dr. Robert Norris on the Frenzy of J. D.* It contained an imaginary report, pretending to be written by a notorious quack mad-doctor of the day, and was anonymous. It cannot be assumed with certainty that Addison was at first aware of the identity of its real author. In any case he directed Steele to write a note to its publisher, expressing Mr. Addison's disapproval of the treatment to which Dennis had been subjected. Thus, to his inexpressible mortification, Pope found himself in the intolerable position of a disavowed champion, reprimanded for his officiousness by the very individual whom he had put himself forward to serve" (Ward). Steele wrote to the publisher Lintot in the following terms: "Mr. Addison desired me to tell you that he wholly disapproves the manner of treating Mr. Dennis in a little pamphlet by way of Dr. Norris' accounts. When he thinks fit to take notice of Mr. Dennis' objections to his writings, he will do it in a way Mr. Dennis shall have no just reason to complain of." Below, at p. 37, l. 5, Pope will be found addressing a remonstrance to Addison, which is evidently modelled on Addison's words here.

l. 4. **this disingenuous hostility.** That is to say, that Pope hated Dennis on his own account, but pretended to hate him on Addison's. So "cant of sensibility," below, l. 10.

l. 14. [**the Guardian**, a daily paper edited by Steele after the *Spectator* ceased. It appeared from March to October, 1713, and Pope was an occasional contributor. C. D. P.]

l. 14. **The ironical comparison between the Pastorals of Philips and Pope.** Pope's *Pastorals* were published in 1709 in a volume of *Miscellanies* which commenced with the *Pastorals* of Ambrose Philips, a writer now forgotten. An anonymous writer in the *Guardian* filled five papers with praise of Philips, and had nothing to say, either of praise or of blame, about Pope's contribution to the volume. Pope wrote, and sent to Steele, the editor of the *Guardian*, a sixth paper, professing to be a continuation of the former series, in which Philips was preferred to Pope after the following fashion: "Mr. Pope has fallen into the same error with Virgil. His clowns do not converse in all the simplicity proper to the country." And again, "After all that hath been said, I hope none can think it any injustice to Mr. Pope that I forbore to mention him as a pastoral writer; since upon the whole he is of the same class as Moschus and Bion, whom we have excluded that rank." At the same time many of Philips' worst lines were singled out for praise, as being better than some of Pope's best lines also quoted. It is difficult to believe that Steele did not see the real character of the contribution thus offered to him, but the story is that, taking it to be a genuine attack on Pope, he showed it to the poet, and obtained his permission to insert it. Johnson does not seem to have any authority for his suggestion that Addison was consulted about the paper prior to its publication.

l. 27. **Jervas.** "Charles Jervas was an early and intimate friend of Pope's, and instructed him in painting about the year 1713. Three years later we find Pope occupying the painter's house during the absence of the latter from London. As a painter, Jervas is spoken slightingly of by Horace Walpole. He is also, says Roscoe, well known by his excellent translation of *Don Quixote*" (Ward).

l. 30. **Betterton.** The famous actor of the name.

l. 34. **some encomiastic verses to Jervas.** *Epistle to Mr. Jervas*, with Mr. Dryden's translation of Fresnoy's *Art of Painting*.

Page 17, l. 3. [**Chaucer's Prologues** were portions of his work, the *Canterbury Tales*. In the first Prologue is a description of the pilgrims who were supposed to travel in company with Chaucer from the Tabard Inn, Southwark, to the Shrine of Becket at Canterbury. C. D. P.]

l. 4. **Mr. Harte.** Friend both to Pope and Johnson. Pope called him "a very valuable young man"; and Johnson, "a man of the most companionable talents he had ever known" (Sharp).

l. 5. [**Fenton.** Pope's assistant in translating the *Odyssey*.

See p. 40. The phrase "by Fenton" limits the verb "were believed," in line 4. C. D. P.]

l. 6. [in the hand, in the hand-writing. C. D. P.]

l. 10. [diffused, made widely known. The verb is unusual, being generally applied only to that which can be poured out, or scattered, and not to a single object. C. D. P.]

l. 13. [religion. See p. 2, l. 7. C. D. P.]

l. 18. **To print by subscription.** Full details of this method of printing will be found in the paragraphs that follow. It has now gone almost completely out of use for the ordinary run of books. Exceptionally costly books, or books that for one reason or another have to be printed privately, are still, however, occasionally published in this way.

l. 21. [Dryden's Virgil was a translation into English verse of Virgil's *Aeneid*. It was published in 1697. C. D. P.]

l. 22. **the Tatlers.** The *Tatler* was a journal edited by Steele. [It commenced in April, 1709, and ran to 271 numbers. C. D. P.]

l. 24. **would be successful.** That is to say, that a sufficient number of persons would put down their name for copies, to warrant the author and the publisher in proceeding with the undertaking.

l. 34. [an English Iliad was of course an English translation, or version, of the *Iliad*. C. D. P.]

Page 18, l. 6. but proposed no means by which he might live without it. Compare below, p. 23, l. 9. "Lord Oxford had often lamented his disqualification for publick employment, but never proposed a pension."

l. 13. **the booksellers made their offers.** That is to Pope, who had still to choose a bookseller, or, as we should now say, a publisher. Bernard Lintot was a great king of the craft of the time. Like some other of Pope's publishers, he found his way into the *Dunciad*.

l. 20. **that the subscription might not be depreciated.** The subscribers, who paid Pope six guineas for each copy of the work, were entitled to expect that the value of their copies should not be lowered by the fact that anybody could go to the bookseller and purchase an identical book at a lower rate. It was therefore stipulated that of the quartos, or first edition, no more should be printed than Pope himself required, either for his subscribers, or as presents for friends. The publisher was to make his profit out of subsequent and differing editions, and the trick of which Lintot is accused is that of having so managed the subsequent editions that, with a little alteration, they could be made to pass for subscribers' copies. It is Pope's account, and ✓ allowance must be made for the inveterate grudge authors have against publishers.

l. 28. [**royal paper in Folio.** The size of the page would be about 20 inches by 12 inches. In a small folio the size would be about 13 inches by 8 inches. Duodecimo would be much smaller, about 8 inches by 5 inches. C. D. P.]

Page 19, l. 5. The notes ... were now subjoined to the text. "This is not quite correct. In the edition 'London: printed by T. J. for B. L. and other Booksellers,' 1718-21, 6 vols. 12mo, the notes are at the end of each volume" (Cunningham).

l. 15. **to be frighted.** We must now say "to be frightened."

l. 30. **He that wants money,** he that is without money. The people referred to in the first clause of this sentence are those who are too poor to subscribe; the second clause treats of those who are too mean to subscribe. Both classes of men conceal the real reason for their refusal under a false show of contempt for the poet.

l. 33. **Addison had hinted his suspicion that Pope was too much a Tory.** In the communication already referred to, at p. 18, l. 7: "You gave me leave once to take the liberty of a friend, in advising you not to content yourself with one-half of the nation for your admirers, when you might command them all." Addison meant that Pope was showing signs of a wish to please only the Tories. He went on: "If I might take the freedom to repeat it, I would on this occasion. I think you are very happy to be out of the fray, and I hope all your undertakings will turn out to the better account for it." On the other hand, the fact that Pope contributed ever so little to Steele's journal was highly offensive to the out-and-out Tories. [Addison was a consistent Whig, and a member of the Whig governments of 1708 and 1714. The *Guardian* was edited by Richard Steele as a strictly neutral paper with regard to politics, but Steele was unable to repress his zeal for the Whigs, and in a few numbers he broke through his professed neutrality. C. D. P.]

Page 20, l. 13. his positions are general. He deals with the broad facts of human life.

l. 23. **the Latin printed on the opposite page.** In those days most editions of the Greek classics had a Latin version printed page for page with the original.

l. 34. **Eobanus Hessus.** This German writer (1488-1540) wrote a translation of the *Iliad* in Latin verse.

l. 35. **the French Homers of La Valterie and Dacier.** "La Valterie, a French abbé in the latter half of the seventeenth century, translated Homer, Juvenal, and Persius; the more celebrated Madame Dacier (1645-1720) translated both the *Iliad* and the *Odyssey* into French prose" (Matthew Arnold's note).

l. 35. **the English of Chapman, Hobbes, and Ogylby.** "The translation of Homer by George Chapman, who died in 1604, is still read. Thomas Hobbes of Malmesbury (1588-1679) translated Homer and Thucydides, but his fame is due to his philosophical work, *Leviathan*. John Ogylby (1600-1676) was patronized by Lord Strafford, and after Strafford's death translated both Virgil and Homer" (Matthew Arnold's note). It has been already mentioned that Pope read Ogylby's version of Homer when a child (p. 2, l. 10).

Page 21, l. 1. **now totally neglected.** There was after this a revival of interest in Chapman's Homer. Arnold, as we have just seen, declares that it is still read. The student will hardly require to be reminded of Keats' sonnet, *On first looking into Chapman's Homer*.

l. 14. **Eustathius.** "Archbishop of Thessalonica in the twelfth century, and famous as a commentator on Homer" (Arnold's note).

l. 16. **I suspect Pope .. not to have been able.** Johnson is here repeating a charge that had already been made by Fenton. "All the crime that I have committed is saying that he is no master of Greek; and I am so confident of this, that if he can translate ten lines of Eustathius, I'll own myself unjust and unworthy" (Broome to Fenton, quoted by Cunningham).

l. 21. **Broome.** Broome and Fenton are two writers of whom little else is known besides the part they took in Pope's translations of the *Iliad* and *Odyssey*. For their share in the two undertakings see below, pp. 21 and 41.

l. 29. **Jortin.** ("John Jortin (1698-1770), known by his *Life of Erasmus*" (Arnold's note). Thirlby was Jortin's tutor at Cambridge.

Page 22, l. 6. **Parnell.** Remembered now only for one poem, *The Hermit*.

l. 21. **but the distance is commonly very great,** etc. There is something autobiographical about the fine passage which follows. Johnson is speaking as much for himself as for Pope.

Page 23, l. 9. [**Lord Oxford.** Harley, head of the Tory ministry, was made Lord Oxford in 1711. C. D. P.]

l. 11. **but never proposed a pension.** Compare above, p. 18, ll. 5-7, and the following from Johnson's *Life of Addison*: "Having yet no public employment, he obtained a pension of three hundred pounds a year, that he might be enabled to travel." Johnson himself had a pension of this sort, as Tennyson had in our own days.

l. 12. **Mr. Craggs.** The friend of Addison. See below, p. 117.

Page 24, l. 1. **Mallet.** Bollingbroke's literary executor. Dr. Maty was secretary to the Royal Society, and one of the librarians of the British Museum.

l. 2. [**reposited,** an obsolete form, now displaced by *deposited.* Cf. repository, a storehouse. C. D. P.]

Page 31, l. 16. [**Halifax** (Charles Montague), a famous Chancellor of the Exchequer and leader of the Whigs. He was Addison's earliest patron. C. D. P.]

l. 20. **gave the following account.** The amusing story which follows is from Spence, p. 101. It is not necessary to believe it.

l. 25. [**Congreve** (1670-1729), a writer of comedies. C. D. P.]

[**Garth** (1660-1719), a doctor, noted in literature for a mock heroic poem, *The Dispensary.* C. D. P.]

Page 32, l. 21. **from a single letter.** This is one of the many letters which Pope published afterwards rather as he would like to have written them, than as he actually did write them. In the present case the original letter is extant, and has been printed by Cunningham. The meaning of the phrase, "if I ever become troublesome or solicitous, it must not be out of expectation, but out of gratitude," has been matter of controversy. How Johnson took it is clear from the passage below, p. 33, l. 5. Pope means that Halifax need not fear his importunate asking, but may be assured of the poet's fervent and almost troublesome gratitude, if a certain favour, which he has some reason to expect, is actually done him. This seems undoubtedly right. The favour cannot have been a light one, if it was to make the difference to Pope of an agreeable life in the town as compared with a contented life in the country. Pope is hinting at a pension, and he did not dedicate his Homer to Halifax because he received no promise of a pension. Ryland, following Milnes, thinks that Johnson "obviously misunderstands Pope's meaning. In saying that he would be troublesome out of gratitude and not out of expectation, Pope means that he will trouble Halifax with thanks and not with requests for help; in other words, that he is quite satisfied with such favour as Halifax had already showed him. 'He could not have meant that he wanted benefits from Halifax before he began to thank him; or certainly he would not have said so if such had been his real feeling' (Milnes)". This does not seem right. Pope means just what Milnes thinks he could not have meant. His letter is really in the style of the little boy in *Punch* who claimed to be helped first "because he had not asked."

l. 32. **but, if I may have leave to add**, etc. The meaning is that all lovers of England at that time must be lovers also of Lord Halifax.

Page 33, l. 12. **Pope looked on Halifax with scorn and hatred.** "This is over-charged. That he disliked Halifax I believe; but compare Pope's posthumous praise of him in the Preface to the *Iliad*. The character of Bufo (in the *Epistle to Arbuthnot*), supposed to represent Halifax, is only true in parts to Halifax's character" (Cunningham).

l. 17. **the two rivals in the Roman state.** Caesar and Pompey. The poet Lucan says that Caesar could not bear that any one should be above him in the state; Pompey, that any one should be as much as equal to him. Addison is the Pompey, and Pope the Caesar, of the comparison.

l. 27. **as Homer says.** *Iliad*, 2. 486.

l. 34. **by his Prologue to Cato, by his abuse of Dennis.** See above, pp. 15, 16.

l. 36. **his poem on the Dialogues on Medals.** *To Mr. Addison, Occasioned by his Dialogues on Medals.* Warburton very absurdly made it the fifth of Pope's *Moral Essays*, in which place it now stands in the editions. "This was originally written in the year 1715, when Mr. Addison intended to publish his book of medals; it was sometime before he was secretary of state; but not published till Mr. Tickell's edition of his works; at which time the verses on Mr. Craggs, which conclude the poem, were added, viz. in 1720" (Pope). Compare p. 117, ll. 17-20.

Page 34, l. 16. **Jervas, the painter.** See above, note on p. 16, l. 27.

l. 19. **Addison once suspected him of too close a confederacy with Swift.** Compare the passage at p. 19, l. 33.

l. 22. **his services in regard to the subscription.** See the next page.

l. 23. **the Tories never put him under the necessity of asking leave to be grateful.** Compare the passage at p. 32, l. 21, and the note there. This jibe at the Tories goes to confirm our interpretation of Pope's meaning there.

l. 25. "**and seems to have no very just one,**" *i.e.* to advise him. This is the reading of editions of 1781 and of 1783. Edd., "and seems to be," etc.

l. 32. **Kennet.** Bishop of Peterborough. His MS. Diary is in the British Museum.

l. 36. **the antechamber.** Either of the Queen or of some great minister.

Page 35, l. 8. About this time it is likely, etc. "'It is likely' is surely a strange kind of fact for a life" (Cunningham). So also Ryland : "It is likely. Johnson seems to be relating a mere piece of gossip, or hazarding an unsupported conjecture," etc. But Johnson's meaning has been misunderstood. By "about this time it is likely" he means that it seems probable that the interview he proceeds to describe as he had heard of it, if it ever took place at all, should be referred to this period of Pope's life. He does not vouch for the story at all (compare the next sentence, and the beginning of the next paragraph), and is free of the reproach of having inserted it because he had come to the conclusion that it was "likely" that the facts were as reported.

l. 9. **officious.** Eager to serve. The word was not in Johnson's time used exclusively in the bad sense which is now its only meaning. Johnson, however, uses the noun in that sense above, p. 16, l. 13.

l. 24. **with the abuse of those qualifications which he had obtained at the public cost.** The meaning seems to be that Addison's pension had enabled him to develop his literary powers, and that he was prostituting his talents in the service of a political party. [In 1699, Charles Montague, the Chancellor of the Exchequer, had procured Addison a pension of £300 a year in order that he might travel and improve his education. The pension ceased in 1702, in consequence of a change of ministry. C. D. P.]

l. 32. **with the name of Tickell.** Johnson is referring to the fact that Pope believed, or pretended to believe, that the version was really by Addison himself. Tickell, a Fellow of Queen's College, Oxford, was one of Addison's following, and eventually edited his works.

Page 36, l. 3. the high-flyers at Button's. Button's was the coffee-house which Addison and his circle frequented. "Addison's chief companions, before he married Lady Warwick (in 1716), were Steele, Budgell, Philips, Carey, Davenant, and Colonel Brett. He used to breakfast with one or other of them, at his lodgings in St. James's Place, dine at taverns with them, then to Button's, and then to some tavern again for supper in the evening: and this was then the usual round of his life." "It was Dryden who made Will's Coffee-house the great resort for the wits of the time. After his death, Addison transferred it to Button's; who had been a servant of his: they were opposite each other, in Russell Street, Covent Garden" (Pope, in Spence, pp. 148 and 199). In making Pope speak of the "high-flyers" at Button's, Johnson is adapting Pope's words rather than quoting them. What Pope said was : "Let Mr. Tickell be proud of

K

the approbation of his absolute lord, I appeal to the people as my rightful judges and masters; and if they are not inclined to condemn me, I fear no arbitrary high-flying proceeding from the small court-faction at Button's." A high-flying proceeding is an extravagant, irrational proceeding. The figure is taken from the story of Icarus, who compassed his own ruin by flying too near the sun.

l. 13. **the four versions of Dryden, Maynwaring, Pope, and Tickell.** Dryden published a translation of the first book of the *Iliad*. Tickell's translation also did not go beyond the first book. The little that is known of Maynwaring ("Maynwaring, whom we hear nothing of now, was the ruling spirit in all conversations at the Kit Kat Club, indeed what he wrote had little merit in it."—Pope, in Spence, p. 257) does not seem to include any knowledge of the translation of Homer by him here referred to.

l. 16. [**Tonson**, chiefly noted as Dryden's bookseller, had a shop close to Gray's Inn, at which he was succeeded by Osborne, who figures in Pope's *Dunciad*. See note on p. 68, l. 36. C. D. P.]

l. 30. **were thus related by Pope.** In Spence, p. 112.

l. 34. [**Lord Warwick** was son of the Countess of Warwick, whom Addison married in 1716. C. D. P.]

l. 35. **to be well with Mr. Addison.** We should now say, "to be on good terms with Mr. Addison."

Page 37, l. 8. **it should not be in such a dirty way.** This is the reading in Spence (ed. 1858). Murphy and Sharp write "it should be not," etc. Arnold and Ryland follow the edition of 1781 in omitting the "not." So also ed. 1783.

l. 11. **what has since been called my satire on Addison.** The lines now stand in the *Epistle to Dr. Arbuthnot*, vv. 193 fg. See the note below on p. 63, l. 1.

l. 18. **to live more by choice,** to live to a greater extent than before according to inclination.

l. 22. **celebration.** We say "celebrity" now.

l. 23. **the vines and the quincunx which his verses mention.**

> "Know, all the distant din that world can keep
> Rolls o'er my Grotto, and but soothes my sleep.
> There my retreat the best Companions grace,
> Chiefs out of war, and Statesmen out of place.
> There St. John mingles with my friendly bowl
> The Feast of Reason and the Flow of Soul:
> And He, whose lightning pierc'd the Iberian lines,

"Now forms my quincunx, and now ranks my Vines,
Or tames the genius of the stubborn plain,
Almost as quickly as he conquer'd Spain."
Imitations of Horace, Satire 1. 122.

The St. John (pronounce "Sinjohn") of this passage is the famous Bolingbroke. The soldier is the Earl of Peterborough. A quincunx is one or more groups of trees arranged like the five of diamonds in a pack of cards.

l. 36. [**he extracted**, etc., he professed to have formed an ornament of that which was only an inconvenience. C. D. P.]

Page 38, l. 4. [**safe in the admission**, they think they may with safety allow themselves to be careless in their indulgences. C. D. P.]

l. 16. [**Waller** (1605-1687), a nephew of John Hampden, was the first poet to teach "the excellence and dignity" of rhyme, and to write couplets with the sense concluded in distichs. C. D. P.]

l. 18. **Pope's voracity of fame**, etc. "The omitted passages were not printed by Pope" (Cunningham).

l. 22. **the character which his son has given him.**

"Born to no Pride, inheriting no Strife,
Nor marrying Discord in a noble wife,
Stranger to civil and religious rage,
The good man walk'd innoxious thro' his age.
No Courts he saw, no suits would ever try,
Nor dar'd an Oath, nor hazarded a Lie.
Unlearned, he knew no schoolman's subtle art,
No language, but the language of the heart.
By Nature honest, by Experience wise,
Healthy by temp'rance, and by exercise;
His life, tho' long, to sickness past unknown,
His death was instant, and without a groan.
O grant me thus to live, and thus to die!
Who sprung from Kings shall know less joy than I."
Epistle to Arbuthnot, vv. 392-405.

l. 24. **gotten.** We must now say "got."

l. 30. **Burnet.** Son of the well-known Bishop of Salisbury of the name. Ducket is said to have helped Burnet in the composition of the *Homerides* and of other works.

l. 33. **Dennis was the perpetual persecutor**, etc. See the passage at p. 15, l. 36. Dennis published in 1717 "*Remarks upon Mr. Pope's Translation of Homer*, with two letters concerning *Windsor Forest* and the *Temple of Fame*.

l. 36. **the "Dunciad."** See below, p. 43, l. 16 fg., and 47, 4 fg.

Page 39, l. 1. this disastrous year. The year of the South Sea Scheme. The £100 shares of the South Sea Company went up to £1000 each, and when the crash came fell to something like their original value. Pope is believed to have made some money out of his speculation. He bought before the great rise, when the shares were from £100 to £175; and he sold out before they had fallen below £400.

l. 13. [**Dr. Parnell** (1679-1717), Archdeacon of Clogher, Ireland. *The Hermit* is the best and the best-known of the poems here mentioned. C. D. P.]

l. 15. [**the frown of a victorious faction.** Parnell had been intimate with the wits of Queen Anne's time, but on her death the Whigs displaced the Tories, and Parnell's hopes of advancement were destroyed. C. D. P.]

l. 28. **Theobald, a man of heavy diligence, with very slender powers.** The editors of the Cambridge *Shakespeare* have made Theobald magnificent amends for this harsh and prejudiced judgment. "Lewis Theobald," they say, "had the misfortune to incur the enmity of one who was both the most popular poet, and, if not the first, at least the second, satirist of his time. The main cause of offence was Theobald's *Shakespeare Restored, or a Specimen of the many Errors committed as well as unamended by Mr. Pope in his late edition of this Poet*, 1726. Theobald was also in the habit of communicating notes on passages of Shakespeare to *Mist's Journal*, a weekly Tory paper. Hence he was made the hero of the *Dunciad* till dethroned in the fourth edition to make way for Cibber; hence, too, the allusions in that poem:

'There hapless Shakespeare, yet of Theobald sore,
Wish'd he had blotted for himself before';

and, in the earlier editions,

'Here studious I unlucky moderns save,
Nor sleeps one error in its father's grave;
Old puns restore, lost blunders nicely seek,
And crucify poor Shakespeare once a week.'

Pope's editors and commentators, adopting their author's quarrel, have spoken of Theobald as 'Tibbald, a cold, plodding, and tasteless writer and critic.' These are Warton's words. A more unjust sentence was never penned. Theobald, as an editor, is incomparably superior to his predecessors, and to his immediate successor, Warburton, though the latter had the advantage of working on his materials. He was the first to recall a multitude of readings of the first Folio unquestionably right, but unnoticed by previous editors. Many most brilliant emendations, such as could not have suggested themselves to a mere 'cold, plodding, and tasteless critic,' are due to him" (Preface to the *Cambridge Shakespeare*, p. xxx. fg.).

Page 40, l. 3. **did many things wrong, and left many things undone.** In his preface Pope professed to have diligently consulted the earliest copies, to have worked "with a religious abhorrance of all innovation, and without any indulgence to my private sense or conjecture," and to have given in the margin all the various readings. "This passage, as one may see who examines the text, is much more like a description of what the editor did *not* do than of what he did. Although in many instances he restored, from some Quarto, passages which had been omitted in the Folio, it is very rarely indeed that we find any evidence of his having collated either the first Folio or any Quarto with proper care. The 'innovations' which he made, according to his own 'private sense and conjecture,' are extremely numerous. Not one in twenty of the various readings is put in the margin, and the readings in his text very frequently rest upon no authority whatever. The glaring inconsistency between the promise in the preface and the performance in the book may well account for its failure with the public" (*the same preface*).

l. 13. **resolving not to let the general kindness cool.** An adaptation of the proverb which bids you "strike while the iron is hot."

l. 20. **patent.** "Apparently the official document by which his legal copyright was assigned to him" (Sharp).

l. 23. **the proposals.** What we should now call the prospectus, issued for the sake of inviting subscriptions.

l. 27. **the memorable trial of Bishop Atterbury.** He was accused of treasonable correspondence with the Pretender. As a conviction could not be got, the Government introduced, and passed through Parliament, a bill depriving him of his bishopric, and exiling him from the country.

l. 31. **Pope answered in a manner,** etc. "After all," wrote Pope, "I verily believe your lordship and I are both of the same religion, if we were thoroughly understood by one another; and that all honest and reasonable Christians would be so, if they did but talk enough together every day, and had nothing to do together, but to serve God, and live in peace with their neighbours. ... I hope all churches and governments are so far from God, as they are rightly understood and rightly administered, and when they are, or may be wrong, I leave it to God alone to amend or reform them; which whenever He does, it must be by greater instruments than I am."

Page 41, l. 1. **and in those few he made several blunders.** "I never could speak in public; and I don't believe that if it was a set thing, I could give an account of any story to twelve friends, though I could tell it to any three of them with a great deal of pleasure. When I was to appear for the Bishop of Rochester, in his trial, though I had but ten words to say, and that on a plain point (how the bishop spent his time whilst I was with him at Bromley), I made two or three blunders in it; and that notwithstanding the first row of lords (which was all I could see) were mostly of my acquaintance" (Pope, in Spence, p. 118).

l. 10. **not over-liberally rewarded.** Pope took £4500 from the public for his *Odyssey*, and set aside only £800 of that for the remuneration of the men who had done half the text and all the notes. Mr. Courthope submits a defence of this, which only leaves the reader in doubt as to whether this was a fraud committed on the public or on Broome and Fenton. "On the other hand, it is to be remembered that the design was all his own,"—as to which compare above, p. 40, l. 18 fg.,—"that its attractiveness depended entirely on the prestige of his name; that the great bulk of the subscribers had been obtained by the exertions of himself and his agents. He had warned his partners from the first that he expected them to perform cheap service."

l. 12. **an account was subjoined,** etc. In it Broome was made to say: "If my performance has merit either in these notes or in any part of the translation, namely, the sixth, eleventh, and eighteenth books, it is but fair to attribute it to the judgement and care of Mr. Pope, by whose hand every sheet was corrected. His other, and much more able, assistant was Mr. Fenton in the fourth and twentieth books."

l. 24. **only one hundred pounds.** In the case of the *Iliad*, the price paid for each volume had been double that. See p. 18, l. 18.

l. 35. **Spence.** The Rev. Joseph Spence. His "Anecdotes, Observations, and Characters of Books and Men, collected from the conversation of Mr. Pope and other eminent persons of his time" have been frequently quoted in these notes.

at that time Prelector of Poetry at Oxford. "No. Warton's father was Professor at this time. Spence succeeded Warton" (Cunningham).

Page 42, l. 12. [**valuable preferments.** In 1728 he became Professor of Poetry at Oxford, but it was not till 1742 that he was made Rector of Great Horwood, in Buckinghamshire. C. D. P.]

l. 20. **Voltaire,** the great French writer (1694-1778). He was in England from 1726 to 1729.

l. 29. **in his own History.** In Bishop Burnet's *History of his own Time.* The Debate upon Black and White Horses was a squib on legal forms and procedure. The question was of a bequest of all the testator's "black and white horses." But the testator had left six black, six white, and six pied horses. The Court with infinite trouble decided that these last must be the horses meant. After which it was discovered that these horses were mares!

l. 34. makes. So editions of 1781 and 1783. Arnold, "made."

Page 43, l. 6. A cat. A civet-cat, hunted for the sake of the musk which can be extracted from some of its glands, and tracked by the hunters by means of its peculiar odour ("winded").

l. 9. the letters written by him to Mr. Cromwell. See above, p. 6, l. 32 fg.

l. 11. [Curll. See p. 7, l. 7. C. D. P.]

l. 12, In these Miscellanies, etc. "The *Miscellanies* contained, among many of Pope's pieces which he had better have left in the obscurity of unauthorized publications, his *Treatise on the Bathos, or Art of Sinking in Poetry*.... It is in my opinion by far the most successful of Pope's prose satires, and evinces the extraordinary facility with which he was able to develop ideas originally suggested to him by other minds. It pilloried the whole tribe of poetasters whose names the *Dunciad* was afterwards to preserve, nailed to the post by quotations from their own works. The chief, or at all events the tenderest, victim was Ambrose Philips, who resorted to the cautious revenge of hanging up a rod in the Whig sanctum at Button's for the chastisement of the offender, should he ever appear there. The *Treatise on the Bathos* would be more frequently read and enjoyed than it is, had not its victims soon afterwards been subjected to another, and yet more classical, castigation. The *Dunciad* seems to have been first published in May, 1728; and the enlarged edition, which followed a few months later, was dedicated to the true foster-father of the work, to Swift" (Ward).

l. 16. Atterbury's advice. See above, p. 37, l. 14 fg.

l. 22. At the head of the Dunces he placed poor Theobald. See above, note on p. 39, l. 28.

l. 27. Ralph.
"Silence, ye Wolves! while Ralph to Cynthia howls,
And makes Night hideous—Answer him, ye Owls!"
Dunciad, Book III. 165.

"James Ralph, a name inserted after the first editions, not known to our author till he writ a swearing-piece called *Sawney*, very abusive of Dr. Swift, Mr. Gay, and himself. These lines allude to a thing of his entitled *Night*, a Poem" (Pope's note on that passage). Ralph was an American.

l. 31. The prevalence of this poem. A phrase which would not be permissible now. We talk of the prevalence of a disease, but not of the prevalence of a poem. Sharp compares Johnson himself, in his *Life of Milton*: "The sale of 1300 copies in two years was an uncommon example of the prevalence of genius."

Page 44, l. 14. **in a Dedication.** The Dedication of a volume, published by Savage in 1732, and entitled "A collection of Pieces in Verse and Prose, which have been published on occasion of the *Dunciad*."

l. 20. **their Miscellanies.** See p. 42, l. 26 fg.

l. 26. **the greatest part of them at random.** Compare Johnson below, p. 46, l. 19, "nobody believes that the letters in the *Bathos* were placed at random."

Page 45, l. 7. **the booksellers would not find their account in employing them.** Compare what has just been said of Ralph's complaint against Pope, p. 43, l. 27. It must be remembered, as has been already pointed out, that the booksellers of Pope's days were publishers as well.

l. 17. [**impression**, edition. C. D. P.]

l. 18. **taken and dispersed.** What is meant is that the "noblemen and persons of the first distinction" bought more copies than one each, and distributed them among their friends.

l. 32. **the author.** Pope or Swift, as it was supposed to be. The book was at first published anonymously.

Page 46, l. 14. **sensibility.** We should rather now say "sensitiveness." Compare the expresssion "cant of sensibility," p. 16, l. 10. There are a great many mistakes, wilful or otherwise, in the preceding account of the inception and publication of the *Dunciad*. Ward well says that "it may fairly be doubted whether the mystification in which every step connected with the publication of the various editions of the *Dunciad* was intentionally involved by Pope, has not answered an end beyond that proposed to himself by the poet, and provided a tangle of literary difficulties, which no learned ingenuity will ever suffice entirely to unravel."

l. 20. **when he thinks himself concealed.** Because he was writing in another name than his own. See p. 44, l. 15.

l. 26. **taken off**, bought up.

l. 31. **without fear**, of being afterwards blamed by the critics for having liked a worthless book.

l. 32. **petty literature**, things written by poetasters and the like.

Page 47, l. 1. Dennis, etc. He published and dedicated to his fellow-sufferer, Theobald, a pamphlet called, *Remarks on the Dunciad.* See below.

l. 4. **published remarks.** Johnson has already referred to this, p. 14, l. 27.

l. 6. **Ducket.** See above, p. 38, l. 32. The following are the lines, as they now stand, in which Burnet and Ducket are pilloried together in the *Dunciad*:

"Behold yon Pair, in strict embraces join'd;
How like in manners, and how like in mind!
Equal in wit, and equally polite,
Shall this a *Pasquin*, that a *Grumbler* write;
Like are their merits, like rewards they share,
That shines a Consul, this Commissioner.'

The expression of which Ducket complained stood in another couplet, which was first altered as Johnson describes, and then omitted altogether. See Roscoe 3. 290.

l. 13. **as diving for the prize.** The Goddess of Dulness has brought all her votaries to the Fleet Ditch and bade them leap in.

"Here strip, my children! here at once leap in,
Here prove who best can dash thro' thick and thin,
And who the most in love of dirt excel,
Or dark dexterity of groping well.
Who flings most filth," etc.

The lines in which Hill is referred to ran thus:

" Then H—— essay'd, scarce vanish'd out of sight,
He buoys up instant, and returns to light:
He bears no token of the sabler streams,
And mounts far off among the Swans of Thames."

Pope attached to these lines the following patronizing note: " A gentleman of genius and spirit, who was secretly dipt in some papers of this kind, on whom our Poet bestows a panegyric instead of a satire, as deserving to be better employed than in party quarrels, and personal invectives." As the passage is now printed, an asterisk has taken the place of the "H——." But Johnson would seem to be wrong in thinking that it was with regard to this passage that Hill addressed his earnest remonstrance to Pope. Compare Cunningham's note: "Johnson has somewhat mistaken the exact point of the controversy. The first *blow* of which Hill complains in his manly letters to Pope is not in the *Dunciad*, but in the *Art of Sinking*. Hill accuses Pope of having attacked him under the initials A. H. in the *Art of Sinking*. The diving scene, which is a sort of palinode on Pope's part, is in the *Dunciad.*" "Hill wrote no less than seventeen dramatic pieces, and was besides, according to Dibdin, 'the projector of nut oil, of masts of ships from Scotch firs, of cultivating Georgia, and of potash!'" (Ward).

l. 20. [**Dr. Arbuthnot** (1667-1735), physician to Queen Anne, and friend of the wits and poets of the period. The fall of the Tories at the death of Anne deprived him of his post as Royal Physician. C. D. P.]

l. 21. **Cleland.** "This Gentleman was of Scotland, and bred at the University of Utrecht, with the Earl of Mar. He served in Spain under Earl Rivers. After the Peace, he was made one of the Commissioners of the Customs in England, in which, having shown himself for twenty years diligent, punctual, and incorruptible, though without any other assistance of Fortune, he was suddenly displaced by the Minister in the sixty-eighth year of his age, in 1741 ... " (Pope).

l. 26. **a poem on Taste.** It stands now as the Fourth Epistle in the *Moral Essays*, with the title, "Of the Use of Riches." In what is now the First Epistle of the *Moral Essays*, Pope endeavoured to make amends to the Duke of Chandos for the attack he was believed to have made upon him in the Fourth (written earlier).

"True, some are open, and to all men known;
Others so very close, they're hid from none;
(So Darkness strikes the sense no less than light)
Thus gracious Chandos is belov'd at sight;
And every child hates Shylock, tho' his soul
Still sits at squat, and peeps not from his hole."

"James Brydges, first Duke of Chandos, for whose splendid hospitality and supposed personal munificence to Pope the latter was accused of having made a base return by satirizing the decorations and furniture of the Duke's house at Canons, in the Epistle *On Taste*. ... Pope denied the pecuniary obligation, and defended himself against the charge of having alluded to the Duke's house. The Duke accepted the explanation; and the line in the text is due to Pope's recognition of the urbanity displayed by his noble acquaintance" (from Ward's note on that passage).

Page 48, l. 6. **The name of Cleland was again employed**, etc. Compare p. 47, l. 21.

l. 14. **an indifferent action**, an action which would have given the Duke no concern.

l. 17. **in one of his Letters.** In a letter which Pope addressed to the Earl of Burlington (to whom the Epistle had been dedicated), with reference to the charge that he made an unbecoming attack upon the Duke of Chandos. As printed in the Letters, the passage runs thus: "However, my lord, I own that critics of this sort can intimidate me, nay, half incline me to write no more: that would be making the Town a compliment which, I think, it deserves; and which some, I am sure, would take very kindly" (Roscoe, 3. 245).

l. 20. **which is a compliment this age deserves.** The meaning is that the age is so bad that it does not deserve that a poet like Pope should write in it. He feels inclined to write no more. Compare the passage at p. 64, l. 22, and the second note there.

l. 25. [**Juvenal,** the great Roman satirist, who lived in the latter part of the first century. C. D. P.]

l. 31. **Gay,** the celebrated author of the *Beggars' Opera*. "Gay was quite a natural man, wholly without art or design, and spoke just what he thought, and as he thought it. He dangled for twenty years about a court, and at last was offered to be made Usher to the young Princesses. Secretary Craggs made Gay a present of stock in the South Sea year; and he was once worth twenty thousand pounds, but lost it all again. He got about four hundred pounds by the first *Beggars' Opera*, and eleven or twelve hundred by the second. He was negligent and a bad manager. Latterly the Duke of Queensbury took his money into his keeping, and let him have only what was necessary out of it; and as he lived with them, he could not have occasion for much: he died worth upwards of three thousand pounds" (Pope, in Spence, p. 161). Compare below, p. 123.

Page 49, l. 8. and found, that is to say, 'and yet they found.' After the lines about his father, in the *Epistle to Arbuthnot*, quoted on p. 2, l. 32, Pope goes on as follows:

"O Friend! may each domestic bliss be thine!
Be no unpleasing Melancholy mine:
Me let the tender office long engage
To rock the cradle of reposing Age,

With lenient arts extend a Mother's breath,
Make Languor smile, and smooth the bed of Death,
Explore the thought, explain the asking eye,
And keep awhile one parent from the sky."

Mrs. Pope died a few weeks after these lines were written.

l. 13. **One of the passages of Pope's life, which seems to deserve some enquiry,** etc. It has led to more enquiry than almost anything else connected with Pope, and the puzzle cannot be said to be solved yet. The following is from Ward: "But since, on a comparison of Curll's with the authorized edition, it becomes evident that both were made from the same original, both presenting in certain cases the same variations from the letters as originally addressed to Pope's correspondents, a choice between two alternatives is left us. Either Curll's mysterious purveyor had obtained access to Lord Oxford's library and transcribed the letters *en masse*; or, Pope himself had supplied Curll with copies. On the latter supposition, the entire proceeding was one of his intricate manœuvres in order to obtain notoriety for his letters, and by the spurious publication to benefit the sale of the intended genuine one. The former alternative involves an obvious improbability; the latter is supported by the circumstance since ascertained, that Pope had withdrawn the letters from Lord Oxford's library in the spring of 1735. This discovery seems at first sight to tend towards the conclusion that Pope had entertained the idea of publishing the Letters *before* Curll's venture saw the light. In this case Pope's edition of his Letters cannot have been brought out in self-defence. The question (which continues to constitute one of the *cruces* of which the life of Pope is so prolific) remains in its original difficulty." Compare the note below, on p. 51, l. 36.

l. 15. [Curll had a shop in Fleet Street, where he published the most disgraceful books and forged letters. In 1716 he was whipped and put under the pump by the boys of Westminster School for publishing a school oration full of blunders. See p. 7, l. 7. C. D. P.]

l. 17. **This volume containing some Letters from noblemen.** Johnson should have written here, " this volume having been advertised as containing, etc." Compare Cunningham's note. "Johnson is here incorrect. The volume complained of does not contain a single letter from any nobleman, and Curll was acquitted, and the copies returned to him, on this ground alone, the Committee finding (15th May, 1735) that the publication was not contrary to the standing order of the House of 31st January, 1721-2, though the advertisement in *The Postboy* expressly mentioned letters from Lords Halifax and Burlington. ... "

l. 28. **offered to sale.** We must now say "offered for sale."

Page 50 l. 1. **Bernard,** that is, Bernard Lintot, the first of the two publishers of the name.

l. 5. **not to pay a porter.** He would not hand over the price demanded for the copies to the man who brought the parcels to his door. He wanted to deal with a principal.

l. 13. **the numbers offered to sale,** etc. The price demanded was very small as compared with the number of copies offered.

l. 22. **filled the nation with praises of his candour.** Compare the passage at p. 8, l. 26 fg.

l. 29. **Mr. Allen.** See below, note on p. 63, l. 36.

Page 51, l. 2. [reposited, modern *deposited*. See p. 24, l. 2. C. D. P.]

l. 3. [See note on p. 49, l. 13. C. D. P.]

l. 5. **the preface to the Miscellanies was written to prepare the public for such an incident.** See above, p. 42, l. 32 fg.

l. 7. **and to strengthen this opinion.** That is "and by way of strengthening the opinion of the falsity of the story, it may be also mentioned that," etc.

l. 25. **Howel.** It is to be feared that Howel's *Letters* have now followed his other ninety-nine volumes into oblivion. His dates are 1596-1666, and he is said to have written more books than any other Englishman of his time. His volume of letters was entitled "Epistolae Ho-Elianae; or, Familiar Letters, Domestic and Foreign." Morhoff, mentioned as having commended this volume, was Professor of Poetry at the German University of Kiel.

l. 27. **Loveday's Letters were printed only once.** Loveday, of whom very little else is known, published a volume of letters on the same plan as Howel's volume in 1659. It ran through several editions, though Johnson apparently had only seen the first.

l. 28. **those of Herbert and Suckling.** The Herbert referred to is Lord Herbert of Cherbury (1581-1648), elder brother of the poet, George Herbert (1593-1633). Suckling is the well-known poet (1609-1641).

l. 29. **Mrs. Phillip's.** Mrs. Phillips (1631-1664) was a woman writer of the Restoration period. [Mrs. Phillips (1631-1664) published nothing in her life-time. In 1669 her poems were published by a friend, and were highly praised by Cowley. C. D. P.]

l. 30. [**Walsh** (1663-1708), a man of fashion, and friend of Dryden and Pope, wrote some verses and prose. C. D. P.]

l. 34. **as connected with the other contemporary wits.** Their letters to him were given as well as his to them.

l. 36. **he had the power of favouring himself.** "And did so. He not only made large omissions, but important alterations, and even additions..." (Cunningham). Johnson, however, is not referring here to the now well-established fact that Pope freely altered his letters before publication, but to the considerations which he proceeds to mention. If Johnson had known that the letters were altered, and that the alterations were the same in both the surreptitious and the authorized editions, he would have had no remaining doubt as to the real character of the mystery attending the publication of Curll's edition.

Page 52, l. 6. in his productions than the rest. In his letters as compared with the letters of his correspondents.

l. 16. **what he persuaded himself to think a system of Ethics.** See this contemptuous criticism of the Essay as a philosophical work elaborated below, p. 104, l. 24 fg.

l. 19. **[eight years.** The first Epistle was published in 1732, and the rest in 1734. C. D. P.]

l. 30. **given,** attributed.

Page 53, l. 7. which they could not afterwards decently retract, as they might wish to do after learning that the poem was written by Pope.

l. 8. **In 1733,** a mistake for 1732.

l. 12. **this design was not discovered in the new poem.** Johnson is continuing the sarcasm of p. 52, l. 16 above.

l. 31. **but having afterwards discovered, or been shown,** etc. This is a third sneer at Pope's reasoning powers.

Page 54, l. 7. In the conclusion it is sufficiently acknowledged, etc.

"Come then, my Friend! my Genius! come along;
Oh master of the poet and the song!...
Thou wert my guide, philosopher, and friend."
Essay on Man, iv. 733 fg.

l. 16. **has been reported.** Compare Boswell's *Johnson,* p. 512. Dr. Blair, in a letter to Boswell, is giving an account of a conversation at a dinner at "old Lord Bathurst's." "The conversation turning on Mr. Pope, Lord Bathurst told us that the *Essay on Man* was originally composed by Lord Bolingbroke in prose, and that Mr. Pope did no more than put it into verse. that he had read Lord Bolingbroke's manuscript in his own handwriting; and remembered well that he was at a loss whether most to admire the elegance of Lord Bolingbroke's prose, or the beauty of Mr. Pope's verse." Johnson's comment on this was as follows: "Depend upon it, Sir, this is too strongly stated. Pope may have had from Bolingbroke the philosophic *stamina* of his Essay; and admitting this to be true, Lord Bathurst did not intentionally falsify. But the thing is not true in the latitude that Blair seems to imagine, we are sure that the poetical imagery, which makes a great part of the poem, was Pope's own. It is amazing, Sir, what deviations there are from precise truth in the account which is given of almost everything." Compare also Spence, p. 108. "Mr. Pope mentioned then, and at several other times, how much (or rather how wholly) he himself was obliged to Lord Bolingbroke for the thoughts and reasonings in his moral work; and once in particular said, that beside their frequent talking over that subject together, he had received,

I think, seven or eight sheets from Lord Bolingbroke, in relation to it, as I apprehended by way of letters; both to direct the plan in general, and to supply the matter for the particular epistles."

l. 22. **philosophy and poetry have not often the same readers.** It was not therefore for some time that the principles of the poem were examined, from the philosophical standpoint, by men who knew anything of the questions in dispute.

l. 26. **did not see what the gay foliage concealed,** did not see the "snake lurking in the grass," as the Latin proverb has it.

l. 32. **Resnel.** This French writer (1692-1761) translated into French both the *Essay on Criticism* and the *Essay on Man*.

l. 33. **Crousaz,** a professor in the University of Berne. He published his *Examen de l'Essai sur l'Homme, poème de Pope* in 1737, and his *Commentaire sur la traduction de M. l'Abbé du Resnel, de l'Essai de M. Pope* in the following year.

l. 34. [**censure,** criticism including both favourable and unfavourable remarks. This censure was published in 1738. C. D. P.]

Page 55, l. 11. **purely rational.** With nothing of the supernatural element in them.

l. 16. [**a necessary ... fatality,** a series of events bound together by laws of nature which are fixed at the beginning, and remain unalterable. "Fatality," *i.e.* the belief in a fixed and unchangeable fate is the feature of many Eastern religions, and enters into the creed of Calvinists. C. D. P.]

l. 21. **He was a man.** This was written immediately after Warburton's death, which occurred in 1779. C. D. P.]

Page 56, l. 1. **oderint dum metuant,** let them hate me if only they fear me. A phrase which, according to Suetonius, was often in Caligula's mouth.

l. 5. **his sentences,** his verdicts on men and things.

l. 7. **pleased himself with the notice of,** been glad to be noticed by.

l. 11. **Concanen.**

"True to the bottom see Concanen creep,
A cold, long-winded native of the deep."
The Dunciad, v. 299.

"Matthew Concanen, an Irishman, bred to the law. He was author of several dull and dead scurrilities in the British and London journals, and in a paper called the *Speculatist*. In a pamphlet callled a 'Supplement to the Profound,' he dealt very unfairly with our poet ... " (from Pope's note on that passage).

l. 14. **the best notes were supplied by Warburton.** There does not seem to be any authority for this but Warburton himself. In a letter, written to excuse his former acquaintance with Theobald and other "gentlemen of the *Dunciad*," Warburton says that Pope once told him that in reading Theobald's edition "he was sorry to find a man of genius got amongst them; for he told me he was greatly struck with my notes." Johnson, whose own edition of Shakespeare was far from being a success, found it hard to be just to Theobald. Compare the note above, on p. 39, l. 28.

l. 28. **to rescue Pope from the talons of Crousaz.** See above, p. 54, l. 32 fg.

l. 33. **who probably began to doubt the tendency of his own work.** Compare the sneering remark attributed to Bolingbroke, p. 54, ll. 10-13.

Page 57, l. 14. **as they say our natural body**, etc. St. Paul, writing of the doctrine of the resurrection of the dead, says of the body, "It is sown in dishonour; it is raised in glory: ... It is sown a natural body; it is raised a spiritual body" (1 *Corinthians* xv. 43, 44).

l. 33. **He once discovered them to Mr. Hooke.** "Pope was much shocked at overhearing Warburton and Hooke talking of Lord Bolingbroke's disbelief of the moral attributes of God. 'You must be mistaken,' said he. Pope afterwards talked with Lord B. about it, and he denied it all. Some time after Pope told his friends of it with great joy, and said, 'I told you, I was sure, you must be mistaken'" (Dr. Warburton, in Spence, p. 281). Hooke is mentioned again below, p. 71, l. 29.

Page 58, l. 8. **Mr. Murray.** The Lord Mansfield of p. 16, l. 31.

l. 9. [**Mr. Ralph Allen**, of Bath, was the friend of many writers of the time. He made a large fortune by providing postal communications between the large towns of England. C. D. P.]

l. 10. **and by consequence a bishopric.** Johnson means that Warburton would never have been made a bishop if he had not, by the kindness of Mr. Allen, previously become a rich and influential man.

l. 11. [**bishopric**, of Gloucester (1759). C. D. P.]

l. 15. **Dobson**, etc. From Spence, p. 135. Dobson was a scholar at Winchester.

l. 16. [Prior. See p. 15, l. 6. C. D. P.]

l. 24. **among the great.**
"Envy must own I live among the great,
No Pimp of Pleasure, and no Spy of State."
Pope, *Imitations of Horace*, ll. 133, 134.

l. 27. [**Bolingbroke, Walpole.** At this time Walpole was Prime Minister, and Bolingbroke one of the chief leaders of the Tory Opposition. C. D. P.]

l. 30. **Mr. Southcot**, a French abbé, who twenty years before had procured the advice of the celebrated Dr. Radcliffe for Pope. The story of Pope's securing an abbey in France for him, through the influence of Sir Robert Walpole, is from Spence, p. 5.

l. 36. **a careless effusion**, a casual burst of interest on the part of the Queen, which she forgot all about as soon as she had said it.

Page 59, l. 3. **Savage**, the poet Savage, author of *The Bastard* and *The Wanderer*.

l. 8. **refusing the visits of a Queen.**
"Hail, happy Pope! whose generous mind
Detesting all the statesman kind,
Contemning Courts, at Court unseen,
Refused the visits of a Queen."
Libel on Dr. Delaney.

l. 12. **it was his intention**, etc. "Mr. Pope's poem grows on his hands. The first four or five Epistles will be on the general principles, or of 'The Nature of Man'; and the rest will be on moderation, or 'The Use of Things.' In the latter part each class may take up three Epistles: one, for instance, against Avarice; another against Prodigality; and the third, on the moderate use of Riches; and so of the rest" (Spence, writing in 1728, p. 36).

l. 14. **the Epistle to Lord Bathurst**, now the third of the *Moral Essays*.

l. 19. **the praise of Kyrl, the Man of Ross.**
"But all our praises why should Lords engross!
Rise honest Muse! and sing the Man of Ross;
Pleased Vaga echoes," etc.

In the passage which follows, Pope describes the many public benefactions of his hero. He attaches the following note: "The person here celebrated, who with a small estate actually performed all these good works, and whose true name was almost lost (partly by the title of the *Man of Ross*, given him by way of eminence, and partly by being buried without so much as an inscription), was called Mr. John Kyrl. He died in the year

1724, aged 90, and lies interred in the chancel of the church of Ross, in Herefordshire." Warburton, in his laborious way, declares that "we must understand what is here said of *actually performing* to mean by the contributions which the *Man of Ross*, by his assiduity and interest, collected in his neighbourhood."

l. 29. **Mr. Victor**, a dramatist of the day.

l. 36. **by ridiculing the ceremony of burning the pope.** A ceremony much in vogue with fanatical Protestants of the time. [Each year, on November 17, the date of Elizabeth's accession, there was a procession by torchlight in which effigies of the Pope, nuns, cardinals, etc., were carried through the streets, to be afterwards burned. C. D. P.] Pope, describing the mad career of the spendthrift son of a miser, has the couplet:

"To town he comes, completes the nation's hope,
And heads the bold Train-bands, and burns a Pope."
(vv. 213, 214.)

Page 60, l. 2. the inscription on the Monument. The inscription on the monument raised by the City of London to commemorate the Great Fire of 1666, expressly attributed the catastrophe to "the treachery and malice" of the Papists. The monument is in the form of a lofty pillar of stone, and Pope's indignant couplet runs:

"Where London's column, pointing at the skies,
Like a tall bully, lifts the head, and lies."
(vv. 339, 340.)

This inscription was removed from the column in the reign of William IV. (December, 1830), after having been removed once before under James II. and restored under William III.

l. 3. **the dialogue having no letters of direction.** [There were no initials to indicate where one speaker ended and another commenced. C. D. P.] As printed now, the speakers are distinguished as P (Pope) and B (Bathurst). "Allen Apsley, Lord Bathurst, a Tory peer, was one of the most intimate of Pope's friends and associates. 'He united,' says Carruthers, 'a sort of French vivacity to English principles, and mingled freely in society till past ninety, living to walk under the shade of lofty trees which Pope and he had planted, and to see his son Lord Chancellor of England.' He died in the year 1774, at the age of 91." Compare the note at p. 54, l. 16.

[l. 7. **Lord Cobham** had been this year arbitrarily deprived of his commission in the army because of withholding his support from Walpole's Excise Bill. He then joined the Opposition. C. D. P.]

l. 8. **his "Characters of Men."** Now the first Epistle in the *Moral Essays.*

l. 11. [**ruling Passion**, a tendency of the mind sufficiently powerful to exercise an influence over all actions. It turns the mind from the first into some particular channel, and is an inborn tendency which influences the mind in a fixed (determininate) and unchangeable direction, acting upon the whole course of our actions, either openly, or more secretly because it puts forward some accidental or less powerful tendency as a means which shall hide its ends. C. D. P.]

l. 24. [**ascendant planet**, a planet which, from its position at birth, exercises a powerful influence on the whole life of a man. This was the belief of astrologers. C. D. P.]

[**predominating humour**. According to an old medical theory the body contained four humours (fluids), and according to the excess of one or other a person's character was strongly marked in some particular direction. For example, an excess of blood made a man sanguinary; an excess of bile made him melancholy. C. D. P.]

l. 29. [**antecedent to reason and observation**, existing before a child is capable of reasoning or of observing. C. D. P.]

l. 30. **independent on.** We must now say "not dependent on," or "independent of."

Page 61, l. 5. [**predestination**, a condition fixed before the birth of the individual. The doctrine put forward tends to produce the belief that the moral character of man is laid down before he is born, and before he is capable of doing anything of his own will to form his own character. C. D. P.]

l. 13. **the Characters of Women.** Now the second of the Epistles in the *Moral Essays*. "Of this Epistle, which was published in 1735, parts had been long before written and even printed. As originally published, it wanted the characters of Philomede, Chloe, and Atossa. According to Warburton's statement, Pope communicated the character of Atossa to the Duchess of Marlborough as intended for the Duchess of Buckingham; according to Walpole, he repeated the experiment *vice versa*. Immediately on the death of Pope, the Duchess of Marlborough applied to one of his executors, Lord Marchmont, with the view of ascertaining whether the poet had left behind him any satire on the Duke or herself. Marchmont consulted Bolingbroke; and it was found that in the edition of the *Moral Essays* prepared for the press by Pope himself just before his death, and printed off ready for publication, the character of Atossa was inserted. If Lord Marchmont made the statement attributed to him by the editor of his papers (Rose), Pope had received from the Duchess £1000, the acceptance of which implied forbearance towards the house of Marlborough. If this be so, it is probable

that the motive which prompted Pope to the acceptance of this
'favour' was the desire to settle Martha Blount in independent
circumstances for life." See the account of this transaction in
Carruthers' *Life of Pope*, pp. 392-396" (Ward). The poet, as we
have seen, fully intended to publish the lines in his lifetime.
He was at the time on good terms with the Duchess of Marlborough, and Mr. Courthope therefore believes that it was Pope's
intention to explain that by Atossa he meant, not the Duchess of
Marlborough, but the Duchess of Buckingham, who had died a
short time before. Johnson's explanation, that Pope had ceased
to have any reason to fear the Duchess of Marlborough, whose
influence and power had greatly waned, is simpler, and agrees
better with the passage itself. It would have been very hard to
convince any one that "the great Atossa" of the lines was not
the Duchess of Marlborough.

l. 15. [**Martha Blount** belonged to a Roman Catholic family of
Mapledurham in Oxfordshire. She was the object of a lifelong
affection on the part of Pope. C. D. P.]

l. 32. **once, as was suspected, without it.** The reference is to
an *Imitation of the Second Satire of the First Book of Horace*,
which was published as having been imitated after the manner
of Mr. Pope. It was included in the collected edition of 1738,
but was rejected by Warburton.

Page 62, l. 3. [**Ennius** (B.C. 239-169), the Chaucer, or father, of
Roman poets. C. D. P.]

l. 4. **Pantolabus and Nomentanus,** two characters in Horace's
Satires.

l. 6. **Oldham and Rochester.** Oldham (1653-1683) wrote a
volume of *Satires upon the Jesuits*. Rochester is the well-known
Wilmot, Earl of Rochester (1647-1680).

l. 12. **Dr. Donne's Satires.** "These Satires, as Pope informs us
in the advertisement prefixed to the *Satires and Epistles of
Horace Imitated*, were 'versified' by him at the request of
Lords Oxford and Shrewsbury, and therefore in the main
belong to an earlier period of his career than the *Satires* among
which they were afterwards inserted. He calls his labour
'versifying,' says Warburton, because indeed Donne's lines
'have nothing more of numbers than their being composed of
a certain quantity of syllables'—a description exaggerated, but
not untrue..." (Ward). Donne was Dean of St. Paul's when
he died in 1631.

l. 16. [**Pulteney** was an active opponent of Walpole, the head
of the Whig ministry of the day. C. D. P.]

l. 20. **The Epistle to Dr. Arbuthnot.** Afterwards placed as the
Prologue to the *Satires*. It is one of Pope's greatest poems.

For the friend to whom it was addressed, compare Ward's note: "John Arbuthnot (born in 1675, died in 1735), besides being a most distinguished member of his profession, the medical, was eminent as a mathematician and a classical scholar. As a politician he was firmly attached to the Tory party, and with Swift became a member of the October Club, established in 1710 by Oxford, Bolingbroke, and their political and literary friends. He was also a member of the Scriblerus Club, and to him is attributed the chief share in the famous treatise of M. S., *On the Art of Sinking in Poetry*, which was published in the *Miscellanies* of Pope and Swift. *The History of John Bull*, *The Art of Political Lying*, and other *jeux d'esprit* of the same kind, were Arbuthnot's own. On the accession of George I. Arbuthnot was deprived of his post as Physician-Extraordinary at Court. Of Pope's sentiments towards Arbuthnot, this Epistle offers the best testimony; Swift said of him that 'he has more wit than we all have, and more humanity than wit.'"

l. 29. [**the Prince of Wales** was Frederick, eldest son of George II. He was for many years an active leader of the Opposition to Walpole's government. He died in 1751. C. D. P.]

l. 32. **seems to reckon with the public**, seems to submit to the public a defence of himself against his critics and detractors. So Ward remarks that the poem "may be almost regarded in the light of a poetical apology *pro vita*, and an attempt for ever to silence the most notable of the poet's detractors."

Page 63, l. 1. the satirical lines upon Addison. The lines are as follows:

"Peace to all such! but were there One whose fires
True Genius kindles, and true Fame inspires;
Blest with each talent and each art to please,
And born to write, converse, and live with ease:
Should such a man, too fond to rule alone,
Bear, like the Turk, no brother near the throne,
View him with scornful, yet with jealous eyes,
And hate for arts that caus'd himself to rise;
Damn with faint praise, assent with civil leer,
And without sneering, teach the rest to sneer;
Willing to wound, and yet afraid to strike,
Just hint a fault, and hesitate dislike;
Alike reserv'd to blame, or to commend,
A tim'rous foe, and a suspicious friend;
Dreading ev'n fools, by Flatterers besieg'd,
And so obliging, that he ne'er obliged;
Like *Cato*, give his little Senate laws,
And sit attentive to his own applause:
While Wits and Templars ev'ry sentence raise,

And wonder with a foolish face of praise :
Who but must laugh if such a man there be ?
Who would not weep if Atticus were he."

(Note that "obliged" in the above must be pronounced, as it was in Pope's day, to rhyme with "besieg'd.") Pope incurred great obloquy for making this attack upon Addison after Addison's death. He attempted to defend himself in the following note on the passage : "It was a great falsehood, which some of the Libels reported, that this Character was written after the Gentleman's death : which see refuted in the Testimonies prefixed to the *Dunciad*. But the occasion of writing it was such as he would not make public out of regard to his memory ; and all that could further be done was to omit the name in the Edition of his Works." The reference is to the story told at p. 37, l. 11, which, however, looks suspiciously like an invention designed to free Pope from a just reproach.

l. 13. **Lord Hervey,** called *Sporus* in the poem :
"Let *Sporus* tremble—What ? that thing of silk,
Sporus, that mere white curd of Ass's milk ?
Satire or sense, alas ! can *Sporus* feel ?
Who breaks a butterfly upon a wheel ? ..."

Ward's note on the passage is as follows : "The original of this famous portrait was John, Lord Hervey, eldest surviving son of the Earl of Bristol, and author of the *Memoirs of the Reign of George II*. At an early age he became a great favourite at the court of the Prince and Princess of Wales at Richmond, where Pope and his literary friends enjoyed high favour. He married Miss Lepell, whom Pope himself greatly admired. Afterwards he attached himself to Walpole's party, and was appointed Vice-Chamberlain to the King (George II). Ultimately he attained to the office of Lord Privy Seal ; and after Walpole's fall continued to take an active part in politics, notwithstanding his miserable health, till his death in 1743. The cause of his estrangement from Pope remains obscure ; but the first public offence was given by Pope, in allusions in his *Miscellanies* (1727) and the first edition of the *Dunciad* (1728). Then in 1734 appeared the *Imitation of the Second Satire of the First Book of Horace*, where Lord Hervey was twice attacked under the soubriquet of Lord Fanny, and his friend, Lady Mary Wortley Montagu, was even more venomously aspersed. They retorted in verse and prose ; and Pope wrote his prose *Letter to a noble Lord*. The *Character of Sporus* followed in 1734 ; and another attack in the satire originally called '1738,' in *Epilogue to the Satires* (1738), brought out a poem, *The Difference between Verbal and Practical Virtue Exemplified*, etc., by Lord H. The original hints for all the insinuations and insults introduced by

Pope into the *Character of Sporus* are, according to Mr. Crocker, to be found in Pulteney's *Reply* to a pamphlet against himself and Bolingbroke (1731), which he attributed to Hervey. The *Reply* brought about a duel. Mr. Crocker can find no evidence for the report that the rupture between Pope and Lady Mary was due to the 'rivalry' between himself and Hervey 'in her good graces.'"

l. 18. **he had written an invective against Pope.** See the last note. At v. 380 of the *Epistle to Arbuthnot* there is the couplet:

"Let the two *Curlls* of Town and Court abuse
His father, mother, body, soul, and muse."

To which Pope attached the following note: "In some of Curll's and other pamphlets, Mr. Pope's father was said to be a mechanic, a hatter, a farmer, nay a bankrupt. But, what is stranger, a *nobleman* (if such a reflection could be thought to come from a nobleman) had dropped an allusion to that pitiful untruth in a paper called an *Epistle to a Doctor of Divinity*; and the following line,

'Hard as thy Heart, and as thy Birth obscure,'

had fallen from a like *courtly* pen, in certain *Verses to the Imitator of Horace*. Mr. Pope's father was of a gentleman's family in Oxfordshire, the head of which was the Earl of Downe, whose sole heiress married the Earl of Lindsey. His mother was the daughter of William Turnor, Esq., of York: she had three brothers, one of whom was killed, another died in the service of King Charles; the eldest following his fortunes, and becoming a general officer in Spain, left her what estate remained after the sequestrations and forfeitures of her family. ..." Compare p. 1, l. 11 fg., and the note there.

l. 25. **His last Satires.** Now placed as an Epilogue to the *Satires*, in the same way as the *Epistle to Arbuthnot* forms the Prologue to the *Satires*. The Epilogue is in two Dialogues, of which the first was published in 1738, and the second in the following year. The first Dialogue came out on the same morning as the poem *London* by the then altogether unknown author of this *Life of Pope*. See Boswell, p. 38. "Johnson's *London* was published in May, 1738; and it is remarkable that it came out on the same morning with Pope's satire entitled '1738'; so that England had at once its Juvenal and Horace as poetical monitors." Pope took a great and friendly interest in the appearance of the new poet. See the note on p. 69, l. 20.

l. 28. **entangled in the opposition.** He had either not chosen or not been able to follow Addison's advice (p. 18, l. 9) that he should steer clear of the two great political parties in the state. He was identified with the Opposition.

l. 36. **Allen.** The couplet in his praise contains one of the countless happy phrases of Pope's which are now in themselves almost part of the English language:

"Let humble Allen, with an awkward shame,
 Do good by stealth, and blush to find it fame."

"Ralph Allen, of Prior Park, and an intimate friend and constant correspondent of Pope's, to whom he performed many kind services. He was afterwards a munificent patron to Fielding. Of his charitable habits there is evidence in Pope's will" (Ward's note on that passage). Allen has been immortalized by Fielding as the Squire Alworthy of *Tom Jones.*

Page 64, l. 6. **took some liberty with one of the Foxes.** In the "First Dialogue" Pope had, in effect, accused Henry Fox of having borrowed from Lord Hervey the greater part of his speech in the House of Commons on the occasion of the death of Queen Caroline. In the present poem he returns to the charge, and uses the following offensive simile:

"Let Courtly Wits to Wits afford supply,
 As Hog to Hog in huts of Westphaly;
 If one, through Nature's bounty, or his Lord's,
 Has what the frugal, dirty soil affords,
 From him the next receives its thick or thin,
 As pure a mess almost as it came in;..."

By "in a reply to Lyttleton" Johnson means a reply made in the House of Commons in the course of debate. Fox's speech on this occasion, and the threatened prosecution of Whitehead and his publisher, are supposed to have effectually deterred Pope from further satire.

l. 22. **attempts of reformation.** We must now say "attempts at reformation," and even that would more naturally refer to attempts at self-reformation. Johnson means attempts to reform other people.

by his commentator. That is, by Warburton. But the note referred to is signed P., by which Warburton means us to understand that it is Pope's own. "This was the last poem of the kind printed by our author, with a resolution to publish no more; but to enter thus, in the most plain and solemn manner he could, a sort of protest against that insuperable corruption and depravity of manners, which he had been so unhappy as to live to see. Could he have hoped to have amended any, he had continued those attacks; but bad men were grown so shameless and so powerful, that Ridicule was become as unsafe as it was ineffectual. The poem raised him, as he knew it would, some enemies; but he had reason to be satisfied with the approbation of good men, and the testimony of his own conscience."

l. 30. **The Memoirs of Scriblerus.** The full title was *Memoirs of the Extraordinary Life, Works, and Discoveries of Martinus Scriblerus.* "The design of the *Memoirs of Scriblerus* was to have ridiculed all the false tastes in learning, under the character of a man of capacity enough; that had dipped into every art and science, but injudiciously in each. It was begun by a club of some of the greatest wits of the age, Lord Oxford, the Bishop of Rochester, Mr. Pope, Congreve, Arbuthnot, Swift, and others. Gay often held the pen; and Addison liked it very well, and was not disinclined to come into it. The Deipnosophy consists of disputes on ridiculous tenets of all sorts; and the adventure of the Shield was designed against Dr. Woodward and the Antiquaries. It was Anthony Henley who wrote 'the life of his music master, Tom Durfey'; a chapter by way of episode. It was from a part of these memoirs that Dr. Swift took his first hints for *Gulliver*. There were pigmies in Schreibler's travels; and the projects of Laputa. The design was carried on much further than has appeared in print; and was stopped by some of the gentlemen being dispersed or otherwise engaged (about the year 1715). See the memoirs themselves" (Pope, in Spence, p. 8). This book was published in 1741, making, along with Pope's correspondence with Swift, a second volume of our author's prose works. "Schreibler," in the extract from Spence, is German for "Scriblerus." "Martinus Scriblerus" is "Swift the Scribbler." "Harley, Lord Oxford, used playfully to call Swift *Martin*, and from this sprung Martinus Scriblerus. *Swift*, as is well known, is the name of one species of swallow, the largest and most powerful flier of the tribe, and *Martin* is the name of another species, the wall-swallow, that constructs its nest in buildings" (Carruthers).

Page 65, l. 15. [**Don Quixote**, by Cervantes, a satire on knight errantry, and the absurd chivalric romances of the Middle Ages. It had the effect of putting an end to that sort of literature. C. D. P.]

l. 16. **History of Mr. Ouffle.** "A '*History of the Ridiculous Extravagancies of Monsieur Ouffle*,' London, 1711. This was a translation from a French work, of which the author, the Abbé Bordelon, sought to do for witchcraft what Cervantes had done for knight-errantry" (Arnold's note here).

l. 18. **his Travels**, *Gulliver's Travels*. See the extract from Spence above.

l. 20. **in a region not known to have been explored**, etc. The reference is to the poets who wrote in Latin long after that tongue had ceased to be a living language. The French poet and critic Boileau held that no poem of the first order would ever be written in a dead language, as also that a writer of the age of

Augustus would probably have detected ludicrous improprieties in even the best modern Latin. Johnson, who was himself fond of writing in Latin, speaks here and in his *Life of Addison* of these views of Boileau's as a bringing into contempt of a meritorious class of writers. The selection from the Italians who wrote in London, of which Pope published a revision, was put out originally in 1684.

l. 32. **injuriously**, unjustly. So in l. 34 of the next page, "injurious" where we should now say "unjust."

Page 66, l. 5. **one of them shall be addressed to you.** A favour which Swift repeatedly begged at Pope's hands. "I have the ambition, and it is very earnest, as well as in haste, to have one Epistle inscribed to me while I am alive, and you just in the time when wit and wisdom are in their height; I must once more repeat Cicero's desire to a friend: *Orna Me*" (Swift to Pope, on the 3rd of September, 1735, quoted by Carruthers).

l. 27. **the laurel**, etc. Cibber was made Poet Laureate in 1730.

l. 31. **he has liberally enough praised the Careless Husband.**

"All this may be; the People's voice is odd,
It is, and it is not, the voice of God.
To Gammer Gurton if it give the bays,
And yet deny the Careless Husband praise,
Or say our Fathers never broke a rule;
Why then, I say, the Public is a fool."
First Epistle of Second Book, vv. 89-94.

Cibber's *Careless Husband* was first acted in 1704, and kept the stage throughout the century.

l. 32. **among other worthless scribblers.** He is mentioned as the first of the Dunces.

"Not with less glory mighty Dulness crown'd
Shall take thro' Grubstreet her triumphant round;
And her Parnassus glancing o'er at once,
Behold, a hundred sons, and each a Dunce.
Mark first that youth who takes the foremost place,
And thrusts his person full into your face.
With all thy Father's virtues blest, be born!
And a new Cibber shall the stage adorn."
(3 vv. 135-142).

The Goddess of Dulness is speaking prophetically, and anticipating the birth and career of the second Cibber. In the first book of the *Dunciad*, vv. 31, 32, Pope had already made a mock of Cibber's father.

"Where o'er the gates, by his fam'd father's hands
Great Cibber's brazen, brainless brothers stand."

The place is the Lunatic Asylum called Bedlam Hospital. Pope attaches the note, "Mr. Caius Gabriel Cibber, father of the Poet Laureate. The two Statues of the Lunatics over the gates of Bedlem Hospital were done by him, and (as the son justly says of them) are no ill monuments of his fame as an artist.

l. 33. **in his Apology.** *Apology for the Life of Mr. Colley Cibber.* Published in 1740. The student should note that in such a title "apology" means no more than "defence," and does not imply any admission of error. The phrase is a translation of the Latin *Apologia pro vitâ suâ*, under which title in our own day the late Cardinal Newman published a defence of his life and career against the aspersions of Kingsley.

Page 67, l. 4. **afterwards.** Both Ryland and Sharp think that Johnson has gone wrong in his dates here, because the two contemptuous allusions to Cibber, which he proceeds to mention, were made before, and not after, the publication of Cibber's *Apology*. But "afterwards" in the text means "subsequent to the praise of the *Careless Husband*." The "submissive gentleness" of l. 2 is the line of conduct which Cibber, as he tells us, pursued when Pope began to attack him without cause.

l. 6. **in the fourth Book of the Dunciad.** The Goddess, when her Dunces have been bewitched by a wizard's cup into other forms, comes to their help as follows:

"But she, good Goddess, sent to ev'ry child
Firm Impudence or Stupefaction mild;
And straight succeeded, leaving shame no room,
Cibberian forehead, or Cimmerian gloom."
(vv. 529-32.)

l. 8. [**ridiculing the Laureat.** The following epigram by Pope appeared in the Grub Street Journal:

"Tell, if you can, which did the worse,
Caligula or Grafton's Grace?
That made a Consul of a horse,
And *this* a Laureate of an ass."

And in the *Epistle to Dr. Arbuthnot*, Pope says:

"Whom have I hurt? has Poet yet, or Peer,
Lost the arch'd eye-brow, or Parnassian sneer?
And has not Colley still his lord . . . ?" C. D. P.]

l. 17. **a pamphlet.** "A Letter from Mr. Cibber to Mr. Pope, inquiring into the Motives that might induce him in his *Satirical Works* to be so frequently fond of Mr. Cibber's name." Published in 1742.

l. 22. **to a very distant cause.** To an incident which happened so far back as the year 1717. "Early in the following year (1717) the production of the farce of *Three Hours after Marriage*, in which Gay had been assisted by Arbuthnot and Pope, occasioned the outbreak of a quarrel between the latter and Colley Cibber. The farce itself (Pope's co-operation in which constituted his solitary dramatic effort) is beneath contempt. Pope, as Gay afterwards admitted, 'never heartily approved of' the piece. Nor can the wit of those parts in which the hand of Pope is clearly discernable, and where Dennis is caricatured as Sir Tremendous, be fairly said to rise above the level of the remainder. The play was however damned on account of the extravagant nonsense of its last act, in which two lovers insert themselves respectively into the skins of a mummy and a crocodile. The *Rehearsal*, a play always used (like its successor the *Critic*) as an opportunity for introducing gag on popular topics of the day, happened to be performed shortly afterwards. Colley Cibber on this occasion introduced an allusion to the unhappy mummy and crocodile. Pope, whose presence in the theatre may have added to the effect of the allusion, sharply inveighed against the actor behind the scenes; and the latter not unnaturally swore to repeat the joke on every future occasion. To this episode Cibber, in his *Apology*, attributes the origin of Pope's animosity against him. There can be little doubt that the production towards the close of the year of Cibber's *Non-Juror* (so successful an attack upon Jacobites and concealed Papists that a patriotic pamphlet of the day desired to see it as common in every house as a Prayer-book or *Whole Duty of Man*) added a worthier cause of anger in Pope's mind against the future laureate of King George II." (Ward, in his Introductory Memoir).

Page 68, l. 6. **if suffered to remain without notice, would have been very soon forgotten.** Compare what Johnson says of the sufferers from the *Dunciad*, p. 44, l. 2 fg.

l. 13. **nobody enquired, but.** Nobody had any other interest in an attack made by Pope on Cibber except the hope, etc.

l. 22. **Silence.** [The silence of Pope was the only means to showing Cibber that Pope despised him. C. D. P.]

l. 28. **he degraded Theobald from his painful pre-eminence.** See p. 43, l. 22 fg.

l. 32. **depraved his poem.** Made his poem worse, as a work of art, than it was in its original state.

l. 34. [**Theobald.** See p. 39, l. 28 fg. and note. C. D. P.]

l. 36. **introduced Osborne,** etc. The *Dunciad*, 2. 167 fg. Pope has the note: "Thomas Osborne. A bookseller in Gray's-inn, very well qualified by his impudence to act this part: and therefore placed here instead of a less deserving Predecessor. This man published advertisements for a year together, pretending to sell Mr. Pope's subscription books of Homer's *Iliad* at half the price: Of which books he had none, but cut to the size of them (which was quarto) the common books in folio, without Copperplates, on a worse paper, and never above half the value." Compare above, p. 18, l. 23 fg., where Lintot is accused of a similar, if it be not the same, trick. Osborne was an old foe of Johnson's. "It has been confidently related, with many embellishments, that Johnson one day knocked Osborne down in his shop, with a folio, and put his foot upon his neck. The simple truth I had from Johnson himself. 'Sir, he was impertinent to me, and I beat him. But it was not in his shop: it was in my own chamber'" (Boswell, p. 49).

Page 69, l. 5. [**fate of Cassandra.** Cassandra was daughter of Priam, King of Troy (B.C. 1200). She was gifted with the power of true prophecy, but her predictions were fated never to be believed. C. D. P.]

l. 15. **his own magpye,** etc.

"Yes, you despise the man to Books confin'd,
Who from his study rails at human kind;
Tho' what he learns he speaks, and may advance
Some gen'ral maxims, or be right by chance.
The coxcomb bird, so talkative and grave,
That from his cage cries Cuckold, Whore, and Knave,
Tho' many a passenger he rightly call,
You hold him no Philosopher at all."
Moral Essays, i. 1-8.

l. 16. [**at a venture,** without aiming at any particular object. C. D. P.]

l. 17. **according to his engagement.** See p. 67, l. 16 fg.

l. 19. [**hartshorn** (ammonia) is used as a stimulant. Pope means that his energies would merely be stimulated by Cibber's pamphlet. C. D. P.]

l. 20. **Mr. Richardson,** a literary man of the time, and son of a well-known painter. It was to this Mr. Richardson that Pope applied when he wanted to find out about the author of the new poem *London* (compare above, note on p. 63, l. 25). "Pope, who then filled the poetical throne without a rival, it may reasonably be presumed, must have been particularly struck by the sudden appearance of such a poet; and, to his credit, let it be remembered that his feelings and conduct on the occasion were candid and liberal. He requested Mr. Richardson, son of the painter, to endeavour to find out who this new author was. Mr. Richardson, after some enquiry, having informed him that he had discovered only that his name was Johnson, and that he was some obscure man, Pope said, 'He will soon be *déterré'*" (Boswell, p. 39).

l. 24. [**writhen**, twisted; an old participle of *writhe*, an intransitive verb now, but here used transitively. C. D. P.]

Page 70, l. 3. has been exhausted. So edition of 1781 and edition of 1783 (Waugh). Matthew Arnold, "had been exhausted."

l. 10. **terminations not consistent**, etc. He proposed, for example, to call a British giant Corinaeus.

l. 23. **While he was yet capable**, etc. Carruthers (p. 387) rightly rejects this story, the evidence for which is unknown, as "quite incredible." Spence (p. 280) has preserved a remark of Dr. Warburton's to the effect that "it was very observable, during the time of Pope's last illness, that Mrs. Blount's coming in gave a new turn of spirits, or a temporary strength to him."

Page 71, l. 10. his death was approaching. The stories of Pope's last days which follow are all from Spence. Johnson has omitted a very characteristic one. The quack doctor, Thomson, had been saying to the poet that he was glad to find him breathing so much easier, that his pulse was very good, and "several other encouraging things." Pope turned to Lyttleton, who was at the moment coming into the room, and said, "Here am I, dying of a hundred good symptoms."

l. 17. **Bolingbroke sometimes wept over him**, etc. "There is so much trouble in coming into the world, and so much more, as well as meanness, in going out of it, that 'tis hardly worth while to be here at all!" (Lord Bolingbroke, in Spence, p. 242). Spence goes on: "His Lordship's melancholy attitude on the morning of the 21st was remarkable, leaning against Mr. Pope's chair; and crying over him for a considerable time, with more concern than can be expressed." "'O great God! what is man?' said Lord B., looking on Mr. Pope and repeating it several times, interrupted with sobs" (Spence, p. 243).

Page 72, l. 11. to solicit preference as the publisher, to ask that he might be employed as the publisher of Pope's papers.

l. 14. **what was 'reserved for the next age.'** A quotation from Pope's *Imitations of Horace*, II. i., vv. 57-60:

"In this impartial glass my Muse intends
Fair to expose myself, my foes, my friends;
Publish the present age; but where my text
Is Vice too high, reserve it for the next."

Page 73, l. 19. **proceeded wholly from his zeal for Bolingbroke.** This was the opinion also of Horace Walpole, a shrewd judge of men and things. "As to his printing so many copies, it certainly was a compliment, and the more profit (which, however, could not be immense) he expected to make, the greater opinion he must have conceived of the merit of the work. If one had a mind to defend Pope, should not one ask, if anybody ever blamed Virgil's executors for not burning the *Aeneid*, as he ordered them" (Walpole, quoted by Carruthers, p. 399).

l. 25. **He brought some reproach upon his own memory**, etc. The piece of gossip that follows is of very doubtful credibility, and is in any case of no importance to anybody. In Spence Mrs. Blount is made to say: "I had never read his will; but he mentioned to me the part relating to Mr. Allen, and I advised him to omit it, but could not prevail on him to do so."

Page 74, l. 5. **accomptant**, accountant.

l. 8. **The person of Pope**, etc. Compare the passage at p. 10, l. 13 fg.

l. 9. **in his account of the Little Club.** An imaginary club of small men. "A set of us have formed a society, who are sworn to dare to be short, and boldly bear out the dignity of littleness under the noses of those enormous engrossers of manhood, those hyperbolical monsters of the species, the tall fellows that overlook us" (Pope). The club was described by Pope in two articles in the *Guardian*. In the following he is supposed to be describing himself. After saying that the most eminent persons of the Little Club are "a little poet, a litttle lover, a little politician, and a little hero," he goes on: "The first of these, Dick Distich by name, we have elected president: not only as he is the shortest of us all, but because he has entertained so just a sense of his stature, as to go generally in black, that he may appear yet less. Nay, to that perfection is he arrived that he stoops as he walks. The figure of the man is odd enough; he is a lively little creature, with long arms and legs: a spider is no ill emblem of him: he has been taken at a distance for a small windmill."

l. 15. **his application**, that is, to his studies.

l. 20. **his life was a long disease.** A quotation from the lines by Pope, quoted above, on p. 2, l. 32.

l. 21. **the headache.** We now speak of a man suffering "from headache," not from "the headache."

l. 27. **sensible of cold.** We should now rather say "sensitive to cold." Compare the note on the use of the words "sensibility," above, p. 46, l. 14.

l. 31. **till they were laced.** "They" refers to "boddice," which is a corruption of "bodies," and was at first always used as a plural. It is now only a singular, with a new plural "boddices." [The "boddice" corresponded to the modern stays, and were looked upon with some suspicion because they gave an artificial shape to the wearer. C. D. P.]

Page 75, l. 5. [**a tye-wig,** a wig tied in a nob with a piece of ribbon. In 1764, owing to change of fashion, wigs ceased to be worn. C. D. P.]

l. 8. [**valetudinary man,** a man of a sickly constitution, hence unpleasing to others by his frequent need of assistance, and his constant anxiety for his own health. C. D. P.]

l. 12. **C'est que.** For the child is always man, the man is always child.

l. 21. [**left no room for another,** he demanded so much attention as to deprive others of it. Hence it was impossible to wait upon anyone else. C. D. P.]

Page 76, l. 10. [**Hannibal,** the famous Carthaginian, who spent most of his life in warfare with the Romans, ended his days in exile; and at last, to avoid falling into the hands of his implacable foes, swallowed a dose of poison, which, according to the common story, he carried with him constantly in the hollow of a ring (183 B.C.). In his victory at Cannae (B.C. 213) upwards of 43,000 Romans were slain, including a consul and eighty senators. C. D. P.]

l. 22. "**He hardly drank tea without a stratagem.**" An adaptation of a line of the poet Young's:

"Nor take her tea without a stratagem."

l. 28. **teazed.** Johnson spells this word "teized."

l. 31. [**His unjustifiable impression.** See p. 72, l. 18. An "impression" is a printed edition of a work. C. D. P.]

Page 77, l. 8. [**apophthegm,** a short, pointed saying. C. D. P.]

l. 11. **horresco referens,** "I shudder as I tell the story," a saying put by Virgil in the mouth of Aeneas when he is relating the death of Laocoon. Johnson is alluding playfully to the fact that, like Patrick, he had himself written a dictionary.

l. 16. **was to be courted back.** We must now say "had to be courted back."

Page 78, l. 23. [**their habitation in the Mint.** The Mint was a district in Southwark, and at this time was inhabited by felons, outlaws, and vagabonds. Its inhabitants claimed the privilege of protection from debt, and the place had become a refuge for the worst characters, so that no bailiff or officer of justice dared to venture there. C. D. P.]

l. 31. [**set genius to sale,** offered his talents for sale; he never allowed the great and wealthy to pay him for writing flattering poems, nor wrote such poems in the hope of pecuniary reward. C. D. P.]

l. 35. **a distich for his Highness's dog.** This is the "Epigram engraved on the collar of a dog which I gave to his Royal Highness":

"I am his Highness's dog at Kew;
Pray tell me, sir, whose dog are you."

The Royal Highness was Frederick, Prince of Wales.

Page 79, l. 14. **Cobham, Burlington, or Bolingbroke.** The first Epistle in the *Moral Essays* was inscribed to "Sir Richard Temple, Lord Cobham." "Sir Richard Temple, created Viscount Cobham by George I., in 1718, and made a Field Marshal in 1742, was on intimate terms with Pope during the latter part of the poet's life. Pope speaks, in his last letter to Swift, of 'generally rambling in the summer for a month to Lord Cobham's, the Bath, or elsewhere...'" (Ward). The fourth Epistle in the *Moral Essays* was inscribed to "Richard Boyle, Earl of Burlington." "Richard Boyle, third Earl of Burlington, born in 1695, died in 1753. He took no prominent part in politics, although his high rank obtained for him a great post at court and the order of the Garter. But he obtained wide fame by his taste in architecture, inspired by a natural love of art, and educated by studies in Italy. Horace Walpole says of him that he 'had every quality of genius and artist, except envy.' It has been doubted whether the architect Kent, who long lived with him, did not owe more to his patron, than the latter owed to the artist. The designs of any notable buildings were made by Lord Burlington; among these the Colonnade of Burlington House (the house itself was built by his father)" (Ward). Of Johnson's aversion to Bolingbroke the *Life of Pope* presents many examples besides the present one.

l. 24. **such were the simple friendships of the Golden Age.** In other words, there never were such friendships between men at all.

Page 80, l. 29. **Pope confesses,** etc. "If in these Letters, and in those which were printed without his consent, there appears too much of a juvenile ambition of wit, or affectation of gaiety, he may reasonably hope it will be considered to whom and at what age he was guilty of it, as well as how soon it was over. The rest, every judge of writing will see, were by no means efforts of the genius, but emanations of the heart; and this alone may induce any candid reader to believe their publication an act of necessity, rather than of vanity" (Preface to the *Letters*).

Page 81, l. 2. **Swift complains**, etc. "My Lord Bolingbroke and Mr. Pope press me with many kind invitations, but the former is too much a philosopher; he dines at six in the evening, after studying all the morning till the afternoon; and when he hath dined, to his studies again. Mr. Pope can neither eat nor drink, loves to be alone, and hath always some poetical scheme in his head. Thus the two best friends I ever had have utterly disqualified themselves for my conversation, and my way of living" (Swift to Mrs. Caesar, July 30th, 1733; quoted by Sharp).

l. 7. [**winter of Forty**, *i.e.* the winter of 1739-40, generally known as "the hard winter." Frost began on Christmas Day, and continued till February. Many people who had lived near Hudson Bay declared they had never known it colder there than in London during this winter. C. D. P.]

l. 11. **that every pamphlet disturbed his quiet.** See the story related at p. 69, l. 20 fg.

l. 17. [**disesteem**, a lack of admiration, with a slight suggestion of contempt. C. D. P.]

l. 19. **he had not much to say**, etc. Horace Walpole tells us that Pope's reply was: "Sir, I own I love the lion best before his claws are grown."

l. 24. [**emmets**, ants, which usually make "hillocks" for nests. C. D. P.]

l. 35. **a fool to Fame.** From the lines by Pope quoted above, on p. 2, l. 32, a fool to fame is one who allows the love of fame to take the full direction of him.

Page 82, l. 4. **falsehood is always in danger of inconsistency.** A Johnsonian turn to the proverb which says that liars should have good memories.

l. 5. **he makes it his boast at another time that he lives among them.** In the couplet quoted above, in note on p. 58, l. 24.

l. 10. **after many deaths**, etc. Pope, referring to a letter from Swift introducing a friend of Swift's to him, says: "To my great pleasure it confirms my hope of seeing you once more. After so many dispersions and so many divisions, two or three of us may yet be gathered together: not to plot, not to contrive silly schemes of ambition, or to vex our own or others' hearts with busy vanities (such as perhaps at one time of life or other take their tour in every man), but to divert ourselves, and the world too, if it pleases; or, at worst, to laugh at others as innocently and as unhurtfully as at ourselves." The picture did not please Swift at all. He replied: "I like the scheme of our meeting after distresses and dispersions; but the chief end I propose to myself in all my labours is to vex the world, rather than to divert it; and if I could compass that design without hurting my own person or fortune, I would be the most indefatigable writer you have ever seen, without reading" (two letters, written in September, 1725). Johnson's second quotation from Pope here is taken from a letter written in March, 1736-37, in which Pope affectionately implored Swift, then sinking into his decay, to come and take up his abode with him. "Would to God you would come over with Lord Orrery, whose care of you in the voyage I could so certainly depend on, and bring with you your old housekeeper, and two or three servants! I have room for all, a heart for all, and (think what you will) a fortune for all. We could, were we together, contrive to make our last days easy, and leave some sort of monument, what friends two wits could be in spite of all the fools in the world."

l. 26. **a glut of study**, etc. "This leads me to give you some account of the manner of my life and conversation, which has been infinitely more various and dissipated than when you knew and cared for me; and among all sexes, parties, and professions. A glut of study and retirement in the first part of my life cast me into this; and this, I begin to see, will throw me again into study and retirement" (Pope to Swift, Jan. 12, 1723). In his reply Swift said: "I have no very strong faith in you pretenders to retirement; you are not of an age for it, nor have gone through either good or bad fortune enough to go into a corner."

Page 83, l. 12. **what is more likely**, etc. Compare, "The writer commonly believes himself," etc., p. 80, l. 16 fg.

l. 16. **his malignity to Philips.** See p. 16, l. 14 fg.

l. 19. **Bentley.** Richard Bentley, keeper of St. James's Library, a great scholar and critic. He was reported to have said that Pope's Homer was very pretty, but was not Homer.

l. 21. **before Chandos, Lady Wortley, and Hill, was mean in his retreat.** For the first and last cases here see p. 47. With regard to Lady Wortley Pope took refuge in the asseveration that the "Sappho" of his *Satire* was never intended for her, a statement which was certainly untrue.

Page 84, l. 2. **His ungrateful mention of Allen in his will.** See above, p. 73, l. 25 fg.

l. 18. **his correspondence with Racine.** This was the son of the great dramatist. Himself something of a poet, he had, in verses called *La Religion*, written of Pope as being obviously no good Catholic. Pope wrote repudiating the accusation.

l. 26. **The positions which he transmitted from Bolingbroke,** etc. See above, p. 54, l. 7 fg.

Page 85, l. 5. **he studied in the academy of Paracelsus.** This writer openly professed his contempt for books, of which he said he never possessed at a time more than six.

l. 10. **Dobson.** See above, p. 58, l. 15.

l. 21. **his verses to Jervas.** See above, p. 16, l. 34.

Page 86, l. 36. [**retrenching exuberances,** cutting away unnecessary parts (Fr. *trencher*, to cut). C. D. P.]

l. 20. [**nor opened a shop,** etc. See p. 78, l. 31. He never offered for sale poems of condolence or congratulation. C. D. P.]

Page 87, l. 19. **He never exchanged praise for money,** etc. Johnson is already thinking of the comparison between Dryden and Pope on which he enters in the following page. Compare the following from his *Life of Dryden*: "We know that Dryden's several productions were so many successive expedients for his support; his plays were therefore often borrowed, and his poems were almost all occasional. ... The occasional poet is circumscribed by the narrowness of his subject. Whatever can happen to man has happened so often that little remains for fancy or invention. ... After so many inauguratory congratulations, nuptial hymns, and funeral dirges, he must be highly favoured by nature, or by fortune, who says anything not said before."

Page 88, l. 11. [**rectitude,** strictness in right thinking (Lat. *rectus*, straight). C. D. P.]

l. 12. [**dismission,** the act of setting aside; a more usual word now would be "dismissal." The power of his mind to think rightly was shown by his putting aside all his personal likings. C. D. P.]

the dismission of his poetical prejudices. The reference is to the "ambition of conceits" which Johnson notes as disfiguring Dryden's earliest poetical works. See the beginning of the *Life of Dryden.*

Page 89, l. 1. **the two satires of "Thirty-eight."** See above, p. 63, l. 25 fg.

Page 90, l. 17. [**dilatory caution,** the carefulness to be accurate which caused him to put off the time for publication. The epithet "dilatory" does not imply waste of time, as it would now. C. D. P.]

l. 31. [**determination,** decision. C. D. P.]

Page 91, l. 11. a line in which, etc.
> "The balmy Zephyrs, silent since her death,
> Lament the ceasing of a sweeter breath."

Daphne is dead, and the zephyrs of spring are not blowing. The lines are not really different from two which precede them, and which have escaped Johnson's condemnation.
> "In hollow caves sweet Echo silent lies,
> Silent, or only to her name replies."

l. 23. **Cooper's Hill.** A poem by Sir John Denham, published in 1642. "*Cooper's Hill* is the work that confers upon him the rank and dignity of an original author. He seems to have been, at least among us, the author of a species of composition that may be dominated local poetry, of which the fundamental subject is some particular landscape, to be poetically described, with the addition of such embellishments as may be supplied by historical retrospection or incidental meditation" (Johnson in his *Life of Denham*).

l. 23. **Waller's poem on The Park.** Waller wrote no poem of that name. Johnson is probably referring somewhat carelessly to a poem, *At Penhurst*, from which he makes the following quotation in his *Life of Waller*, censuring the thoughts as hyberbolical and the images as unnatural:
> "While in the park I sing, the listening deer
> Attend my passion, and forget to fear:
> When to the beeches I report my flame,
> They bow their heads, as if they felt the same.
> To gods appealing, when I reach their bowers,
> With loud complaints they answer me in showers.
> To thee a wild and cruel soul is given,
> More deaf than trees, and prouder than the heaven!"

l. 31. **the order in which they are shown must by necessity be arbitrary.** Johnson makes a similar remark in another field at p. 11, l. 8 fg.

Page 92, l. 5. in his Campaign. A poem written by Addison in commemoration of the campaign which ended in the great victory of Blenheim. The lines Johnson is referring to are as follows:
> "When actions, unadorned, are faint and weak,
> Cities and countries must be taught to speak;
> Gods may descend in factions from the skies,
> And rivers from their oozy beds arise;
> Fiction may deck the truth with spurious rays,
> And round the hero cast a borrowed blaze."

l. 10. **nothing is easier,** etc. Because it has all been done by the Greek and Latin poets already. In *Windsor Forest* Lodona is a nymph chased by Pan. The kind gods change her into a stream.

> "She said, and melting as in tears she lay,
> In a soft, silver stream dissolv'd away.
> The silver stream her virgin coldness keeps,
> For ever murmurs, and for ever weeps;
> Still bears the name the hapless virgin bore,
> And bathes the forest where she rang'd before."

There are a hundred such tales in Ovid's *Metamorphoses*.

l. 13. **as Steele warmly declared.** See above note on p. 14, l. 31.

l. 20. **the concluding paragraph.**

> "Nor Fame I slight, nor for her favours call;
> She comes unlooked for, if she comes at all.
> But if the purchase costs so dear a price,
> As soothing Folly, or exalting Vice:
> Oh! if the Muse must flatter lawless sway,
> And follow still where fortune leads the way;
> Or if no basis bear my rising fame,
> But the fall'n ruin of another's fame;
> Then teach me, heaven! to scorn the guilty bays,
> Drive from my breast that wretched lust of praise,
> Unblemish'd let me live, or die unknown;
> Oh grant an honest fame, or grant me none!"

l. 24. [**the Pollio,** a remarkable prophecy by Virgil which Pope in common with many others considered to resemble passages of Isaiah foretelling the coming of Christ. See note on p. 11, l. 31. C. D. P.]

l. 25. [**from what original.** The Bible. Johnson suggests that Pope's poem excels that of Virgil because Pope had access to the Bible. C. D. P.]

l. 27. **The Verses on the Unfortunate Lady.** See above, p. 11, l. 34 fg.

Page 93, l. 10. **history will always take stronger hold of the attention than fable.** Dryden sang of Alexander the Great and Thais: Pope of Orpheus and Eurydice. But this sentence of Johnson's has not passed without challenge. Compare, for example, Ward's remarks on this Ode. "This famous Ode, written by Pope in the year 1708 at Steele's desire, in praise of an art 'of the principles of which he was ignorant, while to its effects he was insensible,' has been naturally compared by successive generations of critics to Dryden's masterpiece on the same subject. A superiority which few will be disposed to deny has been generally claimed for

Alexander's Feast; but it may be questioned whether in this class of poetry either the choice of historical instead of mythological illustrations, or the unity of the object represented, is to be regarded as an absolute merit. ..." St. Cecilia was the patron saint of Music, and both Odes were written for a society of musical votaries, who met on her day in honour of her and of the art.

l. 20. **numeris lege solutis**, In numbers that owned no law.

l. 35. **Had all been like this—but every part cannot be the best.** Compare what Johnson says with reference to Dryden's poem on the death of Mrs. Killegrew. "All the stanzas indeed are not equal. An imperial crown cannot be one continued diamond; the gems must be held together by some less valuable matter."

Page 94, l. 7. **The conclusion**, etc.

"Of Orpheus now no more let Poets tell,
To bright Cecilia greater power is giv'n;
His numbers raised a shade from hell,
Hers lift the soul to heav'n."

Dryden wrote:

"Let old Timotheus yield the prize,
Or both divide the crown:
He raised a mortal to the skies;
She drew an angel down."

Johnson called this conclusion "vicious"; "the music of Timotheus, which *raised a mortal to the skies*, had only a metaphorical power; that of Cecilia, which *drew an angel down*, had a real effect: the crown therefore could not reasonably be divided." Sir Walter Scott called this "looking for spots in the sun."

l. 15. **the Essay on Criticism.** See above, p. 8, l. 10 fg.

l. 22. **and never afterwards excelled it.** Compare Ward's remarks as to this in his *Memoir*, p. 18: "It is to this period that we must ascribe the first of his preserved juvenile pieces. Though he had no public, the tonic of common sense appears to have been occasionally administered by his father; and the sense of rhythm was a gift which had been bestowed upon him by nature, together with a general correctness of taste in the choice of words and expressions which his preference for poetical over prose reading could not fail to heighten. To these causes must be attributed the extraordinary and perhaps unparalleled fact that there is little vital difference, so far as form is concerned, between some of the earliest and some of the latest of Pope's productions. His early pieces lack the vigour of wit and the brilliancy of antithesis of his later works, but they have the same felicity of expression, and the same easy flow of versification."

l. 28. **the comparison of a student's progress**, etc. In illustration of the point we have just been considering, it may be noticed that the passage referred to begins with a couplet which is as familiar in the English ear as a household word. Few remember that it was composed by a lad of twenty. The lines are as follows:

"A little learning is a dang'rous thing;
Drink deep, or taste not the Pierian spring:
There shallow draughts intoxicate the brain,
And drinking largely sobers us again.
Fir'd at first sight with what the Muse imparts,
In fearless youth we tempt the heights of Arts,
While from the bounded level of our mind
Short views we take, nor see the lengths behind;
But more advanc'd, behold with strange surprise
New distant scenes of endless science rise!
So pleas'd at first the tow'ring Alps we try,
Mount o'er the vales, and seem to tread the sky,
Th' eternal snows appear already past,
And the first clouds and mountains seem the last;
But, those attain'd, we tremble to survey
The growing labours of the lengthen'd way,
Th' increasing prospect tires our wand'ring eyes,
Hills peep o'er hills, and Alps on Alps arise!"
(vv. 215-232.)

Page 95, l. 7. **Perrault.** "Charles Perrault brought out, between 1688 and 1696, his *Parallèle des Anciens et des Modernes*, in which he assigns the superiority to the moderns. He was answered by Boileau" (M. Arnold's note).

l. 8. **In their similes the greatest writers have sometimes failed.** With what follows compare Johnson's remarks of a similar character on Dryden's *Eleanora*. "This piece, however, is not without its faults; there is so much likeness in the initial comparison, that there is no illustration. As a king would be lamented, Eleanora was lamented.

'As when some great and gracious monarch dies. ...'

This is little better than to say of a shrub, that it is as green as a tree, or of a brook that it waters a garden as rivers water a country."

l. 20. **the celebrated paragraph**, etc.

"'Tis not enough no harshness gives offence,
The sound must seem an Echo to the sense:
Soft is the strain when Zephyr gently blows,
And the smooth stream in smoother numbers flows;
But when loud surges lash the sounding shore,

The hoarse, rough verse should like the torrent roar;
When Ajax strives some rock's vast weight to throw,
The line too labours, and the words move slow;
Not so, when swift Camilla scours the plain,
Flies o'er the unbending corn, and skims along the main.
Hear how Timotheus' varied lays surprize,
And bid alternate passions fall and rise !
While, at each change, the son of Lybian Jove
Now burns with glory, and then melts with love,
Now his fierce eyes with sparkling fury glow,
Now sighs steal out, and tears begin to flow;
Persians and Greeks like turns of nature found,
And the world's victor stood subdu'd by Sound !
The pow'r of Music all our hearts allow,
And what Timotheus was, is Dryden now.
(vv. 364-383.)

Page 96, l. 8. Motion however may be in some sort exemplified. Johnson first excludes all resemblances except that between the movement of the action, so to say, and the movement of the lines. All others must depend on resemblances between individual words and individual things, and these, except in the case of the few onomatopoetic words which a language possesses, must be mostly imaginary. In the case of motion the ancients had the advantage over English poets in the artful way in which they could vary dactyls and spondees. Johnson takes however a case in which it is claimed that the cadence is so skilfully altered that in the beginning you have an echo of the slow motion of the stone up the hill, and in the end an echo of its quick fall down. Pope was proud of the passage, and it may have owed something to him, although it stands in one of the books translated by Broome. "I have loaded the verse," says Pope, "with monosyllables, and these almost all begin with aspirates:

"Up the high hill he heaves a huge round stone.'"

Johnson claims that his second line has "lost much of the delay." But it is to be noticed that it first lost all the aspirates. Pope anticipated a good deal of Johnson's criticism here in a passage in his Preface to Homer, which Cunningham quotes. "Homer is perpetually applying the sound to the sense. This, indeed, is one of the most exquisite beauties of poetry, and attainable by very few. I know only of Homer eminent for it in the Greek, and Virgil in Latin. I am sensible it is what may sometimes happen by chance, when a writer is warm and fully possest of his image: however, it may reasonably be believed they designed this, in whose verses it so manifestly appears, in a superior degree to all others. *Few readers have the ear to be judges of it*, but those who have will see I have endeavoured at this beauty."

l. 13. [**Sisyphus**, the father of Ulysses, for his wickedness during life was severely punished in the lower world, where he had to roll up hill a huge marble block, which, as soon as it reached the top, always rolled down again. C. D. P.]

l. 16. [**resulting**, springing back (Lat. *resultare*, to rebound). C. D. P.]

Page 97, l. 3. **Waller was smooth**, etc. *Imitations of Horace,* i. 2. 267 fg.

l. 8. **will find the line of swiftness**, etc. It should not be necessary to point out that the swiftness of the line has nothing to do with its length. A man may run a mile swiftly while another is crawling along quarter of a mile.

l. 13. **the Rape of the Lock.** Above, p. 12, l. 35 fg.

l. 30. [**Sylphs**, according to the Middle Age belief, were the elemental spirits of air. They were so called by the Rosicrucians, from the Greek *silphē*, a butterfly or moth. See p. 13, l. 30, note. C. D. P.]

[**Gnomes**, according to the Rosicrucian theory, were the elemental spirits of earth, and the guardians of mines and quarries (Greek, *gnoma*, knowledge). C. D. P.]

Page 98, l. 29. **the Lutrin,** a poem of Boileau's. [Translated into English in 1708 by Rowe. C. D. P.]

Page 99, l. 4. **the machinery.** See note above, on p. 13, l 30.

l. 11. **the game at ombre might be spared.** In the beginning of the third canto. "From the terms used in the game of Ombre-Spadillo, Basto, Matador, Punto, etc., there can scarcely be a doubt that the other nations of Western Europe derived their knowledge of it from the Spaniards" (Chatto, quoted by Ward). It was a game of cards.

l. 17. **Eloise to Abelard.** Above, p. 15, l. 3.

l. 34. **curiosa felicitas,** a 'thoughtful happiness,' that is, a happy knack of expression, which looks accidental, but is really the result of much thought. The phrase was applied to Horace by Petronius.

Page 100, l. 3. **Essay on the Life and Writings of Pope,** by Warburton.

l. 12. **the barbarians,** as the Greeks called all nations but themselves.

ll. 16, 17. **Anguillara and Salvini.** The one translated Ovid in the sixteenth century, and the other Homer in the seventeenth century.

l. 23. **Tully and Germanicus.** Tully we now always speak of as Cicero. Compare Tully's Offices, above, p. 3, l. 15, and the note there. Germanicus is the well-known nephew and adopted son of the Emperor Tiberius. He translated into Latin the astronomical poem of the Greek writer, Aratus.

l. 25. [**Terence**, Terentius Afer, a celebrated comic poet born at Carthage, B.C. 193. He studied Menander's comedies, and was himself a successful writer of plays in Latin. C. D. P.]

[**Menander**, born at Athens, B.C. 342, wrote comedies which are now lost, but some idea of them can be formed from those of Terence, who was little more than a translator of Menander from Greek into Latin. C. D. P.]

Page 101, l. 20. [**necessitas quod cogit defendit**, necessity defends what it compels us to do. This is freely translated in the succeeding sentence: "that may be lawfully done which cannot be forborne." C. D. P.]

l. 26. **of the same general fabric with that of Homer.** We must now say 'same as.' They both wrote in hexameter verse.

l. 35. **falling into regular subordination,** of an ordered constitution.

Page 102, l. 29. **they were undoubtedly written to swell the volumes.** See above, p. 21, l. 6 fg.

Page 103, l. 6. [**the Odyssey.** See pp. 40, 41. C. D. P.]

l. 11. **the Dunciad.** Above, p. 43, l. 16 fg.

l. 12. [**Mac Flecknoe**, a satire on Thomas Shadwell, the dramatist, who had published a most savage poem against Dryden. Political opposition had changed Shadwell and Dryden from friends to bitter enemies. Flecknoe, whose name is used as the title, was a dull poet who had always laid himself open to ridicule. He died in 1678, and *Mac Flecknoe* was published in 1682. C. D. P.]

l. 25. **An author,** such as one of those whom Pope attacked in the *Dunciad*.

l. 31. **impune diem consumpserit ingens Telephus.** Juvenal begins his first Satire by railing at the way in which the **poets** of his acquaintance insist on reciting their productions to him. In the **present case** he complains that the enormous Telephus of one writer has taken up the whole of his day.

l. 35. **like the javelin of Priam,** thrown ineffectually by the aged Priam at Achilles. The incident is in the second book of the *Aeneid*.

["Pyrrhus
Old grandsire Priam seeks. Anon he finds him

> Striking too short at Greeks; his antique sword,
> Rebellious to his arm, lies where it falls,
> Repugnant to command."—*Hamlet*, II. 2. C. D. P.]

Page 104, l. 5. **such as,** etc. See the *Dunciad*, ii. 85, iv. 371, and iv. 403.

l. 16. **Essay on Man.** Above, p. 52, l. 15 fg.

l. 28. **the poet's Liebnitian reasoning.** Pope took a good deal of his philosophy from the German philosopher Leibnitz.

Page 105, l. 11. **vulgarity of sentiment,** thoughts which are common to everybody. The phrase would now imply a censure which is not in Johnson's mind at all. It is paraphrased immediately as "the talk of his mother and his nurse."

Page 106, l. 5. **felicity of composition,** the *curiosa felicitas* of p. 99, l. 34.

l. 7. [**lines unsuccessfully laboured,** lines which Pope had not succeeded in making perfect. *To labour* is here used transitively in the sense of to work upon, to elaborate. See p. 90, ll. 3-25, for Pope's method. C. D. P.]

l. 12. **The Characters of Men and Women.** Above, pp. 60, 61.

l. 16. [**Boileau's Satire,** *Les Précieuses Ridicules* (1659), a satire on the ladies who discussed polite language and literature in Paris. C. D. P.]

l. 22. **The Gem and the Flower.**

> " 'Tis from high Life high Characters are drawn ...
> Court-virtues bear, like gems, the highest rate,
> Born where heav'n's influence scarce can penetrate:
> In life's low vale, the soil the Virtues like,
> They please as beauties, here as wonders strike.
> Tho' the same Sun, with all-diffusive rays
> Blush in the Rose, and in the Di'mond blaze,
> We prize the stronger effort of his pow'r,
> And justly set the Gem above the Flow'r."
>
> (vv. 135-148.)

l. 32. **Eulogy on Good Sense.**

> " Oft have you hinted to your brother Peer
> A certain truth, which many buy too dear:
> Something there is more needful than Expense,
> And something previous ev'n to taste—'tis Sense:
> Good Sense, which only is the gift of Heav'n,
> And tho' no Science, fairly worth the seven:
> A Light, which in yourself you must perceive:
> Jones and Le Notre have it not to give."
>
> (vv. 39-46.)

Pope is writing of the use of riches. Jones and Le Notre were famous, the one as an architect, the other as a designer of gardens. Johnson writes "Elogy" for "Eulogy" here.

l. 33. **the End of the Duke of Buckingham.** Pope never excelled himself here.

> "In the worst inn's worst room, with mat half-hung,
> The floors of plaister, and the walls of dung,
> On once a flock-bed, but repair'd with straw,
> With tape-ty'd curtains, never meant to draw,
> The George and Garter dangling from that bed
> Where tawdry yellow strove with dirty red,
> Great Villiers lies—alas! how 'chang'd from him,
> That life of pleasure, and that soul of whim!
> Gallant and gay, in Cliveden's proud alcove,
> The bow'r of wanton Shrewsbury and love :
> Or just as gay, at Council, in a ring
> Of mimic'd Statesmen and their merry King.
> No Wit to flatter left of all his store !
> No Fool to laugh at, which he valu'd more.
> There, Victor of his health, of fortune, friends,
> And fame, this lord of useless thousands, ends."
> (vv. 299-314.)

"George Villiers, Duke of Buckingham, the son of the first Duke (the favourite and minister of James I. and Charles I.), was born in 1637. He lost his estates as a royalist, but recovered them by his marriage with the daughter of Lord Fairfax. He is the Zimri of the Absalom and Achitophel of Dryden, whom he had ridiculed as Bayes in the burlesque play of the *Rehearsal.* Thus we have portraits of this typical hero of the Restoration period by Dryden and Pope, as well as by Burnet and Butler, Count Grammont and Horace Walpole. The tenant's house at which he died (in 1687) was at Kirkby Moor Side, near Helmsly, in Yorkshire" (Ward's note).

l. 35. **The Epistle to Arbuthnot.** Above, p. 62, l. 20.

Page 107, l. 7. **the satire upon Sporus.** A violent personal attack on Lord Hervey.

l. 13. **the dignity of vice,** etc. A passage which certainly bears eloquent witness to Pope's courage in attacking vice in high places, of which there was enough and to spare in the England of his day.

> "Vice is undone, if she forgets her Birth,
> And stoops from Angels to the Dregs of Earth :
> But 'tis the Fall degrades her to a Whore :
> Let Greatness own her, and she's mean no more ;
> Her Birth, her Beauty, Crowds and Courts confess ;
> Chaste Matrons praise her, and grave Bishops bless ;

> In golden Chains the willing World she draws,
> And hers the Gospel is, and hers the Laws,
> Mounts the Tribunal, lifts her scarlet head,
> And sees pale Virtue carted in her stead.
> Lo! at the wheels of her Triumphal car,
> Old England's Genius, rough with many a scar,
> Dragg'd in the dust! his arms hang idly round,
> His flag inverted trails along the ground!
> Our Youth, all livery'd o'er with foreign gold
> Before her dance: behind her crawl the Old!
> See thronging Millions to the Pagod run,
> And offer Country, Parent, Wife, or Son!
> Hear her black Trumpet thro' the Land proclaim
> That not to be corrupted is the shame."
>
> (vv. 141-60.)

l. 15. **The Imitations of Horace.** Above, p. 61, l. 30 fg.

l. 25. [**Roman images**, Latin imagery, that is, figures of speech and idioms which were familiar to the Romans, but could not be applied in descriptions of English manners. C. D. P.]

Page 108, l. 15. **the most perfect fabric of English verse.** The Heroic verse, as it is called, of ten syllables, in which Pope's works, with a very few exceptions, are all composed.

l. 30. **without regard to Swift's remonstrances.** "I borrowed your Homer from the bishop (mine is not yet landed) and read it out in two evenings. If it pleaseth others as well as me, you have got your end in profit and reputation: yet I am angry at some bad lines and triplets, and pray in your next do not let me have so many unjustifiable rhymes to *war* and *gods*" (Swift to Pope, June 28, 1715).

l. 34. **To Swift's edict for the exclusion of alexandrines and triplets.** The triplet is a group of three lines with the same rhyme. Swift spoke of it as "a vicious way of rhyming, wherewith Dryden abounded and was imitated by all the bad versifiers in Charles the Second's reign" (Swift to Beach, April 12, 1735). The Alexandrine is an occasional verse of twelve instead of ten syllables. See for example, above, p. 96, ll. 17, 24, 32. "Dryden likewise brought in the Alexandrine verse at the end of a triplet. I was so angry at these corruptions that, about 24 years ago, I banished them all by one triplet, with the Alexandrine, upon a very ridiculous subject. I absolutely did prevail with Mr. Pope, and Gay, and Dr. Young, and one or two more, to reject them. Mr. Pope never used them till he translated Homer, which was too long a work to be very exact in" (Swift in the same letter). The "triplet, with an Alexandrine," by which Swift hoped he had made both expedients ridiculous, occurs in his *City Shower*, and runs thus:

"Sweeping, from butchers' stalls, dung, guts, and blood;
Drown'd puppies, stinking sprats, all drench'd in mud,
Dead cats, and turnip-tops came tumbling down likè flood."

Compare what Johnson says about both triplets and Alexandrines in his *Life of Dryden*. He sums up there as follows: "Considering the metrical art simply as a science, and consequently excluding all casualty, we must allow that triplets and Alexandrines, inserted by caprice, are interruptions of that constancy to which science aspires. And though the variety which they introduce may very justly be desired, yet to make our poetry exact, there ought to be some stated method of admitting them. But till some such regulation can be formed, I wish them to be retained in their present state. They are sometimes grateful to the reader, and sometimes convenient to the poet. Fenton was of the opinion that Dryden was too liberal and Pope too sparing in their use" (*Life of Dryden*, p. 98).

Page 109, l. 2. except once. Perhaps.

"The meeting points the sacred hair dissever
From the fair head for ever and for ever."
(3. 153-4.)

l. 3. **Expletives.** Words put in merely to fill up the line. Johnson's illustration in the next sentence is very curious. The lines referred to might, by the process he suggests, be made to run thus:

"Achilles' wrath, to Greece the spring
Of woes unnumber'd, goddess sing!
That wrath which hurl'd to Pluto's reign
The souls of chiefs untimely slain;
Whose limbs unbury'd on the shore,
Devouring dogs and vultures tore."

As Pope actually wrote the passage, the spring was direful, the goddess was heavenly, the reign was gloomy, the chiefs were mighty, the shore was naked, and the vultures were hungry. It is not commonly known that Burns spoilt one of his finest lyrics by the converse process. His first draft of *Ye Banks and Braes* ran thus:

"Ye banks and braes o' bonnie Doon,
How can ye bloom so fair?
How can ye sing ye little birds,
And I sae fu' o' care?"

and so on. The version we know was altered to suit a particular tune.

l. 14. **Lo, where Mæotis,** etc. *Dunciad*, 3. 87, 88.

l. 17. **Watts.** Dr. Isaac Watts, the hymn-writer.

Page 110, l. 7. his version. His translation of Homer.

l. 14. **Mr. Jodrell.** One of Dr. Johnson's intimate friends. He was a member of the social club which Johnson got up in 1783, and which he vainly endeavoured to induce Sir Joshua Reynolds to join (Boswell, p. 622).

l. 20. [ill, undeserved by the object on whom they were bestowed. C. D. P.]

l. 26. [**Chapman**, a dramatist of Elizabeth's reign. In 1598 he published a translation of seven books of Homer's *Iliad*. C. D. P.]

Hobbes, a supporter of the policy of the early Stuart kings. His first work (1628) was a translation of *Thucydides* from the Greek. C. D. P.]

Page 112, l. 14. **which was printed in the Visitor.** "*The Universal Visitor and Monthly Memorialist*, 1756. This was a magazine which lived for one year only, but to which Johnson contributed" (Arnold's note). There was good reason for not inserting this examination of Pope's epitaphs in the Life, and most readers will wish that it had not even been added to the Life as a supplement. It is a curious reflection that if nothing of Pope had survived but the quotations made from him in this Life, and the present supplement, future ages would have been quite unable to understand his fame. Of the epitaph on Atterbury, which Johnson calls a "contemptible dialogue" (p. 125), Macaulay wrote: "That the epitaph with which Pope honoured the memory of his friend does not appear on the walls of the great national cemetery, is no subject of regret; for nothing worse was ever written by Colley Cibber."

l. 19. **at this visit.** In this paper, called a visit in allusion to the title of the magazine.

l. 29. **Charles, Earl of Dorset.** "A wit and poet, author of the well-known song beginning, 'To all you ladies now on land.' He died in 1706" (Arnold's note).

Page 113, l. 9. **his great forefathers' every grace.** Note that the apostrophe is not used in the possessive plural. Compare p. 121, l. 10:

"Lies crown'd with Princes honours, Poets lays,"

i.e. with honours paid by Princes and lays sung by Poets.

l. 10. **reflected on his race.** Another mistake or misprint in Johnson. Pope wrote, "reflected in his race." Ward, in a note on the words which follow, "Where other Buckhursts," etc., apparently understands them to refer to some of Buckhurst's illustrious ancestors. But the poet has passed from them. The meaning is, that as Dorset was the very image of his "great forefathers," so he himself is imaged in his descendants. Compare Johnson's own words, where he is pointing out that there is no connection between this particular blessing, and the fact that Dorset was a peer. "They might happen to any other man, whose ancestors were remembered, or whose posterity were likely to be regarded."

Page 114, l. 18. **kept.** Pope wrote "keep."

Page 115, l. 1. **Sir William Trumbal.** See above, p. 5, l. 24.

l. 3. **Easthamsted**, a few miles south of Pope's early home at Binfield. C. D. P.]

l. 28. **like an unskilful painter**, who draws the picture of something that nobody can recognize, and has to write the name under it.

l. 36. **an honest courtier cannot but be a patriot.** This is Johnson's opinion; it was certainly not Pope's.

Page 116, l. 11. [**impertinent**, not to the point; this is the original meaning of the word, as the opposite of *pertinent*. C. D. P.]

l. 13. **the poor conspirator**, etc. "Major John Bernardi, who died in Newgate, Sept. 20, 1736, after an imprisonment for forty years on an alleged conspiracy against William III." (Johnson's note).

l. 23. **Who ne'er knew joy**, etc., who never had a joy that his friends were not invited to share in. In the next line Pope may be quoting the words used by Louis XIV. on hearing of the death of his queen. He declared that it was the first grief she had caused him.

Page 117, l. 3. **James Craggs.** See above, p. 23, l. 12. "As Craggs's death alone arrested the inquiry into the charge of peculation brought against him in connection with the South Sea frauds (his father committing suicide shortly afterwards), the praise in the third line of Pope's *Epitaph* is singularly bold" (Ward).

l. 4. **Jacobus Craggs**, etc. "James Craggs, Secretary and Privy Councillor to the King of Great Britain, the darling and the delight alike of prince and people, lived, superior to his honours and to envy, for thirty-five (alas, alas! too few) years, died on the 16th of February, 1720."

l. 11. **Statesman, yet friend to truth**, etc. The lines on Craggs were taken by Pope from his own Epistle to Addison (*Moral Essays*, Epistle V.), with an alteration in the last line, which in the Epistle runs:

"And prais'd, unenvy'd, by the Muse he lov'd."

Page 118, l. 5. **Mr. Rowe.** "Nicholas Rowe (1673-1718), poet laureate, author of *The Fair Penitent, Jane Shore*, and a translation of Lucan's *Pharsalia*" (Arnold's note). Rowe was perhaps modest enough not to have taken any objection to the "chief fault" which Johnson finds in this epitaph.

l. 8. **Beneath a rude and nameless stone he lies.** "The tomb of Mr. Dryden was erected upon this hint by the Duke of Buckingham; to which was originally intended this epitaph:
"This Sheffield rais'd. The sacred Dust below
  Was Dryden once: The rest who does not know?"... (Pope.)

l. 18. **To wish peace to thy shade**, etc. A point on which Johnson felt very strongly. See the passage in his Dryden, p. 68, l. 28 of the edition in this series, and the note there.

Page 119, l. 15. has no name in the verses. See above, p. 115, l. 17.

l. 23. **Robert Digby.** "Robert Digby was a frequent correspondent of Pope's during the years 1717 to 1724. He died in 1726; and Pope laments his death in a letter to his brother, Edward Digby" (Ward). There is only one good line in this epitaph, and, as Johnson points out, it is Dryden's.

Page 120, l. 16. for the greater part of mankind. The words that follow are a quotation from the Epistle on the *Characters of Women*:
  "Nothing so true as what you once let fall,
   'Most women have no characters at all.'" (vv. 1, 2.)

Page 121, l. 5. Sir Godfrey Kneller. "Sir Godfrey Kneller was born at Lubeck in 1648, and after being introduced by the Duke of Monmouth to King Charles II., filled the office of State-painter under that monarch and his successors up to George I., in whose reign (in 1726) he died" (Ward). "I paid Sir Godfrey a visit but two days before he died; I think I never saw a scene of so much vanity in my life. He was lying in his bed, and contemplating the plan he had made for his own monument. He said many gross things in relation to himself, and the memory he should leave behind him. He said he should not like to lie among the rascals at Westminster: a memorial there would be sufficient; and desired me to write an epitaph for it. I did so afterwards; and I think it is the worst thing I ever wrote in my life" (Pope, in Spence, p. 125).

l. 12. **Living**, etc. "Imitated from the famous Epitaph on Raphael":
  "Raphael, timuit, quo sospite, vinci
   Rerum magna parens, et moriente, mori" (Pope's note).

Pope's lines are not so much an imitation as a close translation.

l. 18. **but of very harsh construction.** "Living" is used in the sense of 'while he was alive,' and "dying" in the sense of 'now that he is dead.' So Dryden used "reversed" in the sense of 'when they had been revers'd,' a construction which misled Johnson as to his meaning. (See the Dryden, p. 95, l. 19, and the note there.)

l. 19. **Henry Withers.** "Henry Withers, Lieutenant-General, descended from a military stock, and bred in arms in Britain, Dunkirk, and Tangier. Through the whole course of the two last wars of England with France, he served in Ireland, in the Low Countries, and in Germany: was present in every battle and at every siege ..." (from the prose inscription on Withers's monument in Westminster Abbey).

Page 122, l. 15. **Mr. Elijah Fenton**, the author of great part of the translation of the *Odyssey*. See above, p. 41, l. 9 fg.

l. 24. **From nature's temperate feast rose satisfied**, a reminiscence of Horace. "So rarely can we find the man who, contented with his portion of days, leaves the banquet like one who has had his fill" (*Satires*, i. 1. 117-119).

l. 26. **borrowed from Crashaw.**
"The modest front of this small floor
Believe me, reader, can say more
Than many a braver marble can:
Here lies a truly honest man."
(Crashaw, *Epitaph upon Mr. Ashton*.)

Page 123, l. 29. **the wit of a man**, etc. "Pope had probably in his mind 1 *Corinthians*, xiv. 20: 'In malice be ye children, but in understanding be men.' But Dryden, also, had said of Mrs. Killigrew: 'Her wit was more than man, her innocence a child'" (Arnold's note).

Page 124, l. 16. **The thought in the last line.** Ward compares the following four lines from a recently discovered poem, which has been attributed to Milton:
"In this little bed my dust
Incurtained round I here entrust,
While my more pure and noble part
Lies entomb'd in every heart."

l. 21. **Isaacus Newtonius**, etc. Isaac Newton, whom Time, Nature, and the Heavens call immortal, this marble confesses to have been mortal.

l. 28. **Why part should be Latin**, etc. Compare above, p. 117, l. 28 fg.

l. 31. **he is not immortal**, etc. An objection of the same 'petty character as that which Johnson took to the conclusion of Dryden's and of Pope's Odes for St. Cecilia's Day. See above, p. 94, l. 7 fg.

Page 125, l. 1. Edmund, Duke of Buckingham. "Only son of John Sheffield, Duke of Buckinghamshire, by Katherine Darnley, natural daughter of James II." Roscoe.

l. 25. **The contemptible dialogue between He and She.** An epitaph on Atterbury. See note above, on p. 112, l. 14.

l. 27. **In his last epitaph on himself.**

"Under this Marble, or under this Sill,
Or under this Turf, or e'en what they will;
Whatever an Heir, or a Friend in his stead,
Or any good creature shall lay o'er my head,
Lies one who ne'er car'd, and still cares not a pin
What they said, or may say, of the mortal within:
But who living and dying, serene still and free,
Trusts in God, that as well as he was, he shall be."

Page 126, l. 6. Areosti. "Ludovico Ariosto (1474-1533), one of the most famous of Italian poets, author of *Orlando Furioso*. The sense of the Latin lines in the text is as follows: 'The bones of Ludovico Ariosto lie buried under this stone, or under this sod, or under whatsoever his kind heir chose, or a comrade kinder than his heir, or a traveller lighting by good hap on his remains. For what would befall him he could not tell, but neither did he esteem his empty carcase enough to desire to provide for it an urn in his lifetime: howbeit in his lifetime he provided this inscription for his sepulchre, if any sepulchre he was hereafter to have'" (Arnold's note).

INDEX.

Aaron Hill, in the *Dunciad*, 47.
Addison, praised *Essay on Criticism*, 8; and *Unfortunate Lady*, 13; advice to Pope, 14; disowned Pope's pamphlet to Dennis, 16; jealousy of Pope, 34; reproaches Pope, 35; opinion of *Iliad*, 36; satirized, 63.
Alcander, 5.
Alexandrines, 108.
Allen of Bath, 50, 63, 73.
Arbuthnot, Dr., notes on *Dunciad*, 47; character, 62; one of the Scriblerus Club, 64.
Art of Sinking in Poetry, 43.
Atossa (Duchess of Marlborough), 61.
Atterbury, praised Pope's Letters, 37; his trial, 40; presented a Bible to Pope, 41.

Bentley, 83, 93, 103.
Berkeley, 14.
Betterton, 16, 17.
Binfield, 3; Pope's estate sold, 37.
Blount, Martha, 61, 70, 73.
Bolingbroke, ridiculed Pope, 54; hatred of Warburton, 58; Pope's executor, 72.
Bull, in *Essay on Criticism*, 9.

Burnet, 38.
Button's, 36.

Caryl, request to Pope, 13.
Chapman, 110.
Characters of Men, 60, 106.
Characters of Women, 61, 106.
Cibber, made Poet Laureat, mentioned in *Dunciad*, 66; and in *Epistle to Arbuthnot*, 67.
Cleland, 47.
Congreve, 31.
Craggs, offered Pope a pension, 23.
Criticism, Essay on, 8.
Cromwell, 6.
Crousaz, criticised *Essay on Man*, 54.
Curll, published Pope's Letters, 7, 43, 49; prosecuted by Pope, 49.

Dacier, 21.
Deane, taught Pope, 3.
Dennis, 6, 8, 9; criticised *Rape of the Lock*, 14, 47, 98; remarks on Addison's *Cato*, 15; attacked by Pope, 16; criticised *Windsor Forest*, 91.
Dialogue on Medals, 33.

Dobson, translated *Essay on Man* into Latin, 58, 85.
Dodsley, 64, 71, 72; aided by Pope, 83.
Double rhymes, 109.
Dryden, seen by Pope, death, 3.
Duke of Chandos, 47.
Dunciad, its success, 43; Pope's account, 44; presented to the King, 45; false editions, 46; criticised, 103.

Easthamsted, 115.
Eloisa to Abelard, 15, 99.
Epistle to Arbuthnot, 62, 106.
 ,, Lord Bathurst, 106.
 ,, Lord Burlington, 106.
Epistles of Pope, 51.
Epitaphs, 112-126.
Essay on Criticism, 8, 94.
Essay on Man, 52, 104.

Garth, 31.
Gay, death of, 48; epitaph, 123.
Grotto, Pope's, 37.
Guardian, compared Pastorals of Philips and Pope, 16; Pope contributed to, 19.

Halifax, heard Pope's *Iliad*, 31.
Hobbes, 110.
Homer, 111.
Hooker, quoted, 11.
Howell's Letters, 51.

Iliad, various translations, 100; Pope's, 17, 100; purchased by Lintot, 18; copied in Holland, 18; praised by Johnson, 23; the original, 24; extracts from MS., 24-31; published, 35; criticism of notes, 102.
Imitations of Horace, 61, 107.

January and May, 4.

Jervas, taught Pope painting, 16; tries to reconcile Pope and Addison, 34.
Juvenal, quoted, 48.

Kyrl, the Man of Ross, 59.

Letters of Pope, 7, 49-51.
Lintot, published Pope's *Iliad*, 18, 35; and *Odyssey*, 41.
Loveday's *Letters*, 51.
Lutrin, The, 98.

Mac Flecknoe, 103.
Machinery in *Rape of the Lock*, 13, 97-9.
Man of Ross, 59.
Marchmont, Lord, 70, 72.
Memoirs of Scriblerus, 64.
Messiah, published in the *Spectator*, 11, 92.
Miscellanies, 43, 44.
Monument, inscription on it, 60.
Mrs. and Miss, 13, l. 2, note.
Mrs. Phillips' Letters, 51.
Mummy and Crocodile, 67.

Ode for St. Cecilia's Day, 93; compared with *Alexander's Feast*, 93.
Ode on Solitude, 4.
Odyssey, 40, 103; criticised by Spence, 41.
Orinda (Mrs. Phillips), 51.
Osborne, 68, 69.

Papists, censured *Essay on Criticism*, 10.
Parnell, assisted Pope, 22; poems published by Pope, 39.
Pastorals, 6; printed, 8.
Pastorals of Philips, 8.
Patriot King, 72.
Pindar's *Odes*, 93.
Pollio, 92.

INDEX. 199

Pope, birth, 1; at school, 2; personated Ajax, 2; "lisped in numbers," 2; imitated English poets, 4; studied French, 4; at Binfield, 5; acquainted with Trumbal, 5; Wycherley, 6; frequented Will's, 7; hostility to Dennis, 10; wrote Prologue to *Cato*, 15; studied painting, 16; hindered by religion, 17; offered *Iliad* to subscribers, 17; contributed to *Guardian*, 19; read *Iliad* to Halifax, 31; Letter to Addison, 37; death of his father, 38; criticised by Burnet, Ducket, Dennis, 38; speculated, 39; his edition of Shakespeare, 39; hostility to critics, 39; undertakes *Odyssey*, 40; witness in Atterbury's trial, 40; overturned in a coach, 42; entertained Voltaire, 42; published *Dunciad*, 43; his apologies, 47; poem on Taste, 47; ingratitude to Chandos, 47; mother's death, 49; prosecuted Curll, 49; his *Essay on Man*, 52, 102; Letter to Warburton, 57; his theory of the ruling Passion, 60; challenged Pulteney, 63; follower of Prince of Wales, 63; afflicted with asthma, 66; his drama ridiculed, 67; quarrel with Cibber, 66-9; last illness and death, 71; his person, weaknesses, habits, 74-6; domestic character, 77; contempt for poverty, 78; social qualities, 79; Letters, 80; contempt of the world, 81; religion, 84; good sense, 84; methods, 86, 87; compared with Dryden, 89, 90; invention, imagination, and judgment, 107, 108; was he a poet? 109; Letter to Mr. Bridges, 110.
Prevalence, 43, l. 31.
Prior's *Nut-Brown Maid*, 15; *Solomon*, 58.

Queen Caroline, 58.
Quincunx, 37.

Ralph, in the *Dunciad*, 43.
Rape of the Lock, 12, 97.
Resnel, translated *Essay on Man*, 54.
Rosicrucians, 13.
Ruffhead, 12, 40, 70.

Scriblerus Club, 64.
Sensibility, 46, l. 14.
Simile of Alps, 94.
Sound and sense, 95-7.
Southcot, 58.
South Sea Bubble, 39.
Spence, criticised *Odyssey*, 41; lived with Pope, 42.
Steele, 11, 14, 35, 92.
Swift, promotes subscription to *Iliad*, 34; his *Gulliver's Travels*, 65.

Taverner, taught Pope Latin, 2.
Temple of Fame, 14, 92.
Thebais, 4.
Theobald, criticised Pope, 39; at head of the Dunces, 43.
Thomson, Dr., attended Pope, 70.
Tickell, published rival translation of *Iliad*, 35.
Tonson, refused to publish Pope's *Iliad*, 36; published *Shakespeare*, 39.
Triplets, 97.
Trumbal, Sir William, 5; epitaph, 115.
Tully, 3.
Twickenham, Pope's house, 37.

Unfortunate Lady, 11, 92.
Use of Riches, 59.

Voltaire, entertained by Pope, 42.

Waller, 38, 91.
Walsh, encouraged Pope, 7; Letters, 51.

Warburton, commended *Essay on Criticism*, 11; remarks on *Essay on Man*, 55; defended Pope, 56; on *Rape of the Lock*, 97.
Warwick, Lord, 36.
Whitehead, summoned before the Lords, 64.
Windsor Forest, 15, 91.
Wycherley, 6.

www.ingramcontent.com/pod-product-compliance
Lightning Source LLC
Chambersburg PA
CBHW020824230426

43666CB00007B/1098